# SMALL BOATS
# ᴬᴺᴰ LARGE SLOW
# TARGETS

**Oral Histories of United States' Amphibious
Forces Personnel in WWII**

# SMALL BOATS
# AND LARGE SLOW
# TARGETS

## Oral Histories of United States' Amphibious Forces Personnel in WWII

BY
### Robert E. Witter

Typical scene along the invasion beach, Leyte, 1944.

Pictorial Histories Publishing Co. Inc.
Missoula, Montana 59801

LIBRARY OF CONGRESS
CATALOG CARD NO. 98-65346

ISBN 1-57510-043-6

First Printing June 1998

*Typography Leslie Maricelli*
*Cover Graphics Mike Egeler*

**PICTORIAL HISTORIES PUBLISHING CO., INC.**
713 South Third St. West, Missoula, Montana 59801

# Table of Contents

# Photographs and Documents

For POOK
Elizabeth Jane Witter

# Introduction

One of dozens just like her, the small, gray boat with the squared-off bow, pitched and bobbed as she growled her way toward the enemy shore. Packed tightly within her hold, thirty-six anxious men awaited the scraping of her hull against the sandy beach—a sound that would signal the imminent drop of the ramp and their headlong charge into surf and enemy fire. Although they had practiced this maneuver time and again, the jarring reality of enemy shells bursting about them and bullets cracking the air above forever ended many a youthful belief of invincibility and, all too often, forever ended many a youth.

Most of us today have seen this moment recounted in films and documentaries, or have read of the exploits of the Marines and soldiers who struggled through the surf on an enemy beach to regain territory held by a tenacious foe. The ones nearly forgotten in the passage of time, however, are the men who brought the troops to these shores in the first place—the crewmen aboard the lumbering LSTs and the sailors who guided their small boats to those hellish beaches while enemy artillery, small arms fire and aircraft sought to blast their fragile craft out of the water!

This book is their story; the unvarnished reminiscences of former small boatmen and LST crewmen who, in their own words, tell of their unique participation in the Second World War.

# Acknowledgments

This book is the product of a number of truly nice people who, despite the many failings of an ignorant author, generously and patiently gave of their time and memories. Since I could not possibly list these folks in order of importance, alphabetically, they are: Mr. J.A. Brinkman, Mr. Jerry Chappelle, Mr. Robert J. Dolan, Mr. Leroy Hazel, Mr. Lester R. Jarvis, Mr. Paul Anthony Koeppler, Mr. George W. Leach, Mr. Herbert W. Stamer, Mr. Theodore Stratton and Mr. Carey Surratt.

Likewise, I am greatly indebted to the following people: Mr. Robert Ruman, Articles of War bookstore, Skokie, Il, for outstanding advice, and providing a source for military books that I have yet to see equalled anywhere else; Mr. John W. Pemberton, manager of Photographic Services, and his production staff at the Mariners' Museum, for some really fine photographs of small boats; Mr. Mahlon Groover, for sharing many of this wartime photographs; Mr. E.C. Finney Jr., Curator Branch, Photographic Section, Naval Historical Center, for a number of very nice photographs and some invaluable information; Mr. Carl M. Ploense, III, historian for research I desperately needed, and Mr. Benjamin H. Witter and Mrs. Roberta J. Witter, for always being there.

# Part 1
# The Small Boats

# LCP(L)
## Landing Craft, Personnel (Large)

| | |
|---|---|
| Length: | 36'8" |
| Beam: | 10'10" |
| Draft: | 2'6" aft (light) |
| | 3'6" aft (loaded) |
| Displacement: | 13,000 lbs. (light) |
| Crew: | 3 |
| Armor: | Three transverse 10-pound bulkheads |
| Propulsion: | 150 horsepower Superior diesel, or |
| | 165-225 horsepower Gray diesel, or |
| | 225 horsepower Kermath gasoline, or |
| | 250 horsepower Hall-Scott gasoline engine. |
| Speed: | 8 - 11 knots |
| Endurance: | 50 miles (gasoline) |
| | 130 miles (diesel) |
| Number built for U.S. service during the War: | 2,193 |
| Description: | Based on boat builder Andrew Jackson Higgins' *"Eureka,"* a fast motor boat. It could carry four tons of cargo or 35 personnel. |

An LCP(L) discharging troops during a training exercise. As evidenced by the second and third men from the left, note the awkward manner of getting the troops from the craft to the shore—they had to crawl over the side and drop.

Landing Craft, Personnel (Large). Port view of the craft while beached.

## LCP(R)
## Landing Craft, Personnel (Ramp)

Length:               36'8"
Beam:                 10'10"
Draft:                2'6" aft (light)
                      3'6" aft (loaded)
Displacement:         13,000 lbs. (light)
Crew:                 3
Armor:                Three 1/4" plate; transverse bulkheads.
Propulsion:           105 horsepower Buda diesel, or
                      115 horsepower Chrysler Royal gasoline, or
                      150 horsepower Palmer gasoline, or
                      225 horsepower Gray diesel engine.
Speed:                8 - 11 knots
Endurance:            80 miles (gasoline)
                      200 miles (diesel)
Number built for U.S.
service during the War:    2,631
Description:          Improved version of the LCP(L), this was
                      the first model to feature a bow ramp.

LCP(R) at full speed and unloaded.

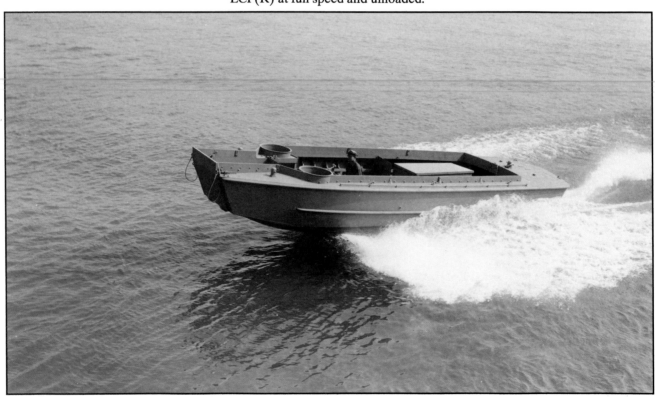

Landing Craft, Personnel (Ramp). Full starboard view of the craft.

LCP(R) on the beach with the ramp lowered.

LCP(R) at the dock with ramp raised.

LCP(R) as viewed from the interior and looking toward the bow. Note the machinegun tubs on either side of the passage, and the coxswain's controls and gauges on the left.

LCP(R) viewed from the interior and looking toward the bow. The white box-like structure in the center foreground is the engine compartment.

LCP(R). Bow on, with the ramp lowered.

LCP(R)—overview of the craft with the ramp lowered.

*USS Gilmer* (APD-11) at the Mare Island Navy Yard, 27 November 1944. Note: 3"/50 D.P. gun. LCPR landing craft and davits.

# LCVP
## Landing Craft, Vehicle/Personnel

Length:                          36'
Beam:                            10'6"
Draft:                           3' aft, 2'2" forward
Displacement:                    18,000 lbs. (light)
Crew:                            3-4
Armor:                           1/4" STS, ramp and sides.
Propulsion:                      225 horsepower Gray diesel, or
                                 250 horsepower Hall-Scott gasoline engine.
Speed:                           9 knots
Endurance:                       102 miles
Number built for U.S.
service during the War:          23,358
Description:                     Featuring a considerably wider ramp than
                                 the LCP(R), it could carry three tons of cargo,
                                 or a light vehicle, or 36 personnel.

Landing Craft, Vehicle, Personnel (LCVP).

LCVP built by Matthews. Photograph dated 31 January 1944.

LCVP built by Chris-Craft. Photograph dated 17 November 1943.

An LCVP about to unload a ___ the beach.

An LCVP being manhandled off a beach.

LCVPs approaching Leyte, October 1944. Note the .30 caliber machinegun mounted on the port side of the craft.

A jeep hitting the surf.

An LCVP
cradled within
an LCM.

This photograph was taken from within the
hold of an LCVP—looking toward the stern
and the coxswain's position. The fellow in
the picture ("Shorty" Connors) is sitting on
the wheel.

# Leroy Hazel, BM 2/C

*Someone sent me this questionnaire one time asking me what my life was like in the service. The first thing the questionnaire asked was, when you got to this foreign port, wherever it was; "How did the people greet you," "What did they say to you?" I don't know, they were Japanese, and they weren't too happy to see me!*

The guy that talked me into getting into the Navy, Bill Mueller, worked with me at Kraft Cheese, down by Navy Pier. I had tried to join the Navy before, but my old man wouldn't let me because I was an only child. Anyway, this guy says, "Why don't we join the Reserves?" It wasn't such a bad idea; two week cruise during the summer, train once a month and get paid for it (I think it was eighteen dollars a month)—we'd have it made! Anyway, I got called out to active service before he did. I was gone and Bill was still sitting in Chicago.

Much later on, at the 'canal (Guadalcanal), we had a destroyer sunk and these guys came across on a Swedish liberty ship. They were coming into Tulagi Harbor and they ran aground on the coral. The Merchant Marine, and I shouldn't knock the Merchant Marine, but when we went aboard, they had all of the matting for aircraft runways and they wouldn't unload the ship because they weren't longshoremen. The Navy on the island had to go on board, rig everything up and unload this ship.

In the meantime, one of the Marine colonels said, "I want that sonofabitch off that reef within twenty-four hours. If it ain't, I'm gonna blow it right out of the water because you're attracting bombers!" Meanwhile, there were the survivors off of this destroyer (an APD—an old four piper), and one of them looked awfully familiar. I said, "Hey, don't I know you?" and, sure enough, it was this guy that joined when I did. He'd got stuck on the *Calhoun* and, when we got the ship off the next day, he went back to Guadalcanal and got on the *Little*. That afternoon they sank the *Little*. He got on the *Gregory* and, two days later, they sank the *Gregory*. So that's why he's called the "Unsinkable Bill Mueller."

As a member of the Naval Reserve in Chicago, we were the first division to be called to active duty—two weeks before Christmas 1940. We went out to Portland, Oregon, where we were assigned to the *Heywood*—one of the very first amphibious APAs. Every division called out after that had to go through Navy boot camp, but I never went.

```
               23rd DIVISION, 6th BATTALION
               USNR ARMORY, CHICAGO, ILL.

                    December 10, 1940

From:          Acting Commanding Officer, 23rd Division.
To:            All Personnel of the 23rd Division

Subject:       MOBILIZATION FOR ACTIVE DUTY.


     1.        This division will leave for Portland,
Oregon on Wednsday, December 18, 1940 at 1:00 PM from
the Union Station, Chicago, Illinois.

     2.        All men will be at the Armory on Wednsday,
December 18, 1940 at 8:30 AM. No man will be allowed to
leave the Armory after reporting for duty.

     3.        All Navy Clothing and Equipment must be
be at the Armory, Monday Night, December 16, 1940 in order
that it can be prepared for shipment.

     4.        All men will be required to carry a
Ditty Box or Bag on the Train, as the Sea Bags will be
stored in the Baggage Car and will not be available
enroute.

                    Walter D. Hantelman
          _____
                    Walter D. Hantelman
```

This is the *USS Heywood* prior to conversion. While Hazel and his shipmates worked on her conversion, they lived on the *Neville* which was berthed beside her.

This was the *USS Heywood*. The *Heywood*, at the time this photograph was taken, had four 3-inch cannon—two aft and two forward. The gun at the center of the stern was a 5-inch "51." The 5-inch was supposed to be a surface gun, a weapon totally unsuited for our purposes. The 3-inch guns were eventually replaced with 40 millimeter guns that were far more useful against enemy aircraft.

U.S.S. HEYWOOD

We had a hundred reservists from Oregon, a hundred reservists from Chicago, and fifty "China Boys" (sailors who had already been in for four or eight years and, because of this, most likely spent some time in China.) One of these guys, a Bosun's Mate by the name of Red Marshall, had sixteen years and was only a Second Class—he kept getting broke (reduced in rank) all the time for things like getting drunk, getting in fights, and so on. As a matter of fact, after getting into port one time at Norfolk, Red decided that he was going to go home to see his folks. His last visit had been twelve years before, so he thought it was time to check in and see how things were going. Well, Red got all decked out in his dress uniform, took off, and it was no more than two hours later that we got a call from the local brig that Red was being held there for destroying a bar!

Red was one of the strongest men I have ever known. As an example, when you would have to put an eye in a ten-inch hawser, you would take a fid (a wooden stick tapered at one end) and drive it through the rope by hitting it with a mallet. Red, on the other hand, would simply twist this massive rope open with his bare hands, jam his thumb in where the strands of the rope separated, and insert the line like threading a needle.

It's always seemed kind of odd to me because they say that war wasn't planned. Here I was a reservist, trained for a destroyer, and I come out to this ship that has landing craft on it. What I mean is, who foresaw that we were going to have to have landing craft, and why was I out here a full year before the war started? I have a big suspicion that they knew a year ahead of time what was going on. I don't think, personally, that the attack on Pearl Harbor was such a surprise. If you remember, after World War I, they said that 'Mother was never going to send her son to foreign soil'—so how better to get your people to go to a foreign soil than to have them come here and hit us first? They attacked us, right? So now we have to defend ourselves—it's alright!

So we went out, we're living in an oceanic terminal, and sleeping in hammocks (everybody was falling out of those things like it was going out of style). We got the ship ready, went up to Bremerton, and picked up provisions; it was a two-week process in which we also had guns put on (.50 machineguns, four 3-inch and one 5-inch gun). Then we came back down the coast, went to San Pedro, picked up all of our landing craft and went out to San Clemente and practiced landing.

At first, the idea was to throw out about 600 feet of line so, when the boat hit the beach, you'd snub the line down so she wouldn't broach. Well, that's fine except when you're backing off you've got to get all of that line back in the boat without it getting tangled up in the screw. Well, we found that didn't work. Then they came along and put a big shield up in the back of the boat, but that didn't work either because it was a big pain in the butt trying to climb over that thing—back and forth—so they eliminated that. From then on, they decided that it would all be up to the coxswain to know how to land that boat and how to handle it. We didn't go to any school except for the training we took down in San Clemente.

There were about twenty guys from the ship that were sent to the Higgins' plant in New Orleans where he showed them what the boat was like, how it was made, what to do with it, and what to expect from it. Then these guys came back and taught us.

Once our training was over, we went through the Panama Canal, picked up the Marines in Norfolk, and proceeded to Iceland. I ended up making three trips to Iceland. We had started out with an old Skipper who was just about ready to retire; he could hardly see anymore, he was getting too old, but he was assigned to the ship. When he finally left, we gave him a gold watch, and he called the whole crew to the promenade deck and said:

"When I first came aboard, I looked at this old rust bucket and thought 'What the hell is this?' I looked over the list of men and I got two hundred feather merchants (reservists) and fifty guys from China, and thought 'What the hell kind of a crew is this going to be like?' Then, as time went on in training, I see all of these guys running around on the deck—deck hands—they got these great big knives in their sheaths, and nobody ever walked on this ship. If they wanted to get from one side of the ship to the other, they swung across on a line, or they'd go all the way up to the top of a mast and come sliding down on a cable—I thought this was the biggest band of pirates I had ever met in my life! Now that I've been on it for over a year, and I'm retiring, this was the best damn crew that I ever had serve under me!"

This made us all feel really good.

I was sitting in the mess hall one Sunday afternoon, writing a letter home, when I heard about the Japanese surprise attack on Pearl Harbor. I couldn't believe it—we were at war, and this was supposed to be a year's cruise for training! Naturally I was really tee'd off that they would pull something like that; in fact, the whole crew didn't know what to think—how they (the Japanese) could have gotten away with something like that. I had been to Pearl Harbor in early 1941—sometime around March or April. One of the things that amazed me was that when you went into Pearl Harbor, all of the ammunition on board the ship had to be removed from the ready boxes and stored below deck in the magazine. With no ammunition immediately at hand, I could see how the guys weren't prepared for the attack.

After we made that first trip to Iceland, we came back and loaded the Army, but when we started back we had engine trouble and pulled into Boston Navy Yard. While we were there, somebody decided that we should get some crabs for dinner. Well, they got the crabs, brought them aboard and, while we were eating them, some other guy thought that we should have something suitable to drink with this fine meal. Believe it or not, the idea they came up with was for us to drink the alcohol mixed in with the shellac they stored in the paint locker on board the ship. Now, the object is to strain the shellac through a loaf of bread—holding the loaf lengthwise—so the shellac goes down through the whole loaf and filters out most everything but the alcohol. Instead, they simply dumped the shellac in a basin, threw some oranges and chunks of bread in with it, and ladled the drink out into cups. Anyway, Red Marshal drank more than his share of the concoction and passed out. He had this big, flaming red beard that jutted out from his face so, because of all of the shellac he had drunk, I would swear that you could have stood on his beard without bending a hair. We had to have Red taken ashore and have his stomach pumped out—he damn near died from what we were drinking.

Once the ship was fixed, and we were ready to go back out and catch up with the convoy, the guy in charge of the Army asked, "Where's our escort?" Well, we didn't have one—it was all up there with the convoy. This guy replied, "You're going to take this ship out, with all those (German) submarines out there, and catch the convoy?" When we said that we were, the Army guy said that they weren't going, so they all got off. Well, this was Christmas of '41, so we were in Boston for Christmas and then we had to go down to New York right away. We went down the Cape Cod Canal in this big five hundred and seven foot ship—it was like going down the Chicago River—I mean, it's just a river! They gave us two Coast Guard escorts, but they couldn't keep up with us, I mean this "Old Man" was going to New York, no matter what—he was going to be "in New York for New Years, come hell or high water!" So, we made it. We then picked up the Army again, went back out, dumped the Army off and picked up the Marines.

While we were up there, we had a North Atlantic storm in Reykjavik Harbor. We had both anchors out, turning one third ahead, but we were still losing ground. We had a couple of boats out, and the officer said, "Go out and get those boats, we're going to take them aboard." We went out, got in the boats—we had a hell of a time getting in them—and we came alongside the ship. Well, one minute we had a thirty-five foot free-board (the distance from the ocean's surface to where we were going to get picked up). One minute I'm looking the guys in the ship in the eye, talking to them, and the next I'm thirty-five feet below them telling them, "I don't think we're going to be able to do this." We ended up running the boats onto the beach, and took out the boats' anchor lines and buried them on the beach so we could wait out the storm.

We went back to Norfolk, delivered the Army to Iceland, took the Marines off and went back to Norfolk again. All of the Marines got off and we went south, down through the Panama Canal again, around to San Diego and picked up those same Marines who had, in the meantime, travelled by land to get there. From there, we took the Marines to Samoa, picked up civilian workmen (they were pulling all of the civilians off of those islands) and took them back to San Diego. About this time, April 1942, we picked up a Marine lieutenant who was supposed to be "off his clock" from battle fatigue. We were bringing him back to the States, so they put him in the brig and he'd take out a light bulb and chew on it, and stuff like that. I don't know if he was trying to prove he was crazy, or what, but one day they went down to let him out of the brig to eat, or something, and he ran out to the main deck and dove overboard. We're underway, no escorts or anything, and there he was out there swimming in the ocean. Right away, we circle and lower the whale boat. We got the whale boat in the water, but it wouldn't start. In the meantime, this guy's swimming around and sharks start appearing. Right away, the Marine contingent on the ship broke out their rifles and started shooting at the sharks to drive them away. They finally paddled the whale boat over to pick this guy up, but now he was frantically swimming for the boat. I'm not sure, but I don't think this guy knew there were sharks around—I think he thought the other Marines were firing at him! Anyway, one of the boat coxswains on board the whale boat was a big guy—he had to go about 230 pounds. As the Marine made a stroke for the boat, this coxswain grabbed him by the hand and yanked him clear out of the water.

When you cross the equator, the ship holds a ceremony and initiates all of those personnel who have not crossed before. The ship flies the "Jolly Roger" from her mast, and the "shellbacks" (people who have crossed over before) initiate the "pollywogs" (new inductees). They'd sit you up on a plank next to a makeshift pool of water and ask "What are you?" As soon as you'd open your mouth to say Pollywog, they'd cram this brush full of all kinds of slop in, cut your hair, and drop you over backwards into the pool. There'd be guys along the sides of the pool who would dunk you in and, when you came up, they'd say, "Say Shellback!" Before you could get the words out, they'd dunk you back in again. From there, you'd go down a slide while they'd beat your butt the whole way with canvas tubes filled with rags and sand, and soaked in salt water for about a week. You then had to go through a chute, and they'd be waiting at the other end to beat you some more. Once you made it through, you were now a shellback. This photograph shows two pollywogs just beginning their initiation.

From San Diego we went to Wellington, New Zealand, where we picked up the First Marine Paratroopers—it was then that we knew we were in trouble! If going into battle wasn't hardship enough, the New Zealand longshoremen chose this time to go on strike. Our ships weren't "combat loaded" (everything prioritized and packed according to what the Marines would need first for the landing) so, before leaving New Zealand, all of the Marines had to fall out on the dock and do the jobs of the longshoremen—empty the ships of everything and repack them—in the rain! Finally, we went up and practiced landings off the New Hebrides for a little under two days, and then they figured we knew enough to go in.

I'm an old John Wayne fan, Jon Hall, Errol Flynn, so I liked the idea of adventure. Anyway, back when we were going into Samoa this, for me, was ideal; great white beaches, coral water, beautiful natives, the whole shot. Well, about eleven guys and I went ashore, but we stayed too long and our ship had already pulled out. We were able to catch a supply boat going out to the ships but, because he was running an errand and couldn't actually stop at our ship, he pulled alongside while we had to jump for the nets. It wasn't really so bad because I sort of thought of myself as some pirate creeping on board. The only problem was, we were caught coming back on board!

The next day they had Captain's Mast (a period of the day set aside for meting out punishment) aboard the *Heywood*, and when he got to the twentieth guy he said, "I have to make an example out of somebody" and he called my name. I stepped forward, and he said, "I'm awarding you a deck court-martial." Gee, thanks. He handed out ten days in the brig on P&P (Piss and Punk—bread and water), no leave in a foreign port, no advancement in rating for one year, and a twenty dollar fine (at that time I was making about thirty-six dollars a month).

Later, after leaving New Zealand and getting underway, they called for boat crews who would stay with the Marines on the island. I figured I haven't got anything to lose, so I might as well volunteer. After volunteering, I went down and packed my stuff—they had told us that all we would need was two days worth of clothing because they would be coming back for us shortly. While I was packing, my buddy came down and said, "What the hell are you doing?"

"Man," I replied, "I got shore duty on this beautiful South Pacific Island, with all these beautiful natives, I'm going ashore!"

This guy left, came back in a little while and he started packing. I said, "Where the hell are you going?"

He said, "I'm going with you, I told your Mother I'd take care of you!"

In the meantime, another buddy of ours came down and said, "Where the hell are you two guys going?"

"Aw, man," we said, "we got this deal where we're going to have shore duty on a Pacific island—all the grass skirts" and all this crap.

Five minutes later, he came back down and he started packing and said "I'm going with you!"

So this was how we got shore duty on this beautiful South Pacific island—Guadalcanal!

U.S.S. HEYWOOD

At Sea,
5 August 1942.

PLAN OF THE DAY

Sea Routine:-

0530 All Hands. Turn on fresh water in crew and troop washrooms until 0630.

0600 Modified General Quarters.
Breakfast.

Sunrise: Lighten Ship.
Secure from General Quarters and set condition 2 Mike Afirm ( 4 20MM forward and 2 aft to be manned in addition to 3" ).

0730 Turn to - routine cleaning
Ship's work as directed. Secure fueling gear. Complete nets.

0900 All boat coxswains, boat signalmen, radiomen and wave commenders report to port side of Cafeteria.

1015 Pay crew semi-monthly money in after crews compartment. Lieut. Comdr. Greene, witnessing officer.

1100 Dinner.

1300 Quarters.
General Drills and Debarkation Drills.

1600 Supper.

Sunset: Darken Ship.
Set condition 2 Mike Sail.

1800 First movie.-- Same as last night ("Passport to Alcatraz").

1945 Second movie.-- As above.

NOTES(A) From Comtaskfor:-

ON AUGUST SEVENTH THIS FORCE WILL RECAPTURE TULAGI AND GUADALCANAL ISLANDS WHICH ARE NOW IN THE HANDS OF THE ENEMY X

IN THIS FIRST FORWARD STEP TOWARD CLEARING THE JAPANESE OUT OF CONQUERED TERRITORY WE HAVE STRONG SUPPORT FROM THE PACIFIC

FLEET AND FROM THE AIR SURFACE AND SUBMARINE FORCES IN THE SOUTH PACIFIC AND AUSTRALIA X IT IS SIGNIFICANT OF VICTORY THAT WE SEE

HERE SHOULDER TO SHOULDER THE US NAVY MARINES AND ARMY AND THE AUSTRALIAN AND NEW ZEALAND AIR NAVAL AND ARMY SERVICES X I HAVE

CONFIDENCE THAT ALL ELEMENTS OF THIS ARMADA WILL IN SKILL AND COURAGE SHOW THEMSELVES FIT COMRADES OF THOSE BRAVE MEN WHO

ALREADY HAVE DEALT THE ENEMY MIGHTY BLOWS FOR OUR GREAT CAUSE X GOD BLESS YOU ALL X R K TURNER REAR ADMIRAL US NAVY COMMANDING

F. A. HARDESTY,
Commander, U.S. Navy,
Executive Officer.

The *USS Heywood*'s "Plan Of The Day" for 5 August 1942. Of particular interest are the notes on the bottom third of the page—the planned recapture of Guadalcanal.

At Guadalcanal they landed with no return fire, because it turned out that the Japs ran. Over on Tulagi, it was a different story: the Japs didn't have any place to run, so they dug in; that's where the Raiders and Paratroopers went in. When we landed at Gavutu, we landed with three hundred and fifty men. We figured that this small island couldn't have that many defenders, but the Marine officers told us "Don't go away, we might have to come back off of this beach!" Now, going in on a landing and putting troops on the beach is one thing; going back in to take them off is something else! Well, they landed and took a hell of a lot of casualties and, after about four days, they finally took the island.

When I was going in there, I passed two destroyers who were firing support fire. On top of this high hill peak I see one of our dive bombers coming down and return fire going back up, and I said to myself, "This ain't gonna be no John Wayne movie, this is for keeps!"

We laid off of the island about one hundred yards, watching the whole show—my coxswain was on the stern, while I was behind the engine. I thought that there were bees flying around, so I said to my coxswain, "Are the bees bothering you?"

"No, stupid," he said, "those are bullets!"

This was how I learned about Jap snipers up in the tops of the palm trees.

In the boat next to ours, a man was standing up smoking his pipe. One of those sniper rounds passed by knocking the pipe out of his mouth. When he bent over to get his pipe, another bullet grazed his back—had he not bent over at that precise moment, the bullet would have undoubtedly cut him down. Another coxswain was hanging over the side of his boat, patching a hole at the water-line, when two bullets struck his boat just two inches to either side of his chest. Our Boat Division Officer was looking through his binoculars when his vision became blurred. He took the binoculars down to see what was wrong and there, in the center of the bridge, was a new quarter-inch hole!

Our ships all left the second day, because this was when we had that big sea battle (the Battle of Savo Island) where we lost four cruisers: the *Quincy*, the *Astoria*, the *Vincennes* and the Australian cruiser *Canberra*. I later heard that many of our boys on the transports began cheering when they saw ships in the distance hit by shell fire and begin catching fire. They didn't know that those stricken vessels were our own! Anyway, our ships all got underway and left us. They had only had time to unload half of what we were sup-

posed to get, so now here we were on this island, and we had virtually nothing. We had four 90mm aircraft guns behind us with enough ammunition for only fifteen minutes—after that it was all over, it would be hand-to-hand. Luckily, the Japs never came back.

The first night after the ships left, we pulled all of our boats up on the beach. We decided we weren't going to sleep in the mud, so we took out our life jackets, laid them down in the well of the boat, and planned on sleeping there for the night.

This Marine lieutenant came down and said: "What're you doing, fellas?"

"Bedding down for the night, sir," we replied.

"Where, in there?" he said, "Did you ever stop to consider there's Japanese on this island, and they have no way off—their best bet is a boat, or blow it up! Do you think you ought to sleep in there?"

I immediately got out and found myself a hole!

The third day we had an air raid, and all these Marines went off in a hole. I was running when some Marine hollered, "Hey, stupid, where're you going?"

"I don't know," I said.

"Well, get your butt in here before somebody blows it off," he replied.

So I went in there with the Marines and, naturally, I'm shaking—I don't know what the hell to do. Well, this Marine gives me a shot of Sake and, after that one, I could have licked the World. Nothing bothered me from then on.

We didn't have any clothes except for what we had on. My uniform usually consisted of blue dungarees, lighter blue chambray shirt, a blue-dyed undershirt, and Marine Corps "boondockers" (boots). While I was on the island, my headgear was a helmet and I'd wear a pistol belt with bandoliers of ammunition for my rifle. I threw away my gas mask and filled the pouch up with ammunition for my .45 pistol. Our diet consisted of roots, green bananas, coconuts and some rice that we had confiscated from the Japs. That went on for about three weeks! For a time, however, we did have our own additional supply of drinking alcohol—courtesy of the Japanese for, when we took Gavutu, we found a number of Jap torpedoes laying up on the docks. Somebody got the bright idea of draining the alcohol out of them, so that's what we did—powerful stuff for the nerves!

After all of these years of reading things, I realize now that the guys that put us on this island couldn't do anything for us and had decided to let this be another Bataan! I learned afterwards from Father Gehring,

"The Padre of Guadalcanal," that the only one who saved our butts was Halsey (Vice Admiral William F. Halsey Jr., Commander of the South Pacific Theater).

Halsey said, "If those guys have guts enough to stand there and fight, then you have guts enough to go back there and help them!"

If it wasn't for him, I probably wouldn't be here today.

After about two weeks, the guys on the 'Canal started finding more Japs coming back—they especially tried to land their forces at night. We got bombed every day at noon, and then we got shelled at night by cruisers, destroyers, battleships, what have you. That went on for a solid month, and none of our ships were coming back except for an occasional APD, a submarine and, once in a while, an airplane. Everything was what you had, you weren't getting any more!

My job was to operate the boat and, when a ship could get in, we'd go out there and unload it. The object was to get that thing unloaded as fast as possible and get it out. Every once in a while an AK (cargo ship) would come in, or maybe two APs (personnel transports), and we would take all of the boats and go across the bay. Usually about noon, most every day, we could expect a Jap bombing raid. We had just finished unloading the ships one day and me and my buddy were out in the boat when they sounded "Air Alert." Well, we pulled out into the Bay and, looking up, we saw the Japanese bombers coming in—there we were, watching and counting them. Something dawned on me; if those Japs drop their bombs and miss the Island, they're going to come right out here in the water where we're sitting! About that time, here come the aircraft dropping their bombs and, sure enough, bombs are landing in the water as well as the land. We hauled out of there, and the concussion from the bombs going off in the water was so great that the deck boards (bilge covers) were blowing up about four feet high each time a bomb exploded. At the same time, our anti-aircraft fire began coming back down all around us. My buddy and I were only wearing our blue hats at the time, and we both dove at the same time for this bucket we had in the boat; he and I had both thought of using it for a make-shift helmet! A lot of good that bucket could do!

One night, after the supply ships had left, my buddy and I were left over on Guadalcanal. We had no place to go, and didn't know what to do, so we took off on foot and came across this medical tent. The people there said that we could stay there if we wanted, so we beached the boat, went back and they gave us a couple of stretchers we could lay on. While we were in there laying down, some snipers started firing at our general location.

My buddy said, "Don't you think we ought to get out of here?"

"You got your helmet on?" I asked and, being a wise guy, I said, "You're in a medical tent, you're laying on a stretcher—what more could you ask for? If you get hit, you're right here!"

We stayed and, just about that time, the first fourteen-inch Japanese projectile came through there—it sounded like the Express; it hit and bounced right off the ground.

The Marines had built foxholes where they covered the holes with a layer of coral, a layer of palm tree trunks, another layer of coral, and another layer of tree trunks, and then covered the whole thing with palm leaves, so it was actually like a little fort. Well, my buddy and I took off from the medical tent and were tearing down through this field when I spotted one of those bunkers. We dove in, doing a half twist, side-by-side, never even touching each other.

When we landed inside, a guy said "There's no more room in here."

I said, "There's always room for two more, and I ain't getting out of here—not with those shells coming in!"

For forty-five minutes two Japanese battleships pounded that place trying to hit the airfield; and yet, I wasn't what you'd call really scared because I was in this foxhole with all of this stuff on top of me and I felt safe. Nevertheless, if only one shell had hit there it would have been all over.

During my time, I saw a couple of guys just break down because of the strain. I just couldn't figure out why they'd go off the deep end. You're trained to do this, you've been doing it for a year—I don't know. Maybe I was dumb, or stupid, or didn't understand, or I was just too young to realize what the hell was going on. One guy I knew a little bit just started more or less hallucinating, he started crying; when he talked he didn't make any sense, and he had this faraway look in his eyes, and we finally got him to a corpsman. That was the last I ever saw of him, but there weren't too many of those, maybe a couple. Maybe it was the fact that they were afraid of being killed. Shelling really didn't bother us all that much because, given the fact that it was flat trajectory, it had to get pretty close to you to do any damage. Bombing, on the other hand, was coming down right on top of you, and that could get pretty scary!

After every sea battle, I had to go out and pick up survivors—now that was bad. The first couple of sea battles during the initial phase of Guadalcanal were really bad, for we picked up guys that were burnt—and I mean to a crisp. We took then back to the island and buried them but, in the process, somebody'd accidentally kick an arm, a skull, and this burned flesh would fall off on the wooden deck and get walked on—mashing the mess down into the wood. After about a week, the smell was something awful. We used salt water, gasoline, everything we could think of to cleanse the decks and remove the smell, but we just couldn't seem to get rid of it. As a result, when we'd cruise down the bay, this smell blew back in our faces the whole time. Our only option was to turn the boats around and run them backwards—we had to do this for almost a month before that smell went away. I had one guy I picked up that had his eye in his hand; it was still attached to his socket by the nerve, so I hope they were able to save it.

One thing that struck me as odd, one time, was when I went out to pick up survivors and there in the water were all of these Pea Coats—hundreds of them just floating on the waves. Here we were in the South Pacific, one hundred degree temperatures, and all of these Pea Coats floating by.

Let's say you were on a destroyer that was three hundred feet long, and a cruiser or battleship was firing at you. There ain't no place to go, you're trapped; shells are coming all over and the only place to go is in the drink! The ship is hit—badly—and going down, and you've got to get off; now you know that that's got to affect you. Jumping off of a ship can be a hell of an experience, even under ideal conditions. I jumped off of one during one of our swimming parties one time, and the height from which I jumped tore my arms back to my sides—despite the fact that I had locked my fingers before jumping. When I struck the water, I went down so deep that I thought I'd never come back up. Now add to that the fact that most times a stricken ship is surrounded by a layer of oil burning on the water. There are two ways you can deal with this: you can either swim under the fire and hope you come up where it isn't burning, or you can swim through the flames using a breast stroke to keep the fire out of your face!

All of those guys that I did pick up, that were mobile, were kind of in a daze—like they didn't know what was happening—but they didn't go off of the deep end. They'd just sit there quietly in little groups, and it was obvious that they were in shock. Now I could see where those guys could be affected by "shell shock."

Our engineer wouldn't ride with us anymore after we once had to play tag with a destroyer. When we'd go around one side of the island, there that destroyer'd be taking shots at us. We'd go back around the other side and there he was, waiting to get us. Anyway, while we were going down the harbor with this Jap destroyer firing at us, my engineer jumped over the side and swam to the beach. After that, he wouldn't ride with us anymore.

This new guy, by the name of Whitney, was the ship's gambler—he always gambled, always had money, and he was nuttier than a fruitcake. He used to walk around with a helmet with a bullet hole right in the front center. He always told everybody that he had it on when the bullet entered, but he didn't, it had actually been hanging on the rail of the boat when the bullet struck. He had a Japanese officer's Sam Browne belt with a pistol, and he wore that all of the time. Whenever a ship would come in, Whitney would go aboard and tell them "sea stories;" get cigarettes, candy, and all, because they wanted to hear this stuff. One day we were going across Ironbottom Bay (the body of water separating Tulagi from Guadalcanal) when this big shark swam up alongside the boat. I'm digging out the '03s to use against the shark when, all of a sudden, this guy puts a knife in his mouth and dives over the side. We had to stop, come back and lower the ramp for him and, when we picked him up I asked, "What the hell do you think you're doing?"

"I'm gonna get me a shark, man," he replied. We had shark meat!

One day, Whitney decided to make some of his own "Hooch." So he got some of our water barrels and filled them with papaya juice, pineapple juice, sugar and some other stuff, sealed the barrels and buried them on the island for about a week. When we dug them up and filtered the contents through some gauze, Whitney was determined to be the first to test the results. He drank about two ounces, said, "This is great stuff," bent over at the waist—and stayed that way. We picked him up, took him to a cot and laid him down, but we couldn't unbend him! When we pushed down on his chest, his legs would come up. When we pressed down on his legs, his chest and head would come up.

We rounded up a corpsman who took one look and said, "This guy's dead!" Whitney wasn't dead but he stayed bent like that for about two days. This was one case where I can say that I saw somebody petrified drunk.

We went alongside one of our destroyers one time that was on fire, and Whitney boarded it and went down below deck to see if there were any survivors. It must have been about August 7th, the ship's crew had just gotten paid, and there was money all over the place because of the explosion. Now remember, this guy's a gambler, he likes money. He said that he couldn't even pick up one dollar for, when he looked around, he saw that the force of the explosion had blown guy's bodies into spaces where a body couldn't fit.

In 1946 there was a train wreck in Chicago, where the train tipped over and people were trapped in the cars. I read it in the paper, or heard it on the radio, that this Navy man was in there carrying people out—it was little George Whitney! I called every hotel in Chicago, trying to find that son-of-a-gun, but I could never find him.

At night time the "Tokyo Express" would come through around two or three o'clock in the morning. We used to call it the "Tokyo Express" because they would come down from Rabaul to bring reinforcements and supplies to the 'Canal. Nine times out of ten it would be cruisers and destroyers but, occasionally, there were two battleships that would come through as well. Even though we only had about five functional aircraft on Guadalcanal, our guys needed aviation fuel; they were out of it. The *Amberjack* (a submarine) took most of her stuff out and filled up with AVGAS. She came in on a Sunday morning when three Jap destroyers were shelling the hell out of us. The Skipper of the *Amberjack* was mad as hell because he had to lay on the bottom; he still had torpedoes, but he couldn't take the chance of surfacing and attacking the destroyers for fear that if he were hit at all the AVGAS and submarine would be gone. That same night I was sitting over at what we called "Government Wharf"—a dock where our main office was, and me and my buddy had the night watch. We were sitting there, B.S.ing, when all of a sudden we got lit up like daylight and thought, "Oh, my God, a Jap destroyer!"

It didn't shoot, or anything, so we thought,"What the hell!," and then the blinkers started. We jumped in our boat, went out, and here was the *Amberjack*—it had come in so quietly that we had never even heard it. Anyway, we went out there, pulled alongside, and those guys gave us everything they had; canned fruit, clothes, toilet paper, candy, cigarettes—they emptied out the whole damn submarine of everything but what they would need on the return trip. I always wanted to see these guys, somewhere along the line, and thank them personally, but she was later sunk up at Vella Lavella. That kind of hit home—it bothered me.

Sometime during October one of our ships pulled in around Tulagi Harbor at night and were going to unload. They had their boats out, their lights on, and they were unloading. I was standing there with my buddy and a Marine and I looked out and the Marine said:

"Oh, look, we got air cover!"

"Uh, uh, can't be," I said, "because we can't put our airplanes back on the Island at night—those are Japs."

"Naw," he said, "see the running lights."

"Those aren't running lights," I replied, "those are exhausts."

Just about that time the Japanese aircraft dropped two bombs; luckily they straddled the ship. This Marine turned around and hit the deck—flat out; I literally ran over top of him! Anyway, this ship got underway and left all of her boats. The boat crews pulled alongside and scrambled up the ropes to get back on board, but all of the boats were left stranded out in the harbor. Later on we went out and pulled them back in; each guy would take one boat and tow it back with his own.

Once, we were coming across Ironbottom Bay with a Marine colonel, his jeep, a couple of aides, and it was by ourselves—unescorted. We got about a mile from Tulagi when the boat just quit running. What were we going to do, we sure couldn't paddle it the rest of the way. Anyway, this buddy of mine who had gone to school in New Orleans to learn all about Higgins Boats went down and discovered that the electric fuel pump had gone out. He took the top off of the pump and moved the valve by finger—that's how we got that boat to shore!

We had this Jap destroyer that came in every morning about dawn, at which point he'd shell the hell out of us. This same Marine colonel called us all together, sailors and Marines alike, and said, "Listen, I want everybody down on the point of the Island with whatever you got as far as firepower."

They moved down some 37s (37 millimeter cannon), some mortars, and whatever, and he said, "We're gonna sink that sonofabitch!"

Here I had a .45 and an '03 and I thought, "What am I gonna do to a destroyer?"

Well, the colonel didn't care, he said, "I don't care

if you just stand there and piss in the ocean – **everybody on the point.**"

So everybody moved down that night and, thank God, the destroyer didn't come in the next morning.

There was a river bisecting Florida Island – the main island on the other side of Ironbottom Bay from Guadalcanal. I was sent up that river one day with a boatload of food and ammunition to re-supply a squad of Marines acting as coast watchers at the mouth of the river. Anyway, when we initially landed at Gavutu, Tulagi, and the rest, the Japs that could escape swam over to Florida and hid throughout the island. Here we were, making our way up this river like we were in our right minds when it dawned on me that those Japs are starving – they need food! What was to stop them from ambushing us right out here in the middle of nowhere? Never once, during our two trips up there, did the Japs ever bother us. It was funny, but the Marines up there in this village looked like they had really "gone native." Since their uniforms had rotted, they had to resort to native dress. It was quite a sight to behold!

Another time the Marines put two 5-inch fifty-ones (something like an 'over and under' pair of cannons)

up and, when another destroyer came in about midnight – shelling the hell out of us – the Navy went up to man those guns because they were naval guns. We went up there and the destroyer was going back and forth at its leisure, firing shells and star shells.

Our Captain said, "OK, the top gun will fire the star shell while the bottom gun will fire armor piercing."

We went ahead and fired and the star shell was just about like a match – practically no illumination at all. When we opened the breech to reload, that Jap spotlight shown right down our barrel. At this point we decided to end this; we closed it down because we couldn't do nothing – it was dark and we couldn't see anything. We found out the next day that there was a cruiser out there, beyond the destroyer, that had come in to draw fire. Had we opened fire, I wouldn't be here now, 'cause he had us pin-pointed. Those Marines had put those two guns up the hill by hand, piece by piece. Talk about tough men!

Whenever I saw the Marines come aboard my boat, I knew it was going to be a tough landing, but I was happy they were Marines because, as far as I'm con-

Troops debarking by means of rope ladders from the mother ship to an LCVP.

cerned, the Army just weren't amphibious landing troops; they didn't have the knowledge or training for that. We also hauled New Zealand Army troops, and they were rugged boys, but they couldn't climb the nets—they'd get about half way on these debarkation nets and freeze. They were powerful, big boys, but there was something about going over the side of the ship and climbing down that net to get into our boats that they couldn't handle.

I don't think the Army got the same kind of training that the Marines went through—the Marines were trained to be more of an individual, everybody knew what he's supposed to do—they didn't need someone to tell them. The Army kind of depended on the sergeant, or the corporal to tell them, where the Marines knew what their jobs were and did it.

When a Marine landed on the beach, they didn't walk to the end of the ramp and step off. No matter how deep the water was, they just jumped off and fanned out—they're gone, I mean they didn't hesitate and, if there's a ridge, the first they'd do was get behind that ridge.

I knew a Marine officer, Major Harry L. Torgerson, the greatest guy in the world, and this guy wasn't afraid of nothing. That fella had gone through hell and high water, 'cause I knew that he knew what he was doing! That guy was something else—nothing scared him, absolutely nothing. We had caves on all of these islands, and the Japs would go in them and we couldn't get them out. We didn't have flame throwers at that time, so we had to either wait them out or go in and get them. This Torgerson used to carry blocks of TNT and sometimes he'd tape two or four together and make the wick only about an inch long. He always smoked a cigar, so he'd go to the opening of the cave, light the wick with his cigar, go in and throw it and then come running out. One time he came out hitting the deck, after having lost all of his clothes—the wick had been too short and the blast had torn his clothing off. The only thing he said was that he'd use a little longer wick next time. Nothing bothered him—there could be snipers shooting at us, shell fire, and he'd just be sitting there watching everything and passing out orders.

I saw Major Torgerson once after the islands down in New Zealand and they had used the First Marines in the fighting in "Bloody Ridge." They came out of there with very few people—they almost lost the whole battalion—them and the Raiders, both.

I saw that he was kind of limping, so I asked him, "What the hell happened to you, did you get hit?"

"Naw," he said, "we came back and I parachute jumped and broke my ankle, and now they stuck me behind a desk."

He survived the war, left the service as a lieutenant colonel with a chest full of ribbons, but died of a heart attack in his driveway in New York when he was only 44 years old.

The same thing at Iwo; the Japs had the guys pinned down on the beach, but our guys just kept rushing. Why does a man do this, because he says it's my job and I have to? My buddies depend on me? What is it that makes you do this? I could never figure out what I had done, I just assumed this was what had to be done and I did it. I never thought to myself, "Am I gonna get hurt,...am I gonna get killed?" My only thought at the time was that I had to get the men on my boat to the beach. If it got me, it got me. I never saw, in all of the landings, a boat that was seaworthy not go in to the beach. To this day I really believe that our landings were a lot like that poem about the "Charge of the Light Brigade"—guns to the right, guns to the left, guns to the front, airplanes overhead, and "into the valley of death" we sailed.

The first two months we were there at Guadalcanal, we were always expecting a landing where the Japs would try to take it away from us, so we always had to stand night watches. They always teamed up one sailor with one Marine—never two sailors, because we sailors didn't know what we were doing—we weren't combat troops. I was with a Marine one night when they called "Condition Black"—they expected a landing at any time.

The Marine said to me: "You know, this ain't gonna be no Wake Island or Bataan Death March, we're here and we stay here until it's over—one way or the other!"

"Oh boy," I thought, "this guy's got a real attitude," so I said, "Don't you think we ought to dig a foxhole"

"Naw," he replied, "After the first shell we'll have enough room for both of us."

We're up there, and it's raining, we're in the mud, and I thought, "This ain't no place for a Navy man to be—in the mud!" So I pulled my blanket over me, and I'm laying there, and I evidently rolled over on my stomach during the night and I'm dreaming that there must be a Jap spider hole underneath me and he's taken his bayonet and run it up underneath me and caught me right in the chest. I woke up and my chest was really hurting; had this been a dream or was it real? I kind of moved my hand over the ground to see if there was a blade sticking up and what I found was a piece of sharp rock that had been poking me in the chest!

While at Guadalcanal, we sailors lived in bamboo shacks formerly occupied by Chinese laborers who had worked for the Japanese. Because of their previous occupants, we called this collection of shacks "China Town." They were built over the water on stilts, out off the island. The Marine Corps had its own foxholes and gun emplacements and everything, but the Navy said, "hell, we ain't gonna sleep in the mud!" We took over those shacks because it had a pier where we could tie our boats up to.

We were in there one night when I heard this guy say, "Oh, my God." I looked out to see what was wrong and, although it was two o'clock in the morning, it was lit up like broad daylight by Japanese flares. Within the next five minutes, a five-inch shell came right through the roof of that shack. If you ever wanted to see eleven guys get out of that shack, cross the causeway and onto the island, in about one minute flat, then you should have been there! We had one guy, I called him Hillbilly all of the time, and he was never able to walk on that causeway without slipping and falling in the water. That night he never even got his shoes wet!

Just prior to our landing on Bougainville, I had Number 1 Boat on Number 1 Hatch; it was the first boat off all of the time and the last one on. Now there was this kid that was going to stay as a member of the boat crew on Bougainville, and he had his choice of any boat he wanted and he wanted mine. I didn't want to give it up because that was my life—I kept it in tip-top shape. I had a Chris Craft and he had a Higgins—both boats were 36-foot LCVPs, but the Chris Craft had gears for the steering, whereas the Higgins had cables and pulleys, so it didn't work as well (the Chris Craft also had a pointed stern, but the Higgins had a rounded stern—the pointed stern handled waves from behind better). Anyway, the officer came up and told me that I had to give up my boat because this other fellow had his choice. Arguing further wouldn't do any good, and the officer said that right after the landing we would have to pull alongside each other and switch equipment—the things I had needed to stay with the ship so, since he was getting my boat, we'd have to swap life jackets, ropes and all of the rest of the crap. I was concerned because I knew that while we were out there in the middle of the ocean trading things back and forth, the ship would get underway and I'd end up with shore duty again, and I didn't need anymore shore duty!

This kid's boat was the fourth one on the bottom—the last one off the hatch. This put him in the first wave, and me in the fourth wave. When we went in we were supposed to be five minutes apart for landing. They'd land, drop the troops off, and I'd come in right behind them.

Well, our guys shelled too long and we got strafed, so everybody was all bunched up all together. Finally, as this kid went in, I saw my boat get hit by Jap artillery and go up sky high. Then the boat to my right got it, and the boat to my left got it, and I assumed the next one was for me. As I was going in I found I couldn't see too well so, like a stupid idiot, I stood up on the engine cover so I could get a better view. The Marines down in my boat were looking back at me like I was crazy and, at this point, the Marine lieutenant said:

"I don't want to go in here."

"What are you talking about," I replied, "this is my spot."

"I don't want to go in here," he repeated, "Back off!"

The artillery was still shooting, so I backed off and turned stern to the Japanese gun figuring that if he hits me I'll never know it. The lieutenant told me that he wanted to go down the beach about a hundred yards and just about this time, I found out later, a Marine on the beach silenced the gun firing at us by diving into the bunker with a live grenade—sacrificing his life for ours!

After a bit, the lieutenant said that he wanted to go in here, so I turned the boat and drove up on the surf. The lieutenant turned to his men and said, "OK, when the ramp goes down I want everybody to do exactly what I do." When I hit, I dropped the ramp and everybody went out on their hands and knees. I thought that this was a little silly, crawling around already, and then it dawned on me that there was a Jap machine gun clearing the ridge. The ramp was down, I was standing up on the boat, and how I didn't get hit I'll never know.

So I backed off and, as I was heading back out, I picked up a couple of crews that had lost their boats and were swimming in the water. Among them were a couple of hillbillies that had lost their boat and couldn't swim but, under these circumstances, they looked like a pair of torpedoes speeding for my boat—they knew how to swim all of a sudden! One of the guys, a coxswain of that boat, thought that he had been stung by a bee. About this time, it was in '43, they decided we should wear life jackets—those Kapok jobs, and a Jap bullet had hit his collar, entered it, and lay on his neck—burning his skin. He thought it was a bee or something and when he reached up his fingers found this hot projectile!

Prior to the life jackets we wore those inflatable belts. We wore them all of the time, but what we didn't know was that over time they'd rot in the creases so, when we inflated them, they'd just fall apart.

When I was assigned to the *President Adams* after leaving Guadalcanal, I was part of the boat division and, therefore, had no assigned gun station on board the ship. Now, I'm no longer what they call "Ship's Company," I'm with the Boat Division—I can't touch anything on the ship, where before I worked the ship, made the landing, and then would go back to work on

the ship. Now I can't do anything; I'm a Second Class Boat sitting on the ship with nothing to do except see that my boats are taken care of—make sure that they're all in good shape. Well, I must have hollered long and loud enough to get someone's attention, for they assigned me my very own gun position—a .50 machine gun post on the side of the stack where the searchlights used to go. This was great except for the fact that, nine times out of ten, enemy dive bombers use the stack as their aiming point!

Later on in the war, they decided that all landing craft had to be unloaded from the ship before the craft headed for the beach. As a result, the first to be unloaded had to travel around in circles next to the ship while the rest were lowered and took on their passen-

The *USS President Adams*.

gers and cargo. In the earlier landings, however, once a boat was lowered and he saw a hole on the shore, he headed on in and dropped off his people—none of this waiting around stuff! At one point, the *Adams* was considered the fastest unloading transport in the Pacific—she used to put all of her boats in the water in eighteen minutes—nineteen thirty-six footers and four fifty-foot LCMs! As soon as the ship dropped anchor, the boats on the hatches were picked up by the booms and lowered over the sides of the ship, and the boats on the davits were lowered over the sides by cables from their positions.

In April 1944, I received orders to go back home on leave—this was the first leave I'd had since 1941. Don't ask me why, I don't know, but somehow I just didn't want to leave my friends and shipmates. We already knew that we were scheduled to make the landings at Saipan, and I just didn't feel comfortable about leaving. I was especially reluctant to leave my buddy from Oregon, for we had been in it together the whole time.

One day he said to me, "You know, we're going to Saipan, and you can't keep this up without getting hit. Don't you think you better go home?"

I thought about it a lot, and I still didn't want to go, but a few of the newer guys started saying, "This guy must be gay, these two guys are together," and all this crap,

"He don't want to go home. What the hell's with him," so, finally, I went.

When I got into port, they gave me a "seventy-two" (seventy-two hour pass) because they didn't have any room. When I returned from the pass they gave me my travel orders and a thirty day leave. At the end of my leave I was sent to Amphibious School in San Diego, and all I could think was, "what the hell is wrong with you people?"

The training took place in Coronado; it's a nice place, but it's all sand—like being in a damn desert. So I went down there and, of course, my attitude ain't too great. We go out for training and they've got a model ship in the sand, and it's got to be a hundred and some feet long. It's got little boats on it and everything, and I get handed a little boat on a string. They told me to "go out to the stern of the model boat and make a circle, and when we raise the flag on ship calling for an LCM, or whatever, you come alongside." Well, that lasted about a half-hour—I threw the boat in the sand and left. I thought, "the hell with you people, you're nuts!"

The next day I go in, and we're going to learn Morse Code. So there's some kid up there, blinking away and, mind you, most of these guys that were undergoing this training had just got back from the Pacific after two and three years. So he's standing there with a flashlight making dots and dashes, and he says, "What will happen if I do this?"

Some guy from the back of the room pipes up and says, "You'll probably get a bullet right between the damn eyes!" Everybody got up and left—we didn't want any part of this crap.

Then we had to go out in the boats so they could show us how to make landings. Well, I was with about ten guys, we all took off the life jackets, laid down on the deck, out in the sun, and this poor kid, he's about a Seaman 1st, and he says: "Somebody's got to run this boat!"

"Well, you're doing a good job," one of the guys said, "just keep doing it!"

"If you guys don't get up and do this," he said, "I'll get in trouble and they'll send me to **sea**!" UH, HUH—that went over real big—we're talking July of 1944. So then he got no cooperation whatsoever.

In the meantime, a control boat pulled alongside and they said, "I want somebody to beach this boat so that we can show you how to get it off." Now it was **my** turn! I caught the perfect wave and not only beached it, but broached it at the same time. So there it was, sitting up there parallel to the surf.

Well, they came out, and they're pulling and trying to pull alongside, and one of the guys came over and said: "You guys will have to get out and push while we pull."

"NINE TONS OF BOAT YOU WANT ME TO PUSH OFF THE SAND!"

"Yeah," he said, "we've got to get this boat off!"

So I took the line and threw it away and said, "Stick around; this is the way they do it in the Pacific," and I backed that boat off. What I knew was that the boat was designed that if you got water by the screw—I don't care if it was only half way—and you got sea suction, that boat would come off. When the boat was in reverse, it brings water up along the bow and back down through the tunnel, washed back down, washes away the sand and, eventually, you'll pull it off. During one of the sea battles in Guadalcanal we had to go out and pick up survivors when the boats were high and dry. Our coxswain dug a hole so that the water would come up and the sea suction pulled our boat off of there.

I finally told another guy with me, 'I've had it, I

can't stand this any longer." So I went down to the main office and said: "When's the next bucket out of here!"

"Well," he said, "you've only been here two weeks."

"I ain't gonna stay here very much longer," I said, "you either ship me out of here, or I'm gonna leave!" So they gave me a division and made me division P.O.—I was already 2nd Class. So I've got this division of 165 guys, all recruits, they just came into the Navy!

They decided to take one of those spoon bow landing craft and put rockets on the side. They made it a foot longer, then they took these little rockets (equivalent to a five-inch shell) and put twelve on each side in a rack. You could elevate the rack and with a control panel, say I pushed button number one, two rockets would fire—one from each side. If I hit my target, I'd just push the button and go all the way around the clock and they'd all go. I thought, "Boy, this is great, it's just like being a destroyer!"

They told me I'd have to pick a volunteer crew, and I said, "What do you mean 'volunteer crew,' I thought we were all in the Navy?"

So I looked for an engineer, and this guy—he had to be ten years older than I was, he was married and had two kids—and he said, "I'll go."

I said, "What are you, nuts? You don't need this job."

And he said, "No, I want to go with you."

So then I found two seamen—we had a crew of four—and we'd go out during the day and practice. I thought it was neat because they built a cabin out of metal with vision slits—something like an armored gun emplacement.

So then we were shipped to Oregon to pick up the *Pickens* (APA 190). About this time they decided they needed a 1st Class (Petty Officer 1st Class), but I turned it down knowing that if they made me a 1st Class I'd be stuck on this bucket, whereas if I stayed a 2nd Class I'd stand a chance of getting off. Then they decided I should become Chief (Chief Petty Officer).

I had heard the Chief say that, "If I can get Hazel to become Chief, then I can get transferred!"

NO, NO WAY! I wouldn't do nothing but be 2nd Class!

We pulled into San Pedro to pick up boats, and the Skipper and Exec on shore said, "Tomorrow morning we're going to get underway with all boats aboard." Well, he came back the next morning and there were three boats on the ship—nobody knew how to pick

them up.

When I had wanted to show them, they said, "Uh, uh, you can't touch this, you're with the Boat Division."

Anyway, we pulled out into the bay because they kicked us out of port, and we're trying to pick up these boats. There was one other 1st Class "Boats" on board with me that came off the *Jackson*, and he was Bosun Mate of the Watch all of the time because nobody else could do it, and I couldn't do it because I was part of the Boat Division. So we were sitting out there shooting the bull, and they used to put the LCMs on first, and then pick up an LCVP and cradle it inside the LCM. So we were standing there and I look up and there goes this thing across the ship, and I said, "Do you see what I see?" And here it comes back again going to the other side. We had a fifty foot landing craft sailing back and forth across the deck because the ship was rolling. The kid running the winch didn't know what the hell was going on; the guy in charge was a cruiser sailor—he had never done this before—so the 1st Class I was with picked the kid up out of the seat, grabbed ahold of the controls and when the boat came back, bingo!—right in the skids in one shot!

Then they were bringing up the LCVP and, as they were bringing it up across the ship I heard the guy say "Should I release the brake?"

Although I yelled "No, No, No," he tripped the brake and the LCVP came down, hit the ship, split in half and went over the side.

The "Old Man" (ship's captain) had done shore duty in England for the past three years and had been given a choice: either relieve the troops up in the Aleutian Islands, or join the Fleet. He joined the Fleet. So, when you go to sea with somebody like this that doesn't know one end from the other, well, you have an interesting situation.

We were making landings and our "R" Boat was

*USS Pickens* (APA 190)

This was my crew of the Captain's gig. Clockwise from the top: Al Varner, my engineer, was the old man of our crew; the man to his left is D. Grady, a deck hand; I am below him; next to me is an Hawaiian girl; next to her is C. Head, our radioman and above him is A. Schield, another deck hand. Hawaii, January 2, 1945.

This is a photograph of my buddy Randy Bates (on the left), and me, taken in Hawaii in 1944. Randy had been a Navy yard workman in Honolulu and, because he got tired of being called a "slacker," he joined the Navy and ended up with us.

This is a P Boat—the Captain's gig. The ship's carpenters made up the superstructure especially for the Captain.

Another view of the P Boat. We'd put these tires on the gig when it became necessary to push other craft when there were no tugs around.

This was the inside of the Captain's gig. We spent a lot of time making this boat look good!

sitting on the beach one night when I looked up and here comes an LCM right behind us. I yelled at the crew, "Go Forward!" and this LCM landed right on top of me. He didn't see me because it was dark and, with no experience, that's what I had to contend with!

This was all during 1944, so we drew the landings at Lingayen Gulf. By this time I had the "Old Man's" boat, the gig, which was either a P Boat or and R Boat with a cabin on it, fancy stuff with window curtains and all like that! I had the repair boat at the time, and the kid goes into the beach and can't back off; he had power but the boat wasn't moving. We pulled him off and I went underneath and found that he had a wire strut wrapped around the propeller and shaft. We got an old shallow water diving outfit—the type with the hand pumps to send oxygen down to the diver—and when I got down there I found that the wire had formed a loop around the blade. I stuck my hand in there and tried to twist this loop so I could free it from the propeller blade. The boat bobbed up, came back down, struck me in the head and I let go—now I've got my hand trapped inside the loop. Naturally, I started to panic, the mask was filling up with water, I'm blowing bubbles, and luckily I had read a lot of books on diving. Remembering what they had said, the first thing I did was relax, breathe normally, and then attend to the problem. I reached up, gave a good strong twisting pull, and released my hand. When I came up, the guy asked, "What the hell have you been doing down there, I was getting tired of pumping!"

At Iwo Jima those Army DUKWs were used and, while we were laying off the island, one of them came alongside at about midnight, and the guy says, "Where's Red Beach?" We were concerned about Japanese suicide boats at the time and, not taking any chances, my engineer jammed his Thompson submachine gun in the guy's face.

Once certain of his identity, and as he shut off the motor, I said: "See that big island over there? It's right underneath it, you can't miss it."

The DUKW driver said, "OK," but when he turned the key the thing wouldn't start.

Because we used to have to take the "Old Man" to the clubs, and stuff, in the gig, and then have to wait for him—a wait that could last two, three, four, five or six hours—I went to the carpenters one day and had them make us an aquaplane that we'd use for water surfing behind the gig. What the hell, we had a 36-foot power boat, why not use it while we waited?

This is me aboard the Captain's gig. I didn't smile a lot because I was missing my two front teeth. After I had been on Tulagi for about three months, the Army came in to relieve the Marines. When we went across to unload the ships, we saw that they had bacon and all kinds of goodies that we hadn't seen for some time. Naturally, I "appropriated" some of this food and, that evening, we intended to feast on pancakes and bacon prepared on an old iron stove that one of our guys had confiscated. When I took my first bite, both of my teeth broke off at the gum—my diet up to this point had left my teeth so soft that I was unable to bite through the bacon.

"What do I do now?" he asked.

"Stay out here with us."

"I can't, it's leaking," he said.

"Come aboard here, let that thing sink and tomorrow you can write your congressman to get you a new one."

"I can't do that," the guy said in a choked-up, breaking voice, "they need the ammunition."

Well, I could understand that. Here he was out here in the ocean; he had a job to do and the damn thing wouldn't run. He couldn't paddle it in—we were about two miles off shore—so I said, "OK, put a line on him and we'll tow him in."

At the time I had my own crew of three, an ensign (who was a shoe salesman in civilian life) and a radioman. Well, we put a line on him and took off.

The cruiser Honolulu was sitting close to the island for gun support so, to let her know I was going in, I pulled up amidships of her and then turned and headed directly into the beach. Just as we were about to hit the beach, I said, "Now look, when I hit the beach you guys grab ahold of that line and pull him in as close as you can get him, then I'll back off the beach and I'll push him up on the beach. From there on, he's on his own." Just as I had backed off and pulled up behind him to push, he started his engine and pulled up on the beach by himself.

I turned around and started back out for the Honolulu. In the meantime, the Marines on shore had called for illumination, so the ship started firing star shells. Now I had a cabin on my boat with all of these windows, and the bursting star shells illuminated me because of the reflection on the glass. The Nips must have thought that I was important, so they tried to sink us. A few shells went over the top, a few landed off to our sides, and this ensign was bouncing around in the boat and says, "What'll we tell the Captain if it gets sunk?"

I said, "I don't think you'll be able to tell him anything!"

The landings we made at Iwo (Jima) were the rough ones. You couldn't get up onto the beach but, when you finally did, you couldn't hold steady on that volcanic ash. You had to keep the engines running forward all the time just to hold it, and add to that the surf that pounded us from behind caused the boats to bob around all over the place.

We lost contact with one of our LCMs one time, so I had to go out about twenty-five miles before I finally found it. This same ensign was with me at the time, and the whole trip out, looking for the LCM, we had been constantly knocked back and forth by the waves; it was really tiring work, and the spray had everyone drenched. Well, anyway, this ensign was flopping about all around me so I turned to him and said, "If you don't sit down, I'm going to knock you down—I need you like a hole in the head!" I went back about my business when, later on, I noticed that everyone had moved back in the stern behind the engine. They were getting wet back there but, if that's what they wanted to do, it was fine with me. I later found out that everybody thought I had gone "Asiatic" (crazy) and, given the fact that I was wearing my .45 on my hip, they were afraid I might blow them away. Fortunately, I never got into any trouble for, had the ensign wanted to, I could have been brought up on charges.

The landings at Okinawa were opposed mostly by

the Japanese suicide planes—kamikazes. That morning we were out in convoy so, after finishing breakfast, I went down to the head and, while there, they sounded General Quarters. Since I didn't have a gun station, I didn't bother responding because I didn't have any place to go. I was sitting there reading a comic book when I finally decided I better go up and see what's going on. I opened the hatch, stepped out to take a look and there, right across from us, one of our ships was on fire. Two guys were standing there, so I asked them, "What the hell's happening?"

"It got hit by a kamikaze," they said. Both of our ships had been travelling in line (parallel to each other) and, had the kamikaze missed them, then he would have hit us—and here I was, down below, reading comic books.

At one point, off of the coast of Okinawa, we had to ride out a typhoon. If that wasn't bad enough, we received a message to be careful, for we had entered a minefield. We stationed Marines along the deck to fire at any mines with their rifles so that they would detonate before we struck them.

I was in San Diego on V.J. Day (Victory over Japan) because our ship had come back in for repairs. I had assumed that I would be eligible for discharge for, even though I was three points short of the number required for immediate separation, it just seemed logical that they wouldn't send me out again only to return after a very short time. This was not to be, and I found myself back onboard for another cruise across the Pacific—this time to Japan. They said that if they saw a ship coming back to the States, they'd transfer me.

During the cruise I saw all kinds of ships, but we kept right on going to Japan. We were carrying Army troops from the *Black Hawk* Division (86th Infantry Division) to serve as occupation troops in the Pacific, and they were mad as hell. They felt that they had already fought "their war" (in Europe), and they didn't want any more. Many of them even went so far as to stand up there on the deck and throw their "Hero Bars" (medal ribbons) in the ocean.

One of these guys was complaining to me: "What the hell, we already fought our war over there, and now we have to go over there and help you guys!"

"Help me?" I said, "I've already been over here for three-and-a-half damn years, and I should be getting off this damn bucket, but I'm going over to Japan with you!"

When we finally entered the Japanese home islands, our ship was ordered to Nagoya to pick up troops who were eligible to return to the United States. The pilot boat that came out to guide us into the harbor was a small Japanese vessel—much like a tug or fishing boat. Because we were underway, the pilot boat had to come alongside ours, and this small, funny looking Japanese fellow climbed up the Jacob's Ladder to get onboard our ship to steer it into the harbor. It was kind of odd to turn the controls of our ship over to a Japanese, especially given the way he looked, but he knew the channel and what to avoid.

This is the Japanese harbor pilot that guided us into Nagoya.

When I finally got back to the United States we berthed in San Francisco, I was discharged, received my travel papers, and the guy said to me: "Well, you're from Chicago. Since New York is closer to Chicago than San Francisco, you might as well go with us through the Panama Canal, up to New York, and then go home."

"I have already been through there twice," I said, "and it's an all day affair getting through the locks—I ain't going!"

During the war, I went from New Zealand to Tokyo, made seven landings, and never got a scratch. I had boats hit all around me, I heard the buzzing of Japanese sniper fire, I was knocked about by the concussion of bombs going off near me, and I saw my other boat blown out of the water when that kid took it over, but the boats I was on never got so much as a scratch. I simply can't understand how I made it.

Mr. Hazel moved from job to job during his postwar time—employed at twenty different places in twenty-eight years. Figuring it was time to settle down (at the age of forty-eight), he went to work at United Airlines—commuting forty-three miles each way from Lake Villa to O'Hare Airport nearly every day by motorcycle!

# Paul Anthony Koeppler, BM 3/C

*I was the coxswain on a small boat during World War II. It was neat—I liked it. As a young kid, it was like a new toy to me. I enjoyed it even though there was a lot of miserable hours.*

Our family moved down to Alabama when I was a kid, and all of the children were put back one year in school. Then, when we came back to Wisconsin during the Depression, my brother, sister and I were put back another year. So, technically, I was two years behind in school and, although I was in the 12th grade at the time, it was 1942 and I would have been eligible for the Draft. Even though I was in school, I went down to Milwaukee twice to enlist—I wanted to go in the Navy, but they wouldn't take me because I was still a student. The second time I went down, I tried to join the Coast Guard, but they didn't want me either. All I could do was sit around and wait for "Uncle Sam" to make up his mind. Finally, one morning I got a draft notice to report to the train station with my bag and baggage—I'm going in the Army! Aw, man, I didn't want to go in the Army. I got down there and everybody got on the train except me, and I spotted the draft board guy who said to me, "You wanted to get in the Navy, didn't you?"

"They wouldn't take me," I said.

In the meantime, I had sort of quit school—I was only going about twice or three times a week—and this Catholic school wanted me to stick around and get my diploma, but I just wanted out. Anyway, this draft board guy told me there'd be a Navy recruiter over in Michigan on Monday, and I should go over and talk to him. I went over, took the physical, returned home and waited. Meanwhile, I attended a machinist's manual training school and, after about two months (January 1943), they called me to go in the Navy. I went to Boot Camp at Great Lakes Naval Training Station and, from there, I went to Amphibious Training School at Little Creek, Virginia.

I started training in March at Little Creek, but that was all brand new. There were thousands of people coming in to Little Creek—it was really not that much training, per se. They didn't have enough of the small boats—LCP(L)s—to go out and we really didn't get to know them; you were lucky if you got to go out and drive them once a week. Little Creek, Virginia, in its growing stages, was just a lot of men with not much to do. The first amphibious base was, I believe, in the Solomans, then they enlarged and went down to Little Creek, just outside of Norfolk. So the training there was more or less just training to be in the Navy.

If I remember correctly, when we loaded or unloaded troops from the LCP(R)s, because of the narrow ramp the men would come on the boat in single file. The first group would line up on the port side, the second group would go to the starboard, and the remaining men would line up in the center. Thus, the first man on would be the last man off.

While I was there I couldn't get enough training on the boats, so I was in the Fire Department. I also worked in the office for awhile—doing a lot of odd jobs and marching a lot. I was on shore patrol at Norfolk. You never knew what kind of duty you'd be performing in Norfolk, but I think for two nights I was assigned to the shore patrol with more experienced shore patrolmen. There were certain areas in Norfolk that were off limits so that was part of the job—there were no problems, we just walked our beat like a cop would walk his beat.

From Little Creek, I was sent to Camp Bradford, Virginia, where we had some special training in signal work and they put us through the gas chamber to see how much gas we could take, and so on. From Bradford I was sent to Pier 92 in New York to be shipped out. They gave us South Sea island gear with khakis, pith helmets, mosquito netting and all this kind of garbage to make us think we were going to the Pacific. Instead, I ended up going across the Atlantic to England on a Liberty Ship in which I was in charge of six small boats. Pulling out of New York Harbor, I heard this tremendous racket and thought "Boy, this is gonna be one long ride!" They had given us quarters down in the fantail of the Liberty Ship (about two decks below), and, when I woke up in the morning, we were still in the harbor—the darn Liberty Ship had run into a submarine net and the net had wrapped itself around the prop. We sat there for a day-and-a-half to get cut loose, then they pulled us in to Brooklyn Navy Yard to repair the damage to the propeller. We had about a week-and-a-half there while they repaired the ship, so we had a lot of Liberty—we only had to report in at seven a.m. each morning to let them know we were still there. Finally, we set sail and I landed in Liverpool, England.

While we were transporting the small boats across country by lorry, there was an accident. For security reasons, the drivers of this truck convoy never knew where they were going to end up, for we were only instructed to go to a particular small town and, when we reported in, we'd learn our next destination. While we were in Bristol, and the drivers were in the office, I was waiting in the cab. The truck in front of mine started rolling backwards—the brakes were slipping, and it struck my vehicle—crushing the cab. Fortunately, I had enough time to duck down on the floor and, when the other truck hit mine, it popped the door open. So then we had to stay in Bristol for about two days. They pulled us into some kind of big horse barn—there were no horses there, but it had a fence around it. Our truck was pulled up next to the fence so we were able to climb up on the boat and jump over the fence—I don't remember how we got back in. Anyway, we got dressed up in our navy uniforms and went into town. We went to a dance and when we walked in the music stopped and everybody was totally flabbergasted to see U.S. Navy—they were dumbfounded. I'll never forget that for it was quite a neat experience for a dumb kid who didn't know just what was going on. We were all miniature heroes that night! Of course, they were asking questions, but, hell, I didn't know.

From there we went to Appledore. I really didn't get into a lot of training in the small boats until I got over to England, but Appledore and Instow were advanced small boat amphibious training bases. The place had only been open about two weeks when I got there, and it was here that I operated my first LCVP, for that was all we used. Basically, we thought it was for training ourselves, but they were also training the U.S. Army and British commandos to give them experience with the small boats. They taught them how to load and unload, how to descend the nets to get into the boats and, as a matter of fact, they also used the boats for firing rockets and mortars. The beach at Instow wasn't exactly like the one we would make our graduation landing on at Slapton Sands—it had the tide, it had bad weather, but it just wasn't the same. I spent about seven or eight months at Instow. We were then sent to another amphibious training base while the group from that base came down and trained at Instow.

Finally, we trained at Slapton Sands, and I don't know if I was carrying Rangers or not during this training, but they were firing mortars from our boat. I also remember trying to keep the boat in place just off these rocks, the waves were bad, and they were trying to shoot these hooks up onto the heights so they could climb the ropes upon which the hooks were attached.

At the time, I thought it was a stupid exercise but, then again, I didn't see the whole picture. They were training for a specific purpose. I remember the soldiers coming in and trying to fire their little mortars off the boat, but they seldom ever hit their targets because of the rocking of the boat.

The beaches were mostly sand, but the angle of the beach was extremely shallow. If you got stuck up there at high tide, you'd stay high and dry for something like two city blocks from the water. If I remember correctly, we had something like a fifteen to twenty foot tide, and these long sloping beaches, something like for every foot the water would come up, there was a hundred yards. Therefore, if you were landing when the tide was going out, you had to be damn careful you didn't hit it too hard. Once you touched the sand you had to start backing down, but you didn't want to back down too fast so that when the soldiers unloaded they didn't walk off into six feet of water. So, you had to know what the tide was doing.

One night during our exercises, I saw a glow in the sky about 10-20 miles away. I don't know what the conditions were, or why we were in the area, these were like on-going small mock invasions; fully loaded LSTs, live ammunition, etc. They'd bomb the beaches and get in different groups, load and unload off the LSTs.

Well, there would have been five, maybe six, LSTs that would start off into the channel as if they were actually going to France, then they'd swing out and come in and land at Slapton Sands. I got the feeling that somewhere in this chain, we were supposed to fit into this whole thing. Maybe we were going to be the next wave, I don't know.

We saw the glow in the sky, saw that something had happened, but we never heard about it. Even the people that were there—that were in it—were sworn to secrecy. If you got caught talking about it, man, they'd..., even the doctors, when they started pulling the casualties in, even the doctors and the nurses were ordered to ask them absolutely no questions. The higher echelon knew that something happened and they were ordered to keep it quiet.

The survivors off the ships were quarantined—they were taken to certain areas and interrogated and not allowed liberty or association with anybody. It was kept quiet until recently.

(Note: On the night of April 27-28, 1944, German patrol-torpedo craft—known as "E-Boats"—slipped in amongst a training convoy off Slapton Sands,

England, and attacked several ships. In all, 749 Americans lost their lives in this attack. Due to the secret nature of these exercises, the incident remained classified until just a few years ago.)

While on board LST 282, my first responsibility was the care and control of the small boats. Moreover, whenever the ship was coming in or going out, they always dropped two of my boats over the side to act as tugs for the LST. LSTs were hard to handle—we were always pushing or guiding her, hauling a line across, or something like that. For General Quarters, my position was on the 20mm cannon on the port bow so, anytime General Quarters was sounded, if I wasn't in my small boat, I was with the 20mm gun crew. One of the other things was liberty parties—I would shuttle personnel to and from the land so they could go on liberty. I don't ever remember the LST being tied up to a pier so the people could come and go as they pleased—mostly we were always tied up in the channels, so we always had liberty boats going back and forth and, if you were on duty, you worked for four hours. I wish I had a nickel for every mile I covered in that darn thing!

Those small boats would really go, I don't know how fast but, on good, clear water, I got a feeling that when they were unloaded they must have been able to do about twenty knots. They had a lot of power—you needed the power because when the boat was loaded down it would actually plow through the water. They were very maneuverable—you could stop the thing on a dime (throw it in neutral for a split second) and you could go from full speed to reverse and bring that thing to a full stop in about thirty yards. As much as I knew them, there's nothing I would have changed on them.

My steering wheel was all wrapped up and knotted—dressed up. The front vision port (on the ramp of the boat) could be dropped half way, or all the way, to permit the coxswain to see forward through the ramp. It was made of two sections that were hinged at the bottom and at the middle. Sliding bolts secured it in place when closed up. You wouldn't leave it open when the boat was loaded. When the boat was loaded, it was nothing like this (indicating a raised front end). The steering wheel had little holes in the side of the column, and I remember that it had a little pin that you could pull out and lift the steering wheel, so that when you were empty, the front end would raise up. The steering column was made up of two tubes—one inside the other. The locking pin went through holes in the steering column and was attached to a chain so

you couldn't lose it. I would say that the column could be extended about 20 inches. The throttle came out of the control box and there was a little compass right in the front of the box so the coxswain could look down at it.

When the boats were empty they were fast—could go "bat out of hell." Rather than striking the water with the ramp as when we were loaded, the bow keel would cut through the water. The ramp could be lowered very quickly. It had a trip on the gears, so you'd take the crank out—get it started and just let the ramp fall—they didn't recommend that either. This was done when you'd get up on the beach and just let it drop—and watch that your keel didn't go any further up on the beach than it was supposed to. They wanted them cranked down.

Generally, they didn't lash down vehicles inside of the small boats—I never had them lashed down in mine. Underneath one of these center deck plates they had a hook that they would use to lift the small boats up. It used to be a son-of-a-bitch getting the boats back aboard—they were rough. That big hook—you had to hook them both at the same time. She was riding up and down, bouncing on the waves, and you had to be really careful 'cause it was easy to take your finger off.

All of the boats were painted a dark gray. There were a number of different outfits that made these boats, so it may be that there were small differences between boats.

In order to keep the boat dry, there was a big rubber gasket between the ramp and the hull. But if you were empty, the water line would fall beneath the bottom of the ramp. The nose rode so high in the water that, if it were calm, you could crank it down so the ramp would actually touch the water.

We coxswains were regular cowboys, you'd like to get it going—just like a motorcycle. You might be slow with it when you first started out, but after you got to know it you'd do things like come roaring up to the dock and then throw it in reverse to stop just in time. The throttle was the forward and reverse, and the handle twisted to increase speed.

We'd open the rear hatch of the engine cover, take a life preserver and/or a life vest and sit right down on top of the engine with the life preserver between you and the engine. It would keep you warm. It used to get cold out on the water—colder than a son-of-a-gun.

Everything was at night—they'd call you out at one and you'd go sit out—all the small boats were tied up in the channel. Sometimes they'd have them up on the

Here, a small boat is pulled up alongside LST 49. Of particular interest is the method shown for attaching the davit cable to the stern of the boat.

beach. When they were tied up in the channel, you'd have to get into the DUKWs and they'd take you out to the small boats. You'd get into the boats, warm them up, peel off and circle and circle.

The next boat bigger than the LCVP was the LCM—a two engine job. They had a square box in the back and a bigger ramp—they were bigger, they'd take a tank. In fact, LCMs crossed the channel by themselves—they had patrol craft that took them across. Well, they got out there and the whole thing got delayed and then they had to go into this circle. There was a saying that when a coxswain would go back into civilian life, he'd have to go around the block six times before he would know where he was.

On some of the bigger ships, deck hands wouldn't associate with the black gang. You didn't know anybody on the con. We were kinda clique-ish too. The deck hands stuck together.

Our LST would carry six of these small boats. Twenty-four guys plus two officers. We had watches when we weren't in the boats—we'd have gun stations, etc.

My signalman (communications specialist), Ray McGee from Cleveland, was a pretty sharp guy—he was better than most. He'd use both the flags and the lamp. He was a little older—maybe a little sharper.

The motor machinist's mate (diesel engine specialist) was Lester Leaper. He was kind of an odd guy, but I guess he knew his job. His job was keeping the engine running. I used to always think he was, but I got to talking to another coxswain last year, or the year before last, about the fact that my boat had swamped out because of a faulty bilge pump, and he said, "Paul, there was no reason for you not to be able to pump it out, because the water could have been pumped out through the engine." So there must have been a trick there that I didn't know.

There was also a bow hook man—he was usually a seaman 2nd class or a seaman 1st class, if he had achieved a rate, he would probably be a gunner's mate because he was supposed to know something about the guns...he had a little bit more training on the machine guns. My bow hook man was Thomas Lee Rowe—a fellow out of the hills from West Virginia. He was 100 percent hillbilly—I don't think he had shoes until he came into the Navy. He was a real hardnose, he didn't like it and he didn't care who knew it. He didn't like the officers—he had no respect for officers, in fact, he was summary court-martialed when one officer by the name of Wagner told him something and he responded by saying, "Someday you'll be on the beach all alone...". Well, that was enough for the officer to say that he was being threatened. Well, they fined him. I don't think that all the time I knew him that he ever drew a full pay check. When we got over (to Europe) he was always broke, you know. Over the time, I loaned him two hundred and some dollars, and I just kissed it good-bye. Well, the first thing he did when we got paid up was he paid me back. I never saw him after that.

In memory, even though we had a crew of four, most of the time only one man was working—the one driving the boat. So we'd switch off driving.

The only times we had the guns was when we went into Normandy. We didn't have any gun shields—just the dinky little .30 caliber machine guns.

At least two people rarely had anything to do until it was time to come in and tie up. You always needed one or two men to help with this. Generally, when we were practicing, the four men would just sit in the back.

Sometimes a captain would be a little more lenient—even on the LSTs. Some captains were total pricks—I got a friend of mine, he says, "that son-of-a-bitch, everybody wished he was dead," strictly military, be in uniform, everything had to right up to Navy Code. Our captain was the other way around—he didn't care, as long as you were there when the ship was going out was the main thing—it you've got liberty, fine. He was just a good, easy-going guy. Of course, if you're too easy-going somebody takes advantage of you.

In the small boats, we were freer—we didn't have the discipline. We had no respect for the officers—we had so many ensigns that were just kids like us, except that they had a stripe—you had to salute 'em. This got to be a big joke down in Little Creek, Virginia—'There comes one,' and we'd spread out instead of all saluting at one time, and this would cause the officer to keep saluting each and every one of us. This sort of thing kind of flowed on all the way through the war.

Our destination was Utah Beach. The small boat

people were well-trained, they knew exactly what they were supposed to do. Looking at it from my perspective, there were people that were definitely scared out there but, in my case, I'm always curious and afraid I'm going to miss something. There were people out there who were so scared they probably would have gone AWOL that morning without ever batting an eye.

There was so much happening that morning, and it all happened so fast, that I know I missed a lot of what was going on; its probably like going through a big museum in half an hour—you notice things here and there, but you miss a whole lot. On top of that, you have to remember that there was a lot of confusion at the time and I was fighting to try to get the boat to the beach.

I never got sick, not even going across channel. But there was a lot of people that were sick. If a Navy man gets sick he can go to bed, but there was a lot of sick Army boys that couldn't get off the ship quick enough. Being delayed like it was for 24 hours, some of those boys were so damned sick that they didn't care if they were jumping off into a hornet's nest—they were glad to get off the damned thing. That sickness would take some of the life out of you, it'd wear you down and you couldn't eat, what you did eat you'd throw up. On an LST it was rough, but I'd say that 75 percent of the Navy people on the LSTs would be able to handle it. At the same time, I'd say that about 50 percent of the troops aboard suffered some ill effects from it. On the other hand, you take those LCMs that went across the channel—those boys must have suffered! You see, they'd get out there and circle, didn't know where they were going, waiting for orders, and then they'd have to come back in—they were already half-way across the channel. Then, when it was delayed, they got orders to come back in. So I would imagine that there was some of them boys that were pretty damned sick. Those LCMs were big enough that they wouldn't just ride out the normal waves, they'd get caught in these troughs and just pound the sea and everybody on board would get a shock. It seemed like Mother Nature was trying to get you to bring it up. Bigger ships could ride out these short, choppy waves without much movement, they'd just cut through it. But the LCMs would feel everything. If you met the waves head on, it wasn't so bad, but if you got the waves broadside, you'd get this side-to-side motion that'd roll you back and forth. Since these boats had to circle the larger ships, you'd go from one series of jarring motions to the next—first back-to-front for a while, and then side-to-side for a while, over and over again.

I remember that at the time of the invasion, I was wearing Army-style fatigue pants, a U.S. Navy olive green jacket – it had something like a mohair lining. I'd been issued a .45, the bow hookman had a Thompson submachine gun, and the motor machinists mate had a carbine. I don't remember what the signalman had. When I got back to the LST, I had to turn the .45 back in. Then, of course, the steel helmet – it was painted green, and the greenish-blue 'Mae West' life jacket. I was probably wearing high navy shoes, but that's a guess. Our captain was not very restrictive on uniforms, so, in the long run, over the years, when we finished up training and went out, you'd say that we were some kind of rag-tailed southern confederate outfit because there was everything – everybody had all kinds of different clothes. There was Navy dungaree pants, or you might have a big, turtle neck sweater that you got some place along the line. I know that one fellow had a beret from when we were training with the Canadians. The whole amphibious force was basically like this because you trained with the Army and you almost became the Army.

We unloaded from the LST at about 2 o'clock in the morning and finally hit the beach (after a lot of circling and a twelve mile ride) at 9 a.m. We were supposed to get there at about 7, but we were delayed because of taking on the water. After unloading from the LST, we circled and the object was to look for the florescence created by the spinning screws and also gauge your distance from the ship by sound. I believe that many of the original coxswains were picked for their good eyesight – being able to detect that florescence. You don't necessarily have to have the rate to be a coxswain of a small boat.

The people I was bringing in were personnel attached to the beach party. With the half-track jeep we were carrying, it had to be people with something to do with communications so they could go up and down the beach. The half-track had to have something to do with the beach. We wouldn't have been bringing infantry in that early in the morning until they've got a place to land. They were probably Navy personnel, but you couldn't tell by the uniforms – the Navy wasn't out there with their Navy Blues on, the Navy looked as much like the Army as the Army did.

I got the boat to shore. It was impregnated into your brain – you got a load of troops that you had to get to shore – you got to put them where they were

supposed to go. Well, I was swamping out, it was all I could do just to keep the engine running – keep moving, but I couldn't apply any speed to it. The fact is that we did hit the beach. I didn't know where I was, I couldn't find a place to land. We were loaded with a half-track jeep, about a foot of water in the bottom of the boat, she was already so darned heavy that when I hit bottom, I was still so far out that they had to go through about a hundred yards of water. I know that they were able to get the vehicle off, and I would say they got off into water about three-and-a-half feet deep.

I wouldn't have any idea how close I was to my landing; I saw the beach and I tried to pick out a place where I would get in. I knew they were worried that they weren't landing where they were supposed to but, by the same token, they didn't seem to know where they were supposed to be either. Before we left, they had shown us a picture of the beach but, by the time we got there, the whole beach was covered in smoke, and we couldn't make out any of our landmarks. All we could see was about two hundred yards of beach, the obstacles, and trucks and "Jack Straws" (I think they called them) and concrete pyramids and poles that you had to kinda sneak in between.

(Note: "Jack Straws" were steel beams welded together at their centers to form tetrahedrons – obstacles designed to prevent the safe beaching of landing craft and ships.)

I did what I was supposed to do, part of what I was supposed to do, I got them in, and that was it. When I got into the beach, one of the LCVPs that had been hit – in fact I pulled in right alongside of it – when I got up closer there I figured well, he's in there, I'll go in. I remember that he was on my right hand side and they had either hit a mine or ... because the front end of the boat was all blown apart and I remember that one of the crew was lying across the engine compartment.

One of the patrol craft (they were designed to stay off the shore – about a thousand yards – and they would control the whole wave) was hit – the bow was the only part sticking up. So we lost our control. I don't know when they got hit, but there was about four or five guys sitting up there, and I couldn't go over and help them out – my job was to get them soldiers in!

When I got in there, we run that vehicle off and then the whole boat filled up with water – the water inside the boat nearly reached the top of the bulkhead in front of the engine compartment. It was ready to sink, but the engine was still running. It was a weird thing, but it was running – just barely. Anyway, I don't know where this other small boat came from, I have no idea, but it pulled up alongside and the coxswain yelled "Get the hell out of there." I remember seeing my seabag floating around in the swamped hull of the boat—my crew and I were supposed to go ashore and be attached to the beach party. So I just got out of my boat, jumped into the other one, and this other boat had a whole load of UDT demolition charges. Instead of immediately jumping from ours to his, we were trying to save our gear. The coxswain on the other boat yelled "Leave it go." "Get the hell out of there." It didn't dawn on me at that time, but German 88s were shelling our area and, if they had hit that boat loaded with the demolitions, there wouldn't be much more than toothpicks left. The UDT people never did signal for their charges, so we returned to the LST.

At the part of the beach where I landed, the biggest problem was enemy machine gun fire and the mines on the beach. I know there were mines going off on our beach, because the shelling should have stopped by the time we got there.

I was supposed to go in on the fourth wave, but when I got in I have no idea. I suppose I actually arrived around the time of the fifth or sixth wave, but I went in by myself. I remember explosions on the beach, I remember small arms fire, you could see the machine gun fire walking across the water. The only experience I had with the German 88s was when I realized that they had zeroed in on our boats.

Whatever happened to my boat, I don't know—there was a good chance that it sank because it was damn near under that rough water when I last saw it. Its probably something I shouldn't have done, maybe I should have left the ramp down and sunk it—at least to get it out of the channel.

Part of the training was, say that you got a company of a hundred men that you had to get to the beach at a certain spot. Well, you couldn't take the whole hundred in, you had to take 36 here, 36 there, and then that particular wave would be maybe eight boats, ten boats, or twelve boats, whatever it took to get this unit ashore. Well, you want this unit to hit there all together, not some down there and some up here. So that was basically what the training was all about. Being in the fourth wave, each wave would have a Navy officer, and he was supposed to know where to land, what time you were supposed to land, and the other boats followed what his instructions were because we didn't know—we did what he told us. I was the lead boat in the fourth wave. I had an officer in my boat

but, when I was swamping out because of the malfunctioning bilge pump and holding the whole wave up because I couldn't get my speed (actually, the whole wave was taking on water as well), so the officer got out of my boat and got into another one. He abandoned me and told me "Do the best you can." Well, it ended up that the boat he got into swamped out. I didn't know this until a couple of years ago when I met up with him at a reunion.

After the D-Day landings, our LST converted to a hospital ship to shuttle wounded and prisoners back to England. On our second trip back to the French coast, we landed on Omaha Beach at high tide. When the tide went out, the ship settled down on dry ground and we set down on one of them damn cross beam obstacles the Germans had planted along the beach. The steel beam tore up through the port shaft, flooded the shaft alley, and we couldn't use the engine. After the tide came back in, they towed us back to England where we went into drydock for repairs.

While the ship was being worked on, I went on liberty in London and, of course, they had an air raid when we got there. Naturally, we were cocky veterans, so when the sirens sounded we didn't even bother looking for an air raid shelter. A Bobby (British policeman) camp up and told us we better find a shelter and get in it, but he couldn't even force us to go for we wanted to see this. Some of those buzz bombs (German V1 rockets) came in that night—of course none landed right near us—but you could hear them and a lot of flak.

Once the ship was repaired, we took a load of British soldiers to Gold Beach. We once again loaded up with casualties and prisoners, came back to England, but as we arrived we ran into a damn buoy that bent the shaft—back into drydock again. We only made three trips across the Channel, but after the third trip they refitted us with some kind of new special radar. From there, we went down to the Mediterranean.

On the way to the Mediterranean, we ran into a bad storm that spread the convoy all over God's creation. We ended up in Bizerte, North Africa, where we did some training with the LST. From there, we went up to Naples, Italy, where we loaded up for the invasion of Southern France—Operation Dragoon.

Everything was pretty well-organized in Southern France—at least we could see where we were going. The only thing about Southern France, where I had reached that morning, it had a very steep cobblestone beach that you could take the Army up so far that

This is LST 282 on Omaha Beach, D+5. Here you see it up high and dry on the beach where, once the tide went out and the ship settled on its flat bottom, you had plenty of time to unload the cargo. The small boat you can see hanging off the starboard side wouldn't start on D-Day. My boat would have been hanging in the davit right behind it, but mine was lost and we didn't get another to replace it until we got down to Africa.

arm up, and I replaced the prop. I used to be a half-assed ship's barber and, that afternoon, while I was cutting this guy's hair, I got the word that the Captain wanted my boat and another one to standby to guide the LST into the beach. When I was in the water, the Captain ordered me to man the port bow (of the LST) so that we could guide it like a tug. The ship was underway, and I was gonna swing off the stern and go up to the port bow. I was off about fifty yards from the ship when I looked up and saw what I thought was a flare in the sky. This "flare" was dropped from a plane, so I thought it was an indication that it was a friendly plane. I looked up a couple of seconds later, and this "flare" had turned into something like a miniature airplane. This thing was coming off the starboard bow and looked like it should have passed over us. Instead, it veered toward the ship and made its dive—hitting the port side just in front of the quarters and penetrating the deck. I think everybody in the engine room was either killed instantly, or died soon after.

The ship, prior to being hit, was supposed to have gone an additional quarter mile, then make a right turn and go on into the beach. Well, because of the explosion, the ship never made the turn and went straight ahead and ran up on some rocks where it rolled over a little and burned for at least the next five days. The fire was so bad that no one could even get near it! I went back on board six or seven days after the explosion, and there were still hot spots.

My boat was still underway when the LST went up and, because I was petrified looking at the ship, I almost run over this guy when I heard someone screaming "Help!"

I picked up five survivors in all. The first two was a colored messman and another fellow he had saved who had been blown out of his shoes! The third was a lone sailor, and then there was this Army guy who was floating around. When we got closer, we saw that his

they wouldn't even get their feet wet. In this invasion, I was carrying Army infantry—no vehicles or anything and, when I hit the beach, I hit it too fast and slid right on up—it almost seemed that when I touched the shore, it increased the speed. I knew I was up too high, and I had to move the wheel back and forth so I could snake it back off the beach. There was a German machine gun firing at us, so I poured the gas to it and tore up the prop getting it back into the water. I backed down to where I thought I was a safe distance to put it in forward and make the turn and, as I pulled the pin on the steering shaft to raise the wheel, I noticed that there was blood all over the steering wheel and my left hand. That must have been when that machine gun zeroed in on me, for a splinter from the fire that struck my boat had cut across my arm like a razor, and it bled like a son-of-a-gun. It didn't hurt, and I wouldn't have even noticed had it not been for the blood.

Because of the damage I had done to my prop back on that cobblestone beach, the speed of my boat was reduced quite a bit. I finally got back to the LST, we hoisted the boat aboard, the ship's Doc patched my head was blown off and we couldn't get him aboard—we didn't know where the crank was to lower the ramp—in the excitement, maybe it was right in front of us. We ended up having to pull him up over the fantail. The dead soldier, and this sounds strange, but I swear his helmet and head was floating right along beside him! We picked up a fourth guy, and then the last fellow we picked up was a corpsman who had been left on our ship from when we were a hospital ship. We could hardly get him aboard—his legs were totally smashed—they were like rags. We gave him two shots of morphine, and I decided to get him immediately to a hospital ship. Here, another quirk occurred because, when we got there, one of this corpsman's friends was the first one to meet us. Of the hundreds of places we could have gone, it just happened that we chose this ship at this time. A few days later, I stopped by the ship and inquired about the wounded guy and found out that he had died.

I didn't really know what to do—this ship had been my home and, hell, everybody had abandoned ship! The next day, however, they attached us to the Navy Beach Battalion. They signaled us to come ashore and, from there on in, we were hauling casualties, personnel and prisoners out to the ships. We were there for almost two weeks with our small boat.

In the meantime, we picked up some cots and stretchers to sleep on and, one day, we pulled up alongside a PT boat to get something to eat. We didn't know it, but there were ships out there assigned to feed people—almost like floating restaurants. Well, the PT boat didn't have anything but, before leaving, we spotted this great big canvas tarp all rolled up on their boat. I quietly told one of my guys to grab it and throw it in our boat, so we did—we stole the doggone canvas off the PT boat, went ashore and cut it up to make a cover for over the top of our boat to give us some protection at night. About two days later this PT boat sends a blinker to us to pull up alongside and I thought 'Hell, we can't, he'll see the canvas,' so my signalman sent back that we didn't know what they were talking about. They knew we had stolen that goldarn canvas, and there's no way we were gonna get tied up with them! At the end of our beach duty, we were assigned to LST 284 for a couple of months before I came home.

Once I arrived stateside, I went to Scouts and Raiders training at Fort Pierce, Florida. The classes would start out with a big group—like maybe a couple, three hundred people—and it ends up, when they're all done, that so many remaining had to be eliminated. I was one of those who flunked out because I was late for muster one morning so, for a time, I went back

Paul Koeppler having just returned home for his thirty-day survivor's leave after the loss of his LST during the invasion of Southern France, November 1944.

into business giving free haircuts. Before I flunked, I trained with the small boats to be used with the Scouts and Raiders—I'd operate the boat to take them out and sneak them in to shore, they'd go in to infiltrate another camp, and so on. I later found out that had I stayed with my group, I would have ended up in China like they did.

Later, I was shipped to Shoemaker, California, to be reassigned. One day, while I was there waiting in

These are the huts we lived in at Fort Pierce. Today, you sure wouldn't recognize it—shopping centers and so forth. The Commander of the base was Clarence Gulbranson. The guys nicknamed him "C. Gulbranson" (pronounced Seagull Branson). I remember that every time you saw his car coming down the road, you had to stand at attention and salute the damn car—whether the Commander was in it or not!

line to get something to eat, I met Bob King, a guy who was in Europe with me. We renewed our old friendship, and his dad and ma lived only about fifty miles from Shoemaker. So I went home with him a couple of times, met a gal—his cousin—and between that, and the fact that I really didn't want to go overseas again, one night Bob told me that he wasn't gonna go back and that his dad said that if Paul wants, he can stay and not go back to base. So, just out of the clear blue sky, I thought that I would go AWOL for a couple of days, but it ended up that I was gone for twenty-eight days.

I didn't have anything with me except the clothes on my back and a ditty bag, but Bob's brother was my size, so I dressed in civilian clothes—which was highly illegal. During the time I was away from the Navy, Bob and I went up to Kit Carson Pass to do some trout fishing and camping. We came back after a few days and then left again for Yosemite National Park. It was real touch and go there at Yosemite, because at that time they had a Navy hospital there, so we kind of stayed away from the interesting part of the Park to avoid the SPs and anyone else who might catch on to us. While I was there, they sent a reward notice to my Dad that promised twenty-five dollars for my apprehension. Bob's folks never got nothing like that.

When I got back and turned myself in, naturally I was thrown in the brig. I was given a summary court marshal, and fined $236. I was in the brig when they dropped the first atomic bomb. Later, they hand-cuffed me, took me to my barracks, I got my gear and they shipped me to Treasure Island where they put me in another barracks and I was assigned to another small boat crew. I knew it, but it was too late—there was no way of going AWOL from Treasure Island.

The ship I finally departed on was scheduled for the invasion of Okinawa, but when they dropped the second bomb, instead of going to Okinawa, they sent us to Guam. The war was finally over for me—they didn't need another invasion with small boats, so we got side-tracked, sent to Guam and there it was a matter of just sitting and waiting until I got enough points to get out. While I was there, I guarded Japanese prisoners, worked with the SeaBees and, after about four weeks of doing that, I ended up with the Naval Air Transport Squadron repairing seats on C-47s and anything to do with canvas. I was also classed as a parachute rigger at that time and, when I wasn't on duty, I went into a little private business of making little duffel bags for all the guys going home. So, actually, when it was time to go home, I really didn't want to go—I was getting ten bucks apiece for these bags I was making.

Upon his discharge from the Navy, Mr. Koeppler worked at a ranch in Northern Wisconsin, went trapping with his brother, worked on road construction, worked as a logger, and sailed the Great Lakes with the Coast Guard. He finally "put down anchor" in Wisconsin and, after half a dozen other jobs, he went to work as a tool and die specialist—the job from which he retired after twenty-nine years. He currently resides in Milwaukee, Wisconsin.

Following an investigation which included supporting letters from both his former Captain and the doctor who treated him, Paul Koeppler was awarded the Purple Heart for the arm wound he received during the landings in the south of France—forty-seven years after the event!

45

# Robert J. Dolan, BM I/C

*As far as I'm concerned, the LCVP and the LST combined was the best duty in the Navy. Since I get seasick, duty on board the LST was great because you're not out all that long—you're never more than a week or two away from land. As long as I was driving that LCVP I didn't get sick, but when I'd sit back and watch somebody else drive it, I'd get a little bit queazy.*

I was born on February 1st, 1923, in Wisconsin Rapids, Wisconsin. I went to school there, finished grade school and high school, and graduated in 1940. I was at the movies when I heard about the Japanese attack at Pearl Harbor. My brother and I (he was a year older) went to the local hangout—a pool hall—to talk about it, and he said, "Well, maybe we'll go in together" but my dad didn't want that (he would have had to sign for me), so my brother ended up going in a few months before me. Anyway, I got a job in the ship-yards as a tack welder and Uncle Sam started getting pretty close to my tail (and I didn't want to go in the Army), so I joined the Navy on January 17th, 1943.

I went through Boot Camp at Great Lakes, Company 161, and graduated in April. While there (it was during the winter so we didn't get much outdoor training), we drilled and did our physical training in the gymnasium. We always had inspections—goddam, we had inspections all the time—it was discipline more than anything. Everybody wanted to get into this fight (the war) and just clean house.

I was transferred to Little Creek, Virginia, for our small boat training with the Amphibious forces—at that time, we didn't even know what the hell amphibious force was, and we didn't know what we were getting into. I never heard about "amphibious duty" before I was assigned to it. I had wanted to be in aviation, but of all of the guys in boot camp, I can't remember even one who got into that field. Two things probably happened: they didn't need another aviation mechanic right then, or my marks weren't good enough. My marks weren't all that bad, but some of the guys got submarines, some got sub chasers, and the rest of us got "Amphibs," whether we wanted it or not. Personally, as it turned out, it was the best damned duty in the Navy. Our Navy didn't have all that much experience in amphibious landings, and the officers were just as much green behind the ears as we were.

When we got to Little Creek we were formed into crews—four men to a crew; you had your coxswain, your signalman, your bow hookman and your engineer, and we trained in LCVPs until July 1943. My initial training as a signalman, such as it was, took place at

Little Creek. Basically, they taught us how to use the two signal flags when we would be going in to the beach. If you put the one flag straight up above your head, the small boats would form a line. If you spread both arms out to your sides at shoulder height, with a flag in each hand, the other small boats would form up in a line abreast. Another one was to take a flag in one hand and circle it above your head—that meant for the boats to form up in a circle. I never really did get any formal training as a signalman, and I don't believe any of the small boatmen that I knew did either, until we finally got aboard the LST over in England. Once there, if you really wanted to be a signalman, you'd get with the ship's company and they'd take you up on deck where you'd get training with the signal lamp, the sema-phore flags, and all of that where they would work with a regular signalman, standing watches, and so on.

The engineers for our boats joined us there at Little Creek; they had already gone through diesel mechan-ics school and then they were shipped to Little Creek to be the motor machinists for our small boat crews. Most of the boats had the Gray Marine diesel engine in them, and some had the Chrysler gas engines, but I never saw any gas-engined boats after we left there.

The LCVP could haul thirty-six Army personnel with gear, or a jeep, or maybe a little weapons carrier, but once you got your load, your bow went down and you were pushing a lot of water when you took off. They would go approximately nine to ten miles an hour—unloaded—and they were fun to drive. Kids like us—seventeen-, eighteen- and nineteen-year-olds, somebody'd turn us loose out in that great big old bay out there and you could open it up and let her go. You'd catch hell for doing it, but it was worth it. The thing was to get the troops ashore without broaching because then you couldn't get back off. You'd try to get as far up on the beach as possible so that when you let the personnel off they wouldn't drown—you wanted to be able to drop the ramp and they could step off on dry land.

You had to train with the tides—if the tides were coming in early, you're going out early; if the tides were coming in late, you're going out a little later. They

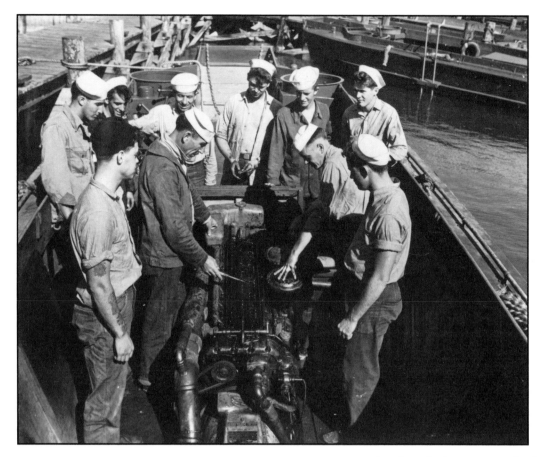

Navy personnel receive instruction on an LCP(R)'s 225-hp Gray Marine diesel engine at the Amphibious Training Base, Fort Pierce, Florida, 29 December, 1943. Other LCP(R)s are in the right background.

had an old ship out there that you had to pull up alongside to simulate loading and unloading—we travelled empty most of the time, but we learned how to get our signals straight about going in and coming back. You had to pull alongside this old wooden sailing ship, pull the nets inside and a guy would say "O.K., you're loaded," and you'd pull out and go circle until it was time to go in to the beach. When it was time to move toward the beach, we'd all turn around and go back out to the ship for another run. During our training there, we didn't have any leaves—it was a seven-day-a-week operation. You didn't have any time on your hands because they kept you busy.

I started out on the LCVPs as a signalman and, eventually, by hook and crook, I became a coxswain (I was better at that than I was a signalman). A coxswain of one of the other crews had a problem—I don't know whether it was he couldn't run the boat, or the crew couldn't put up with him, or whether he had a personal problem, but they took him off the boat and needed another coxswain to take his place. Well, the coxswain of the small boat I was on and I were pretty good buddies. He went and told someone, "Hell, Dolan can handle that job" and, the next thing I knew, I was the coxswain of that other crew. I finally got the stripe

after I took the test—we had a test for coxswain—but I had already been a coxswain for some time prior to the test. The group that I was tested with took it at Instow, England. It was basically a test on seamanship—nomenclature on some items, tie a few knots, what was port, starboard, bow, stern, fo'c's'le, and a little bit about signalling. It was all oral, administered by officers in a classroom. I passed the test, but I don't know whether some of the guys that took the test failed it or not—they needed coxswains as much as they needed anything else. If you could stand and breathe, and get the boat in and out, you probably got the job. The engineers were the only ones pre-selected for their duties because they had gone to school for that specialty. The rest of us—the coxswains, the signalmen, and the bow hookmen, were chosen randomly for their duties.

Our boats were mostly all plywood—the only armor plate that it had was on port and starboard from the bow back to the engine housing (to protect your passengers), and the ramp was armor as well. After the ramp was dropped, and the boat was unloaded, you'd manually crank the ramp back up and return back to your designated area for another load. All we did was practice, practice, practice, and we got pretty damned efficient at it. From there we were transferred to the New York Port of Embarkation for shipment out.

New York was nice. At that time, you could go any place without getting into trouble. We would sometimes go out and get half-soused and nobody would take you or roll you. You'd get on the subway and tell the guy to "get me off at such-and-such at stop," sack out for a while and the guy would wake you up when you got to where you were going. While we were there in New York we had all kinds of different duty, but I wound up in the "Spud Locker" (mess duty). I stayed there a little longer than most of the crew, for what they did was assign certain crews—and my crew on the LCVP was one of them—to go across the Atlantic with LCVPs on the topside of a freighter.

Our vessel was a Liberty Ship named the *Henry S. Foote*. We were with the armed guard, and what a duty that was; we ate better than we ever ate in our lives. We had fresh milk for about the first four or five days out, and their food was much better. We had about four or six LCVPs on topside, and all we had to do was look at them and make sure they didn't fall off. Three of us went over there together with the small boats on topside. All we had to do was maintain them and, hell, when you're underway, what was there to maintain? We greased the rudder, and a few of the exposed parts, and that was all our duty. We didn't have to stand a watch, or anything, 'cause the ship had its own regular gunnery crew, and they did the watch. It was rough for awhile—I didn't like that worth a damn—but we had nice quarters, nice bunks with night lights so we could lay up there and read, and we ate anytime we wanted. The duty was great—oh, the weather got rough sometimes, but we could always go inside to get out of it. I don't recall of any warnings about enemy subs, or anything like that, and I don't think any of the ships got hit. There may have been some sightings, or warnings, but they sure as hell didn't come down and tell us about it. It was very uneventful, as far as wartime goes, but it was a nice ride. We got along with the merchantmen real well—there was no inter-service rivalry, or anything like that. We played cards together, slept together, and ate together.

We weren't out of sight of land yet, and I was sick as a dog from seasickness. I never did feel real good at sea, but I managed to get across. They'd let me lie down a lot and, fortunately, the water was pretty calm most of the way.

We went around the northern part of Scotland, came down through the North Sea and landed in London. When we got there, we took the small boats off the freighter, loaded them on trucks (English lorries) and transported them overland down to Bideford in Devon County. Bideford was a resort town before the war, and the military came in and took over all of the hotels and homes in the area for our use. The hotels weren't like you have today, but the military came in and took them over to house us. It was just a little old spot, and I can't remember seeing many civilians. The rest of the crews were already there, so we began our training with them and with the Army.

That particular area had a pretty damn rough surf, and we trained there until the end of April. We'd pick up the Army on the beach and take them over to Willoughby Beach where we would drop them off. Willoughby Beach supposedly resembled Normandy—to a point—but the water up there was awful damn rough. We lost three LCMs and, one stormy day, we lost seventeen Army personnel there, and some of our sailors were hurt. As a matter of fact, coming off of the beach that particular day, as we had turned the boat around and were heading back out, we hit one of those waves head on and it bent the ramp, broke the two pieces of plywood down the sides, and popped both of the dogging hooks that held the ramp up. When we crested the wave, we went down at about a thirty-five or forty degree angle. The bow hookman was standing next to me by the steering wheel and he ended up rolling all of the way up to the ramp. It was damned rough that day, but I feel that we got some of the best training of any of them that were out there.

While I was stationed at Bideford, I got two seventy-two hour passes to go to London. There were areas that were pretty well blown up. The people were good and they had their USOs, they had their dances, they had their pubs, and they had their women. It was nice for that time of the year—especially considering all that they had gone through—some of those buildings were completely shot.

One of the times I went to London I found two old schoolmates of mine that had gone into the Air Force and they were stationed at Berry St. Edmonds—north of London—and I just went up there and spent some time with them shooting the bull and drinking a few. Oddly enough, I never went any place that I didn't meet somebody from the old hometown, and my hometown was only about 11,000 people. On one of our maneuvers out of Plymouth, there was another guy from my hometown. I didn't know him—he looked familiar—and I asked him who the hell he was. He told me and it turned out that I knew his family. I knew his sister—in fact, I used to double-date with his sister and another fellow. I had to go to this converted LST repair ship (ARL-1) one day to take some things to the machine shop and there was a guy there, as well, from my hometown. Even when I got over in the Pacific, I ran into two fellows there in Saipan from my old hometown. Later still, when we were travelling between the Philippines and Okinawa, another kid from my hometown who had joined the Army got on the ship. In the Pacific they'd let us go ashore for a beer party when they had a chance. This was for relaxation and they'd let us go ashore and have so many beers, I think the limit was about three beers. They'd have what was called a Port and Starboard Liberty. If you were assigned the port side, then you'd have liberty with the port crew and, if you were on starboard, then you'd have liberty with the starboard crew. So half of the crew was on board all of the time. Anyway, there were times when not all of the guys wanted to go—and the officers didn't want to go so, since I was the ranking man, they handed me the Liberty List, the list of who was going, and told me, "Dolan, you take the crew in there and make sure they get their beer." Only half of the port side came, so we had more than our share of beer that day. When I was standing in line to get my beer, I looked over and there was an officer I recognized. He wasn't from my hometown, but he was from a town I used to work in when I went to high school, so he and I had a few together.

From Bideford, we moved down to Plymouth, England, on the southern coast, and that's where small boat crews boarded the LSTs. Everyone from the base went down there, and we were then assigned to a particular LST. Here we trained with the LSTs—making practice landings—until D-Day.

When I was assigned to LST 47 at Plymouth, I hadn't even seen an LST before. Upon boarding the ship, they gave us our quarters, and I had just barely gotten my gear stowed in the locker, when they called out "Small boatmen—man your boats"—we had to go pick up the liberty party. I had boat number 1 so, naturally, I had to go in. I went in, and picked them up, and it was dark. They had an air raid that night—it wasn't near us—it was right in Plymouth, itself, but, when I got back to the ship, the alert was still on and we had to stay in "officer's country." While there, you're closed in and it was all black—you couldn't see anything, or go out and see what was happening. You don't know whether you're blind, or what's going on. It was too confining for me, and I didn't like that at all.

I ended up with a gun station topside on the 20 millimeter. You had the pointer, and ammunition handler, and one guy on a walkie-talkie for communication, on each one of those guns. At least we were topside so you knew what was going on—you had fresh air. I was the pointer—the gunner—but this was once again a matter of just where they put you. They'd have a gunner's mate show you how to handle the gun, then they'd just turn it over to you and hope that you could hit something.

We hit Utah Beach at H+30 (a half hour after H-Hour) and it was wet, windy, and nasty when we made our run. It was too damned rough to land the LST, and I don't know if any of them landed on Omaha, or not. The first day, we anchored about ten miles off shore, and they tried to off-load onto a Rhino barge and an LCT. The LCTs were made to where you could marry them up LCT stern to LST bow. The LST's bow doors would open, the ramp would come down, and the LCT Mark 6's rear would open up and they would mate up to your ramp so vehicles could drive directly from the LST to the LCT. Because of the weather, we couldn't even do that—we couldn't keep them tied up close enough to unload. The next day, however, it calmed down enough so we could unload. Actually, we didn't see anything. I drove right up there onto the beach and didn't have any problem. Now I did see some little splashes in the water—it looked like a guy throwing a rock in there or something, and I didn't know what the hell they were. Come to find out, it was probably rifle or machine gun fire, but it wasn't that close to us. So we dropped our troops off there, in the water, and we backed down off and turned around.

At that time, I had an officer with me, and we turned around from the shore where we could see the big guns firing. After making our turn we looked where we were going, because we had to go out and pick up more troops and come in again and, some distance away, an LCT had been hit. I don't know whether it hit a mine, or a shell from shore hit it, or what, but it got hit. The officer said, "Well, let's go pick them up." So we floor-boarded her and went out there. We were probably about two miles away from the LCT so, when we got to it, the ship had already sunk, the only thing there was the guys floating around in the water. In this particular area, the water wasn't too rough, and we picked up nineteen survivors—I don't know how many dead were still in the water, but we didn't pick up any of the dead ones. Luckily, we didn't hit any of them with the prop of our boat—we just maneuvered around there and hauled the guys up over the fantail, because that was the lowest end of the boat. For a couple of them, we tried to lower our ramp, but it was too rough—the ramp was all metal and, when that goes up and down because of the waves, it would hit these guys trying to crawl into the boat. We hadn't seen too much of the war up until this point. We had seen a couple of ships go down, or get hit, but nothing as bad as when we picked those guys up out of the damn water. They were hurting—they were hurting, goddamit, and they were bleeding all over the place and floating around in that damned old salty water—that has stuck with me continuously to today! These guys were all hurt pretty bad and, if I remember correctly, only one of them was able to get on the hospital ship under his own power—the rest of them had to be hauled up on litters and one of the survivors died on the way to LST 282. It took a long time to transfer these guys from the boat to LST 282 (it had been converted over to a hospital ship), for these big swells would come along and the LCVP would drop down from under you, or it would raise up in the air just as you were putting someone on a litter. The whole thing wasn't that gory to me because I was too busy trying to handle the boat so the guys could get unloaded. I remember one guy that they picked up at the heels and shoulders, and his knee bent the other way when they picked him up. By now it was pretty late in the afternoon, so we didn't make any more runs. We went back to our ship and made a couple more runs the next day to pick up a couple of boats that didn't make it in—the crews had left, and they were broached or beached and had gotten away from their ships.

We couldn't unload our LST the first day because the sea was too dang rough, so the next day they brought in Rhino barges and LCTs so they could unload onto them and they could take the equipment and personnel to shore. On about the second day there we had to pick up about a thousand prisoners and take them back to Portsmouth. The German officers got the quarters where some of the ship's crew were assigned—they didn't kick me out, but they kicked out some of the guys on the port side who had to move in different areas until we discharged the prisoners. They only had about eight or ten German officers, but the guys that

Robert J. "R.J." Dolan

had to give up their berths for them sure weren't happy about it. These officers were kind of arrogant. We had to guard them if they went to use the head, and all of that, and here we were taking care of the guys that were, not too long ago, shooting at your buddies. Most of the enemy enlisted men were there because they had to be; they didn't have any choice in the matter, and it wasn't their damn fault. They probably wanted to get captured so they could get out of that damn mess—I know that some of them did. The enlisted got stuck on the tank deck down below, and we had to stand guard over them (I don't know where the hell they were going to go) until we got to Portsmouth.

We made about nine trips in all across the

Several members of the LST 47 crew. R.J. Dolan is in the front row, fourth from the right.

Channel—back and forth—taking supplies over and bringing wounded or something back. Finally, they got us loaded and sent us to the Mediterranean, where we passed through the Strait of Gibraltar and wound up in Bizerte, North Africa. We spent some time in that area ferrying supplies, and then went up into Italy where we made a few trips across the 'Med' and practiced dropping off troops. We then proceeded to Southern France to participate in Operation Dragoon. As it turned out, our LST, rather than hitting the beach, was designated the good duty of being a "Mother Ship." We just laid out there in the bay and took care of the LCVPs and made sure that the crews had food and supplies. We took crews that maybe lost their boat, or whatever.

After LST 282 was destroyed by a German guided rocket, my crew went on her and, like the others, we'd steal stuff off of it. Since the 282 was no longer usable, they'd send a mechanic over there and, if he found something good, he'd just take it off—all of the ships were doing this. My crew went over there about a day

or two after the explosion and the ship was still smoldering and bodies were laying all around. We stayed there as the Mother Ship for over a month and, on one of the trips that our ship made back to Africa, four of us remained behind on shore to crew LCVPs that had no ship. On their trip back the Med was rougher than hell and one of the mess stewards—a colored guy that served the officers—fell overboard. They dropped a small boat in the water to try to get him, but the water was so rough that they couldn't get close enough without taking a chance of running over him. I don't know exactly how he got picked up, but they did get him back and said that he was as white as a damn sheet when he got back on board. He had been in that rough water a good twenty minutes to a half hour before he was rescued. That water was so rough that the ship actually cracked just forward of the officer's quarters—the quarters above the main deck—on port and starboard about three or four feet inland from the outboard side, and then down the sides. They had to get it welded, so a shipfitter came out there and welded it. What had happened was that the bow had gone up and down so much in those damn waves that it had just broke the top plates. Fortunately, we didn't lose anything and nobody got hurt because of it.

We travelled along the coast of Africa, from Bizerte to Oran and, right after Christmas, we headed back to the States. It took us about two weeks to get back, and it got pretty damned rough out there as well. We finally landed in Norfolk, spent about two days there, then went on up to New York and from there to Boston. When we got to Boston, that's when we got our leave. I think about two-thirds of the ship's company got off for leave, while the remaining third stayed aboard for re-fitting at the shipyard. I went home on my leave for thirty days and had a pretty good time. Everybody in town was great. All the kids, of course, in my age group, were gone and, if they were home on leave, they were having a ball too. Everybody tried to do what they could for you—buy you a drink, get you this, or get you that, get some extra gas, coffee or cigarettes—I didn't smoke, so I gave the extra cigarettes to my dad. My brother was stationed right there in St. Louis at the time, and he came home while I was

there. I didn't know he was coming, and I was upstairs, sleeping, when he came running in about a hundred miles-an-hour and landed right in the middle of the damned bed with me. I don't think the folks knew he was coming home, either. He was AWOL when he came in—I think he was too far away from the base—but, after a few days, he went back and I don't think he was caught. Everybody was real good, you didn't have any problems with anybody. They were glad to see you were home, glad to buy you a drink, get you something, or listen to your war stories. When we went back to the ship, the third who had remained behind took off on their leaves. This last third was replaced by other people, so we lost that group.

After some more work, including getting some more fresh water tanks and removal of the two forward small boat davits, we got under way and proceeded down the coast to Norfolk where we picked up some more personnel. We went down through the Panama Canal, laid out in the lake partway through it, then went through the locks on the other side of the Pacific. We travelled up the Pacific coast to San Diego, spent a day or two there where I had liberty, then on

LST 47 debarking German POWs in England.

up to Washington to a naval yard in Bremerton. Here we picked up a load of colored troops to take to Saipan. From there we crossed the Pacific, stopped off at Hawaii for a day or two, went on to Guam for only a day or less, then on to Saipan where we dropped off our cargo and picked up some supplies. We then made trips from Saipan, into the Philippines, and then on to Okinawa. We got into Okinawa shortly after D-Day—it was getting near the end, and it was fairly safe—we weren't getting shot at or anything like that. We didn't have to beach—we unloaded onto other smaller ships and they took the cargo on in.

We went back and forth from the Philippines to Okinawa about three or four times, just hauling in supplies and personnel, and taking personnel back out. We were anchored in Okinawa the day the Japanese agreed to surrender. Everybody got the word, of course, and every damn ship out in the harbor was firing—shots going up all over the place—you could follow the tracers and, the hell of it is, everything that goes up has got to go down. As a result, some of the people got hurt. I remember that they wouldn't let us fire, and we were a little bit perturbed about that. Our Captain was a pretty smart old guy—he was an old Navy Chief Boatswain's Mate and, when the war broke out, they made him a captain. He was an old "Rum Hound" but, dammit, he knew how to sail.

From Okinawa, we went back to the Philippines and were in Batanga the night they actually signed the surrender. Shortly after the treaty was signed, our next stop was Japan.

The first thing that I can remember, when going ashore in Japan, we got into an old brick building there that was like an NCO club or Airmans Club of today. The Japanese waited on you, and they were still in uniform—or partial uniform—and they were just as good as they could be. They'd bring you the beer, make sure you had enough—we didn't have any trouble with them at all—at least I didn't. The ones that we ran into knew the war was over, knew they had lost, and that was it. I'm sure there were some that didn't, but the ones that I ran into were very helpful—very friendly. They did all the work of loading and unloading the ship, they were the stevedores on shore while we did our share aboard.

I got some leave time there, and it was a treat—up to a point. I was surprised by the way the Japanese acted—like nothing had happened! The ones we saw were going to wait on you, they served you your beer at the clubs where they worked; they were bowing,

bowing and bowing to you all the damn time and there was no animosity from any of those that I saw. It amazed me, but we gave them a hell of a good parking lot (devastation) in some of those areas. I'll tell you, we were in the Tokyo/Yokosuka area and we went ashore one night, four or five of us together, and we didn't know where we were and couldn't speak the language. Well, the ship moved from its dock and going from town to the ship we had to catch a trolley. Well, hell, the trolleys were full and we got on the back of the darn thing and when we wanted to get off we simply pulled down on the electrical connector and brought the car to a halt. The guy driving had to get off and put the thing back up himself—he wasn't too happy about that.

We hung around for a while and I picked up a few souvenirs—got a Jap rifle that I brought home. From Honshu we went up to Hokkaido—the northernmost island—where I pulled small boat duty ferrying the guys ashore. I accidentally left an officer up there on shore one time. I caught hell when I got back to the ship and had to turn around and go pick him up. Not too long after that I had enough points to return home. I got off the LST sometime just before Christmas, boarded a troop transport and thought that when we crossed the International Dateline I'd have two Christmases. Anyway, we didn't hit it on the right date, so I didn't get my second Christmas.

When we got back, we landed at Bremerton, got our medical exam and all of our crap together and they put us on trains. I arrived back at Great Lakes and got discharged two years, eleven months and twenty-two days from the day I enlisted. One of the things I thought was pretty funny was that when you went in the service you had all of these physical checks and everything else where you had to be just so. Your hearing tests, for example, were individual. When you got back, however, they'd run you in with about fifteen or twenty at a time, and would whisper into some kind of a machine. Anybody that didn't hear it had to stand up, or sit down, or whatever. Well, everybody's ears were in great shape, boy, let's get the hell out of here! That's the way they operated and I was glad—got you out of there a couple of days sooner probably.

When Mr. Dolan received his discharge he joined the "Fifty-two Twenty Club," (unemployed servicemen were guaranteed to receive twenty dollars a week for fifty-two weeks) but this only lasted a single week before he went to work at the local paper mill. After a while he joined the Air Force (he couldn't stand being seasick anymore) and retired with just a little over twenty years.

"I would," he said, "like to mention one duty during my twenty-three year career that was one of the toughest yet most rewarding. Shortly after enlisting in the U.S. Air Force while stationed at Westover Air Force Base in Massachusetts, I volunteered for Body Escort Duty. This program was set up by the government to return the remains of those killed overseas back to their families and loved ones in the States. This was tough on the families to receive the remains and not be able to open the caskets. It was worth it when you could see the relief on their faces knowing now that their loved one was home and they could visit as often as they would like and spend time with them. This was a big expense to the government, but it was worth every penny—one thing we did and did right. I am proud to have been chosen to be a part of that program if only for a short time."

Following his retirement from the Air Force, he went to work for McDonnel-Douglas and retired the second time in June 1986.

Ironically, while Mr. Dolan was with the Air Force in Da Nang, Vietnam, in 1965, he saw his old LST 47. Twenty years after he stepped off her deck for the last time, she was now owned and operated by the Japanese!

LST 47 in Da Nang, South Vietnam, 1965.

# Lester R. Jarvis, BM 2/C

*I wouldn't have missed those three years in the Navy for ten years of my life.*

I was born in 1921, on Pearl Street in Martins Ferry, Ohio. I grew up there, went to Martins Ferry High School and, after graduating, I went to work at a factory making twin 40s (40 millimeter guns) for the Government. I think I was there about six months before joining the U.S. Navy.

I was at home when I heard about the Japanese attack on Pearl Harbor, and enlisted in the Navy on February 1st, 1942. A group of us kids went to Pittsburgh for the Air Force, and only one of the six made it. We took the test for the Air Force, and they wanted us to take the job of transports, so we said no, and then we all went in and signed up for the U.S. Navy. We didn't know whether we'd be taken or not but, of course, the Navy would have taken anything as long as it was live meat. I'm not regretting it—I had three years of wonderful, wonderful fellas, we got together like brothers, and we still talk together after fifty years.

I took my Boot Camp training at Great Lakes Naval Base at Chicago, Illinois. The only thing I really remember about Great Lakes was working in the galley, picking up garbage at six in the morning, and getting out on the grinder and exercising. It was just basic training to straighten out an individual.

We had two boys shot off of the water tanks because they were trying to get out—escape. They tried to get them down, but those MPs didn't give a damn—Marines—they kept you in line! It was tough on some kids, and not too bad on others—I really didn't have a problem with that at Great Lakes. They had a prison there—not really a prison, but guys that had gone "over the hill," or guys not coming back from leave on time, and the Commanding Officer would put them in the brig for a week. But the quarters they were held in were guarded by Marines. We didn't like that, but the Marines were part of the Navy, so you couldn't fight it too much. We had the same problem at Pier 92, in New York. At Pier 92, when you did something there, they brought you out with fixed bayonets and stood you in line to pick up your meal. They didn't take any crap. You know, being a young guy and seeing this, it'd scare the hell out of you, so I didn't get in any trouble.

From Great Lakes, I was shipped to Little Creek, Virginia. I think we stayed there at Little Creek for about twelve weeks. That was a rough old base—ninety percent of the sailors there were prisoners at large; they were in the brig, but they were walking around with the "P" for prisoner stamped on the backs of their uniforms because there wasn't enough room for them in the confinement area. When I arrived, there was probably about five thousand sailors getting off the train, and we had to walk about three miles to the camp. As you went through the gate at Little Creek, the one whole side of it was fenced and, in that fence, was all these prisoners—all the guys that were over leave, or causing trouble, whatever. Well, that area was full of prisoners. Most of the people that I knew were in the brig, and they'd beat the hell out of you in the brig. One of the guys I knew—he was from my hometown—was getting out of the brig that day, and he was hollering at me through the fence. He said that he was getting out in the morning, and I didn't get to see him—he was kind of a rough old kid and, about a week later, he came back to my hut to see me, and I asked him where he had been. Well, you see, they'd get them up every other hour in the brig—wake them up—have them muster, and then put them back to bed. Well, he was one of these kinds of guys that would shoot off his mouth, and they whipped him. They put him over a barrel and used a cat-o-nine-tails on him. He took his shirt off and showed me his back, but he was tough, he wasn't crying about it. I think he had made some remark during one of the wake-ups about, "Let's get over this thing—quit screwing around," and that's all he needed; a Master-of-Arms just put him down and showed him who's boss. What this was, was all these kids couldn't stand this treatment in the sense of being away from home. You're awfully, awfully depressed when you're laying in your bunk and thinking about your home, and mother and dad, and apple pie, and ice cream, and your girl friend. The way you get around this is you talk to your buddies about your girl, and his girl, and your mother and father, and you grow out of it after a while. Little Creek was tough. They were living on gob piles that were dredged out of the water and, as it hardened, they'd put another quonset hut up.

At Little Creek they trained us with an old wooden ship out in the harbor. They used this old ship for us to learn how to control our boats—bring them alongside. They had rifle ranges, exercising, and LCVPs, but they didn't have enough boats to train their people, so maybe they'd take ten of us out on a boat, and there was an old, wooden hulk out there. The problem was that we were to train each other on moving towards that hulk. On an LCVP you speeded up real good, and then you'd twist it, and you'd bring it in alongside of a ship, or you'd back it off of a ship. Well, the boys, when we first started, were spending a lot of time taking chips out of that wooden hulk. After a while—it took a while—you'd get better at it, but you didn't have enough training there to really give you the experience that you needed. When the training period ended, it ended; they'd just ship you out to make room for the next group coming in.

After Little Creek, they shipped us to New York on a train and we were in Pier 92 for a period of about seven weeks. That's where we had a problem where the Captain of the Pier had a wife, and he was letting her control this base of about ten thousand men. The barracks there had men on bunks stacked three to four high. The guys would be undressing, they would be changing clothes, and she'd come walking down through the middle of the building with all of these men here. We had a thing called the grinder, down on the driveway off the pier, where we used to muster every morning at 6 o'clock. She'd come out there and stand while we were being brought to attention, mustered, our names called out—and all that crap; she was controlling that base, and I know there was a lot of resentment about it. So Walter Winchell picked it up—about this Commander that let his wife do all the sailor work, and the Commander ended up getting transferred.

When we left New York on a ship, there was so many men—we were on the grinder at that time when they mustered the LST people, and how this happened was, say, there was three guys in a line, and they'd say: "You're a coxswain, you're a gunner, you're a bow hookman," and this was how they set it up. They didn't give you any test or anything. I didn't get to be a coxswain then, but they put us on a Liberty Ship with four boats on each ship.

They took us to Liverpool, unloaded us and our boats on trucks—with each man on a truck—and it took us a week to go from Liverpool to Instow, England. When we landed in Liverpool, here we were—a bunch of American sailors who had never been in England before, we didn't know what Liverpool was, but we had a lieutenant that was in charge of this flotilla crap, and he gave each one of us a Pound Note. We didn't know what a Pound Note was, but at that time it was worth about $4.25. Well, we got into those trailer trucks to drive about three hundred miles. We got only about two hundred miles, or less, and we were flat-assed broke. The guy driving the truck spoke a cockney language, and you couldn't understand half the time what he was asking you, and he didn't understand you. But these truck drivers got to be pretty good guys, and they were buying our meals, and we were sleeping on hammocks in the boat on the trailer trucks—'cause we didn't have money for a hotel. When we arrived, I wanted to get this one guy a carton of cigarettes—American cigarettes—because, hell, he paid for most of our trip down there, but the skipper wouldn't let us do it. The poor guy didn't care, he said, "Don't worry about it, Yank, I'll take care of it—don't worry about it." That's when they put our boat in Instow, England, and assigned us a room in one of those mansions in what was a resort town before the war.

Because they were big rooms, they put maybe eight to ten guys in each room. We lived in these mansions, so to speak, on the beach, with so many men to a room. When I arrived there, the other crews were there, and you'd see our kids coming up the road with high hats on, tuxedoes on, fancy women's dresses on; these people that had left these mansions locked their clothing in closets—which was stupid.

We were living in these rooms—had a big fireplace—and we had a mess hall where we went to eat. Well, there were guys standing in this line one day that didn't have Navy uniforms. We got acquainted with them, and it so happened that they were Rangers—I mean, they were mean and tough boys, and they needed a place to stay, so we took them back with us to our room so they could sleep there. What they were assigned to do was: they were supposed to stay up in the hills until it got dark, and their operation was to take over our base. Now, these four guys were from Detroit, or Toledo, and, honest-to-god, I think they were all racketeers—they must have all been hit men, to be honest with you. They were about our age, but they were a lot bulkier—a lot stronger. These guys looked like a bunch of Detroit or New York gangsters. When we got back to the room, all they did was sharpen their knives on their leather boots, and I mean they were sharp. They always carried these knives on their legs and, if they had to use them—they'd use them—no ifs, ands, or buts about it. Well, what their operation was: in the morning, at daylight, they were gonna knock into the Captain's offices and get all the information on how many boats we got, how many men were there, how many weapons we got, and take it back to the Ranger division. So, about five in the morning, they took off and they did—they got the Captain and tied him up, they got the secretary tied up and whoever else was in the office, they got everything they wanted to know and stole a small boat and took off. When I say Rangers—they were a tough bunch of boys. I'd hate like hell to meet them on the street somewhere. The Captain was all up-tight, because they got all this information and, had it been the Germans, they would have known how many men were there, how many boats were there, what we were using them for, and the Rangers had all of this. Naturally, we never said anything about it—we just let it go.

We worked there in Instow for about eight months. What we did there was we'd make our runs out to the ocean at night, from our base to a small inlet. The Army used to bunk there and, about eleven o'clock at night, we had to get in our boats and we would follow a lead boat for maybe twenty-, twenty-five miles to a long beach and, about daybreak, we'd have the Army guys on board training for assault. We'd line up the LCVPs in their one, two, three, four, five, six lines—twenty boats in a line—then they'd give you a signal to come full speed ahead into the beach.

On December the 18th, 1943, my birthday, we were in the second assault wave going into the beach. When we picked up our boats in a group—forty or fifty boats—they'd signal you by light to come in and pick up your crew. Well, the tide was so strong there that you had to hit that beach on a forty-five degree angle in order to keep yourself from getting ripped and thrown out. So every one of the small boats had to come in at a 'forty-five' and then you'd give it speed so you could hold your bow into the beach so these men could unload. Well, at that particular time, I was in the first wave, but the thing called a ramp crank (the handle that lowers and raises the bow ramp)—I didn't have one. I told the lieutenant next to me and he said, "Borrow it from the guy next to you." Well, that's stupid, because I had to raise it and lower it when I unloaded out at sea. I told him I couldn't do that, so he said, "Well, you're going to have to go back to port there and get yourself another crank." So, after I went back, they signalled me for the second assault wave and I went off the shore, loaded my men, and what we did was we follow a light out to sea until it was almost daylight—almost out to the ocean. It was a calm, nice day that day and, as I was going back in, what they did was give you a speed boat that comes out there to signal you,—"Break in , Go!" We had a speed boat that day but, as we were heading into the beach, he cut us off. He said, "Stop, go back." We didn't know what happened. When we went back, we had to wait for our tide to go in to get us in to shore—we had to unload those men that we had onboard our wave.

Something happened that day that we never found out. There was one hundred and eighteen soldiers, and about ten of our people, killed. Now, you've got to understand, LSMs, LCMs, LCVPs, LSIs—but these big ones were carrying tanks with full crews. We didn't know how bad this was, because they didn't tell us. When we got back into the beach, our commander told us about the losses, but we never got an explanation why. The question that went out was: What happened, what happened? Now the story they gave us was, that on every wave there was a certain amount of water, but there's always another wave that's got three times as much water in it—in the wave itself—as the ones in front of you. What they claimed was that one huge wave, a massive wave, flipped the whole line of boats over—flipped the tanks over. Guys got caught with their heads in the engine room of a tank, and couldn't get out. A couple of them got hit with the turret...there were so damn many stories about this but, to this day, no one has been given the story about this. We were in back of this first wave—we were coming in—and we didn't see any huge waves! We just saw a normal ocean roll.

From what I was told, there were a lot of Army boys hurt in that wave—put in the hospital—and the major in charge of the Army people chewed our people out for killing his soldiers—which wasn't our fault. Our Navy commander went out after him, and there was a little bit of a scuffle, or argument about it, but they just shut it up. Our job was to go out there and head out into the ocean to train the Army in high surf, but we're talking about the ocean now—we've got surf. But you don't have that kind of surf that can kick over an LCM with a tank inside of it! Think about it; you're going into a beach and all of a sudden something comes along and just flips you over like a tin can in the water.

On an assault, one time, a kid froze and wouldn't get off of my boat. We had gone out to sea, it was a nice sea, and we had these photographers and Congressmen up on a hill watching this practice assault. We had twenty or thirty boats in line, coming into that beach, and you'd hit that beach as hard as you could, and drop that ramp. Well, everything was fine, we were going in like you wouldn't believe, and one kid with a flamethrower on his back grabbed the cable that raised the ramp, and I couldn't break him loose. We were backing out, and the ramp was down so I couldn't turn around to get in the water, and pretty soon it swamped me. The kid was still hanging on—he was scared to death—he was scared of jumping in the water and running with that flamethrower. With all of these admirals and everyone standing up there on shore, ten minutes later I'm sitting on the sand because the tide went out so fast. I don't have any idea what happened to the kid, but two soldiers came down and got him and, once he was on dry land, he didn't care. A bulldozer came out about two hours later, shoved me out into deeper water, and I went.

When we were in Ireland, it seemed that the Irish wanted to fight all of the time; they'd fight you in the street, or fight you in an alley, and even fight you in a parade. We were there one time when they had a big parade going, and these guys came up and said, "How do you like the parade?"

"Pretty good," we said.

"What's good about it?" Well, see, what they were doing was playing games with us. Had we said, "I think it stinks," they would have come back with something like, "Well, what stinks about it?" As it usually turned out, we would end up fighting and get the devil beat out of us and, sometimes, we'd beat the devil out of them.

From Instow, England, we went to Plymouth. Prior to becoming a coxswain, I was a bow hookman. For some reason or other, I think the man we had as a coxswain just wasn't there—hell of a nice guy, but I think that half the time he was scared to death. Certain times on an LCVP, you could be in pretty good danger. You're exposed up there, and you've got a gunner behind you that's scared to death to fire. But it gets to be just as customary as driving a car, only you're on water.

When we went to Plymouth to pick up our LSTs, we went with a complete new crew—we didn't know these fellas because they only put six boats and crews on each LST. I was assigned to LST 49. There were three LCVPs hanging on the right side, and three hanging on the left side, and your boat was your boat—you took care of it, you had a motor mac', you had a gunner/bow hookman, and you had a signalman with his flags. All the boys we had worked with for a year, a year-and-a-half, were all spread out on these LSTs, and

you were a total stranger onboard. The crew, I say the crew in terms of the ones that brought it over from New York, were all "old salts," in other words, they had been out on the ocean. Our LST was made in Pittsburgh, it came down the Ohio Valley River—they made it up in Pennsylvania, got a small crew of twelve guys and sailed it down the Ohio River and then brought it over to Plymouth.

Lester Jarvis aboard LST 49.

My General Quarters station was with the fire division. My position on the ship was close to my boat but, if there were a fire, I'd be available to help put it out. Now, if the fire was too much, we'd evacuate, but if the fire were manageable, I was there.

When you first get onboard an LST, or any ship, you're kind of homesick, or lonely—you don't feel really comfortable. As time goes by, a week or so, the first thing you know you talk to this guy, you talk to that guy, he's asking you what you're doing, he's asking you how you do it, and the small boats were new to them. There weren't any on board this LST until we got there. Well, you've got your own LCVPs, and you're heroes and all that crap. You grow so tight together, as a unit, I mean you'd worry about one another—you'd love one another (that sounds strange as hell, but you get so close that that's your little group—that's your buddies). You'd get so tight together that, if you got in trouble, they were behind you. The other crewmen were just as friendly toward you, but there were certain groups of guys that get so tight together, they worry about whether the others are O.K., or not, and so on.

and say, "Tell him to get me a fresh pot of coffee and bring it up." One time I heard a noise from the stern of the ship and here was another one of the mess stewards with a fishing line in his hand—and we were underway. I asked him what he was doing back there, and he said, "The Captain wants fish for breakfast, and we don't have any, so I've got to catch some fish for breakfast." The crew were damn good to these guys, and so were the officers, but this Captain was a Georgia boy whose father was a Rear Admiral, or some

Normandy Invasion, June 1944. An LCVP from *USS Thomas Jefferson* (APA-30) pulls away from the shore with a full load of troops who will be carried to invasion shipping in the harbor. Photographed at a south English port during pre-invasion loading operations, circa early June 1944.

Our Captain was a nut. He was from Georgia, and hated blacks, and whenever he was on the conn he'd call one of the Officers of the Deck up and say, "Wake up that nigger and have him bring me a cup of coffee." Now these kids (the mess stewards) were really good kids—we got along fine with them, but we'd have to go down and wake this black kid up—his name was DuBois—a fantastic kid, a nice kid, but that skipper would make him go into the galley (the officers had their own galley and dining room) and make him a pot of fresh coffee. With a saucer and a cup, climbing a ladder fourteen feet high, the kid had to do this. We couldn't cover for him, and that Captain would wake him up at three in the morning, four in the morning,

damn thing. We used to show movies when we were underway, and he wouldn't let the movie start until he was there. He'd come out of his cabin with a pair of shoes with no backs in them, and a yellow raincoat, and he'd sit in the front seat, and then he'd run the dirt off of his feet where the shoes were open—he was a crumb, a real crumb.

The only thing that saved our tail was that later, while we were off the coast of Okinawa, he broached our ship on a reef and got transferred. You know where he went? To a hell of a big job in Washington, D.C. They would have court martialled anybody else—you broach a ship, and you're in big trouble. Well, they pulled him off of that and, next thing you know, he's gone. We asked about where he went, and found out that because of his father he got some hellacious job.

While still in England, we used to have to use our small boats to act as tugs to keep the ship from broaching when the tides would come in. I burned an engine up on my boat one time—my oil turned to water—and the Old Man was going to court martial me for burning up the engine. "Well," the Exec said, "how the hell was he going to do anything about it? Did you want the ship to hit the shore, or did you want him to hold the ship there?"

The skipper was the kind of a guy that if he was going south, he'd lower a small boat and have it push the bow around to go to the north. He wouldn't start the engines, he'd use the small boat to push him around so he'd be going in the right direction.

Now, when we left Plymouth, we had to skirmish out in the ocean because we were in a flotilla, and they were protected by some of the destroyers. We were headed to Normandy for the invasion. We come in there at about twelve o'clock at night, and we anchored out and, when we got up in the morning, you couldn't see water for ships! There were ships as far as the eye could see in any one direction. There were a lot of LSTs—hundreds of them. The skipper asked me to go to the flagship, and I didn't know where the hell it was, and he didn't either. He said, "Well, find it," and I said, "What if I don't find it?," and he said, "Just go find it." It was almost dark time and I said, "Christ, Skipper, I could get my brains shot out," and he said, "That's your problem." Well, he sent me out there to take the orders to the flagship, and the problem there was everybody was on edge and I was afraid that they'd see us coming through the ships and they'd open up on me and I ain't gonna be around anymore. I made it to the flagship, and made it back—the flagship wouldn't let me stay overnight—I wanted to stay rather than run back around those ships again.

When we got to the beach it wasn't that bad—the day was fine, and the ocean was great. But when that storm arrived, the waves were so bad they were touching the deck of the LST. They were trying to lower our boats in the water, but the ocean was so goddamn bad that when they dropped them in the water, they came back above you and would maybe snap the cables of the davit. Now, I've got these guys on the deck that have to get into the boat, and they had to be careful going down because the waves would be bringing the LCVP up and they could break their legs. We've got these thirty-six guys with forty- to fifty-pound packs

on their backs, and they were trying to go down a rope ladder and get into the LCVP—I'd see some of these guys drop in the water and never come back up. From the LST in front of us, we'd see guys come floating by face down, and that bothered me because we couldn't pick them out—they were too heavy. I wanted the lieutenant to have the guys take off their gear, take off their guns, and come down the ladder and then drop their gear to them on a rope, but he wouldn't do it. We fought our boats for two or three hours, and we were in the second assault wave, but we couldn't get enough boats full of men because the water was coming over the bows so goddamn bad that the guys were waist deep in water in the small boat. I was scared the whole damn time, because I didn't think we'd get out of that.

Now the first assault wave that went in on Utah—the Germans had erected a lot of steel rails in the water that would rip the bottom right out of their boats. Well, these guys were left off with about three hundred yards of water to walk through to get to the beach. On the second assault, we were told about the steel barriers and, as a result, could only get in so far—we couldn't make it any further. It's a terrible, terrible feeling to throw out a soldier in waist high water when he's got a forty pound pack on his back and the waves are beating the hell out of him. The soldiers were scared to death: he's got a gun in his hand, he's wet, his clothes are all wet, his pack's all wet, and he's got to jump in this waist deep water. You know, they'll just shoot the guy if he doesn't get off the boat. We never did that, but I heard it happened when a guy would get scared and grab on to something—what he was doing was endangering everybody else.

We were so damned glad to get back to the old LST because we thought the small boats were gonna drown from the amount of water we were taking onboard. We've got pumps on them, but the water was coming in too damn fast to keep up.

When I got back to the LST, they brought me onboard—they weren't going to send another crew out in that sea. All you could see of the enemy beach defenses were a bunch of flashes. They weren't really bothering us, they were firing at the airplanes—we had so damn many airplanes that if you threw rocks up in the air you could have knocked a couple down! You'd see five - six hundred airplanes at one shot. You never think about it when you're a young, dumb-assed kid, you just think, boy, this is a lot of excitement. We got through that thing pretty decently, but I was concerned because the waves were so massive. When I was in my small boat, one moment I'd be down in a trough, and the next I'd be up in the air on the top of a wave, and I've got this crew of soldiers that are scared to death—they think they're gonna drown without getting shot.

The next day we lined up twenty or thirty LSTs on the dry beach, and the Army came along with German prisoners and began putting them on our LSTs. Our LST was waiting for a group, and the MPs waited for the tide to come in about waist high before sending out five or six hundred of these people. I don't know why they didn't put them on with dry pants on, but they waited and then made them wade out to our ship. At the end of this line was a German lieutenant—now German officers were immaculately dressed, they looked right out of *Esquire*—and this lieutenant tells two of his men to make a ladder that he can sit on so that he doesn't get wet. Well, he rode out there on these two other fellas and they were in up to about their knees, and that MP put a bayonet into his ass about three inches. That lieutenant shot off those two men like something out of a Donald Duck cartoon.

Later, the MPs were sitting on benches on the tank deck of the LST—the tank deck would hold all of the equipment and soldiers—and there were four of them sitting at each corner and holding machine guns. They had fifty of our sailors down there searching these Yugoslavians, Czechoslovakians, what have you, that had been impressed into the German Army. The Germans had placed them in the front line to get blown up, but they were giving up so fast that we didn't have enough room. Anyway, we were down there searching these guys with a guy standing beside us with a Thompson sub machinegun while we searched some poor slob who didn't have nickel one. These were just common, ordinary people, and they didn't even want to fight. Well, our crew searched them for about five hours, and then we had about 15 Jewish doctors—they were interns more than anything else—and they were taking care of anybody who was wounded. This one Jewish doctor had a German officer by his head—under his arm—and he was pulling shrapnel out his head with a pair of pliers; this was a German and he wasn't about to get any royal treatment.

Pretty soon, these Yugoslavians and Czechs were running around the ship like a bunch of kids—we didn't have a hell of a lot of trouble with them at all. After the invasion, we were constantly going back and forth between England and France, carrying nurses, tanks, trucks, and so forth.

When we went into southern France, after the invasion was over, they designated me to take my crew ashore and stay there to pick up any stragglers, or wounded. They put me under English command, but they didn't get us any groceries so we had to scrounge for food. There was a town above us where an American soldier had rolled out a wine keg—big as a house—in the middle of the street; every time we went through we filled up our canteens. We sat on the beach for a good four or five weeks, and all we did was maybe take our .45s out and try to shoot at something in the water—a tin can, or something—for entertainment.

I remember that one time we went into town—a little village—and we went into this bakery. This man in there was a pretty nice fella—I couldn't speak his language—and he wanted us to try something he did. He took a lump of sugar, put Annisette on it, and we ate it. Well, that was all that he had to eat, there wasn't a hell of a lot to eat in the whole town. While we were sitting in there, this soldier came in. He was a paratrooper, and he was trying to find where so-and-so was. He had been behind the lines, and they were given orders to get anything—whatever they had to—to get back to their division, so he had stolen an American motorcycle and sidecar. They didn't care what they had to take—had it been the admiral's car sitting there with the engine running, he would have taken it. Well, we got to talking, and he asked, "Where're you from?"

"I'm from Ohio," I said.

"What part of Ohio?"

"Oh, you wouldn't know it," I replied, "Martin's Ferry."

"You're kidding!" he said.

"No, why, do you know where Martin's Ferry is?"

"Hell, yes," he replied, "I live in Bridgeport! Tell you what," he said, "If I can't get this motorcycle started, I'll give it to you."

Well, he couldn't start it, so he gave it to me, and we couldn't get it started. There were a bunch of Frenchmen there with a moving van, so we told them that if they gave us a tow, they could get us started and, if we couldn't get it started, we'd sell it to them for four bottles of wine. That was the wildest ride I've ever had in my life! When I got up on the hill, the Free French wanted the motorcycle—and they got it. We got the four bottles of wine, but they wanted that motorcycle, so we gave it to them.

We walked back down to the beach, where our LCVP was, and our LST had come back into the harbor. We thought we'd be going back on board, so I went flying back out on the LCVP and there, up on deck where my buddies were, were about forty of the most beautiful French nurses you'd see in your entire life. They were gorgeous looking! Well, what they did was they'd picked them up in, I think, Paris. My buddy, up there on topside, said, "Yeah, these are all French girls, and they can speak English!" Our Captain, I understand, had two of them in there for about two weeks, and never saw daylight. I asked the Exec if he was gonna let us stay aboard the ship, and he said, "Nope, get any kind of material you want, any food you want, load up and get out." So they went on to North Africa, and my crew and I went back to the shore in Southern France.

On our last trip out from the beach we picked up a wounded German officer to take him out to the hospital ship. When he was on board, I asked him, "Lieutenant, are you glad it's over with?"

"It's not over with," he replied, "When the Panzer Division gets down here, we'll throw you back into the ocean, and drown the whole damn bunch of you!"

One of my crew—a pretty good-sized kid about 6'4" and weighing about 260 pounds—said, "Let me throw this sonofabitch overboard." We didn't do it, but let me tell you something about a German soldier. If he's an officer, his clothes are immaculate—he had a pair of boots on that you could comb your hair in them. He may have been captured, but he hated the goddamned Americans—he still thought they were gonna win.

When we pulled into Southern France, we docked at the harbor in Marseilles. The Army had an area fenced-off for us where we could dock safely and, later, we could go into town. We really didn't do a lot in Marseilles. One time, however, the Captain wanted a jeep, so he sent John Culley out to get one for him. John found one with the engine running, but it was sitting there by the door of the SP's offices. Well, John jumped in it and took off, and the SPs took out after him. Fortunately, the skipper had planned ahead because, when John arrived with SPs not too far behind, the doors to the LST were open and the ramp was lowered right down to the edge of the dock. John came off the street doing about sixty miles-per-hour, tore down the length of the dock and sailed right in without slowing down. Once he was inside, they raised the ramp, closed the doors, and the SPs sped right on by.

After Europe, we went back to New York, and got a thirty day leave. I went home, saw the family, raised a little hell and, after getting into a disagreement with Louise (my high school girl friend), I reported back to the ship a week early. Once there, we were told that we were going down through the Panama Canal. We sat on the eastern end of the Canal for about a week where we had liberty at Colon, then pushed through and across to Hawaii.

We sat in Hawaii until our orders were cut, and then headed for the islands. The third island we landed at was Okinawa, where we arrived on D+1 (the day after the initial invasion). Our job was to deliver supplies so, like always, the ship would pull up as far as possible on the beach, wait for the tide to go out, then open the bow doors, lower the ramp, and unload the supplies. One of the ships that accompanied us—I think it was LST 281—was hit by a kamikaze. Now, whenever an LST goes into a beach, they drop off all of the small boats—like a mother duck with her ducklings behind her. One of the reasons for this is just in case the ship gets hit, we're out there to pick up survivors and assist in any way we can. What happened with the 281 was she was kind of racing us into the beach to be the first one in—they were even gunning the engines of the trucks and jeeps onboard her in preparation for getting off. This was when the kamikaze dove down and struck right in the center of the LST—blowing the hell out of it. They tried to get it out for a long time—nine hours, I think it was, and we went aboard and it was a hell of a mess. There were charred skeletons hanging from the wheelhouse, hanging over the rails—it was a terrible sight.

After that we spent our time just transporting material back and forth on Okinawa. The Marines did a hell of job on that island, because there was a lot of dead there—dead, in the sense that, "If you cut me up, I'm gonna cut you up" and, boy, they cut them up! They had no mercy on the Japanese on that island.

While I was over in the Pacific, we went through a Typhoon. It was so bad, that it blew all of the quonset huts off of the island of Saipan. We were notified about the storm about three hours before it hit, and they sent all of the ships—fifty to a hundred of them—out to sea. Anybody on deck was roped-off so he wouldn't be swept overboard, and there were only nine of us—of the entire crew—that weren't seasick. The others were so ill, that they were down on their backs. When the storm hit, and we were out there in the sea, you could look up in the air and see the bottom of another LST; in the next five minutes, that ship would be looking at the bottom of your LST—it was a strange feeling. The next morning, we saw things like a destroyer with the whole bow ripped off, or the bow doors of an LST gone. That water was so powerful that you had no control over the ship—the waves were so massive that it just threw you one way, and then another and, fortunately, we didn't land on anybody or have anybody land on us.

Once we were finished with Okinawa, we hit several of the islands. Some of the crew got off before we left for Hawaii, because we were told that the war was over and we were going home. Then they notified us that they needed a mail ship in Tientsin, China. They were sending us there full of plywood to set up a Marine post office—which never materialized. We stayed there, in China, until my number came up.

From China, I went back across the Pacific on a troop transport. All you did was sit on the deck, go to breakfast, lunch and dinner, and talk to your buddies. It was heart-wrenching to leave the LST but, at the same time, all you could think about was going home. We landed in San Francisco and took a train for about seven days to Great Lakes Naval Base where I was discharged. They gave us our mustering-out pay, all of our papers, and said good-bye.

I caught another train to Wheeling, and the trains were carrying coal from here to Pittsburgh. Well, if you had any white on, by the time you got to where you were going, it was coal dust black. We didn't mind it for, as long as we were going home, we didn't care. It was colder than hell, and the roads were all clogged up, but some guy in a truck saw me standing there on the side of the street and asked me where I was going. I told him I was going home, and he had chains on his truck, so he said, "C'mon, get in the truck," and he took me all the rest of the way home to Martins Ferry.

When Mr. Jarvis arrived home, he secured a job with the local newspaper, married Louise, and bought his present home for six thousand dollars. The house was "beat up and sitting idle," but Mr. Jarvis, who "had never had a hammer and nail in my hand all my life" remodelled it, and lives there to this day with Louise.

# Theodore M. Stratton, BM 2/C

*Simmons pulled the friction igniter fuse on the homemade depth charge and kicked it off the stern of the boat. Immediately, I revved up the engine to full throttle and headed upstream as fast as possible. The depth charge detonated ten feet behind the boat with a tremendous explosion. A geyser of muddy water shot twenty feet in the air and lifted the stern of the boat out of the water. The boat screw, biting at the empty air, set up a vibration that threatened to rip the shaft out of the engine bearing. When the boat settled back in the river, I turned to Simmons and said: "Goddamn, this river is a lot shallower than the Army expected!"*

*Nitro, the nickname given to the Army Demolition sergeant assigned to our unit, had been sitting on one hundred of these depth charges nestled in the well deck of the boat. He looked at me ashen-faced and, with a touch of irony in his voice, said: "Had that charge gone off under the boat, we would have changed the course of the river and they would have picked up our remains with a blotter. The charge must have landed on a sandbar. I'll reduce the charge by twenty blocks—that should correct the problem. Let's hope we don't have that happen again."*

### "Updike's Raiders"

The crossing of the Rhine River had been orchestrated as carefully as that given the preparation for the Normandy Invasion. Precise coordination between the various tactical groups to ensure the timing of air, ground, and naval forces was initiated. The Navy was called upon to furnish boats and experienced crews to make the initial assault crossing of the River. The Air Force was to pound the enemy's rail lines, roads and troop concentrations in an effort to isolate the assault area. The field artillery was to lay down a barrage on specific strong points. The Army was to furnish spearhead forces carefully trained in amphibious operations.

In most cases, battle-hardened Navy and Army veterans of the Normandy Invasion (and subsequent battles) were chosen for this spearhead force. LCVPs (Landing Craft, Vehicle, Personnel) and LCMs (Landing Craft, Mechanized) were the Navy's choice for this inland water operation.

This story relates some of the experiences encountered by one of these Navy crews.

My saga begins in England, where the British had temporarily turned over the Royal Naval College at Dartmouth for the use of the U.S. Naval Amphibious Forces. The purpose of this station was to establish a pool of small boat crews for the upcoming invasion of Europe. The station designation was "United States Advanced Amphibious Base Dartmouth Devon" (USNAAB). To man this station, the Navy sent out a general bulletin to all amphibious ships for volunteers. The quota from our ship was three boat crews consisting of four men each.

At the time, I was a striking quartermaster on LST 508. Gordon Thomas Simmons, my shipmate since

duty at the Naval Technical Training Center in Memphis, informed me he was going to volunteer. I wasn't really interested in joining him but, after a talk with my skipper, I volunteered. I was assigned as boat coxswain and Simmons was assigned as my motor machinist mate. Consequently, we were assigned to Dartmouth Naval Station.

Many of the men who served at this station will recall its infamous "Burma Road." The road into the college ran from the main gate, uphill to the main entrance, then returned back downhill to the main gate—creating a circle of approximately one-half mile. Men who disobeyed minor Naval Regulations were sentenced to carry a full seabag, lashed sea-going fashion, around this circle driveway. Ergo; the "Burma Road." A "Captain's Mast" could sentence you to four to eight hours on the road depending on your infraction. This punishment usually embittered a man more than it disciplined him.

The Dartmouth Base was not homogeneous in the normal way of a U.S. Naval ship or station. It was used as a replacement depot for small boat crews and other amphibious personnel. Men were coming and going individually, and in groups, without really knowing one another or having anything in common but the uniform.

Prior to D-Day, the allies determined that they had insufficient landing craft in certain areas to accomplish their goals, so they called on the U.S. Navy for help. My boat and crew were assigned to the Canadians for landing on what we later found out was Juno Beach. We worked the beach from D-Day until late September. During this period we did everything from assault boat to messenger boat, gun boat, tug boat, rescue boat, etc., etc.

After completing our tour at Normandy, we were returned to Dartmouth for further assignment. We hoped this would be to the United States. We based this hope on the belief that the Navy had accomplished all the assault landings required in Europe. We soon found out how naive we were.

Shortly after arriving, we were ordered to fall out on the parade ground where we were introduced to Lieutenant William Wenker (who was to become our new commanding officer), Lieutenant Sydney Wright (our executive officer), and the other men who were to become our division officers. We were divided into six units consisting of four boats per unit. My boat was assigned Boat Crew #1, Unit #1, under the direct command of Division Officer Lieutenant (Junior Grade) Archyball P. Updike.

Returning to the United States was soon dispelled when our new Commanding Officer said:

"Gentlemen, erase any illusions you may have about going home. I'm not at liberty to disclose at this time your next assignment, but I will tell you that—in all probability—you will earn another Battle Star to wear on your ETO (European Theater of Operations Ribbon). You are to return to your quarters and stow away all of your Navy gear with the exception of your 'dog tags' and your Navy foul weather gear. Any indication that you are naval personnel is not to be carried on your person or within your personal belongings. Any disobedience to this order will be dealt with harshly."

After stowing all Navy gear and donning Army uniforms, we were told we would be taking LCVPs back to the Continent for a secret mission.

The following morning we picked up our boats on the Dart River and proceeded to the inlet where an English LSD (Landing Ship, Dock) was waiting for us. The LSD lowered her stern ramp and pumped water into her stern ballast tanks which flooded the cargo deck. The ship in this configuration allowed our craft to proceed aboard under our own power. Once all twenty-four of our boats were aboard and secure, the LSD pumped the water out of the cargo deck and the ballast tanks, closed the ramp, and we were ready for sea.

The LSD put to sea around 0400 (4 a.m.) and we arrived off the harbor entrance to Le Havre, France, at about 1500 (3 p.m.). We learned that the harbor was secure, but the sweeping of the entrance for mines had not been completed. The English captain of the LSD did not wish to jeopardize his ship so we were informed we would disembark two miles out. The skipper called us together and set down the method we were to follow on entering the harbor. The lead boat was to lower its ramp to approximately forty-five degrees and three of the crew members were to "belly down" on the ramp and peer over the top for mines. In the event a mine was noted in our path, the men lying on the ramp were to take a boat hook and push it out of the way. The remaining boats were to follow in single file at twenty-five yard intervals. In the event the lead boat were to strike a mine, the second boat would take over. Lt. Archyball Updike (division officer), Theodore Stratton (coxswain), Gordon Thomas Simmons (motor mac'), Roy Stull (signalman), and John Alger were chosen for this task. Very cautiously, we threaded our way like a giant serpent through the mine field with no loss of personnel or equipment.

As we entered the inner harbor, we passed many ships and boats sunk at their piers—both by Allied bombers and scuttling by the Germans. Among these was the giant ocean liner *Paris*. She was lying on her port side like the carcass of an enormous whale beached upon a shoal. We were told that the Germans, in an effort to blockade as much of the harbor as possible, had scuttled her prior to retreating. We secured our boats to a quay near this "leviathan" and the skipper went ashore for further orders.

With a clap of thunder, the sky opened up and caught us in a cold, drenching downpour. In our open boats we had no protection against the weather, so we all tried to seek cover under the aft gun tubs. The canvas we had stretched over the gun tubs offered little protection so we finally decided that we would just have to make the best of the situation. It rained all night and, as we had been ordered to remain with our boats, we understood how an infantry soldier in a "fox hole" felt.

At dawn the Army started backing large weapon carrier trailers up to the dock. For the first time we realized that our boats were to be carried overland to some distant point. However, we were still in the dark as to where this point was to be. After the Army cranes had laboriously loaded our eight-ton boats on the flatbed trailers, we were told that arrangements had been made to quarter us in a half-bombed out building that had once been a gymnasium. That evening we were told our assignment was to take assault troops across the Rhine River.

In the deepest of secrecy, our unit moved into Belgium and Germany with our LCVPs. Movement of these large landing craft was an arduous task accomplished at night to avoid detection by the enemy. One of the headaches encountered was the movement of these vessels through towns and over blasted-out roads in a blackout. On one occasion, while going through a small town, a house at a turn in the road became an obstacle. The owner was roused out of bed and told to vacate the premises immediately. The Army officer's words were: "We gotta blow up your house. It's in our way." Shortly afterward, dynamite and a bulldozer cleared a path for the Navy boats.

After a week of travel over bombed-out roads and towns, we arrived at an old wool dyeing mill in Limburg, Belgium. This was to be our station through Thanksgiving, 1944.

The enemy still held the ground a short distance east of Limburg. In this area the Germans had a launch site for the V-1 guided missile. During the day, four or five of these missiles could be seen and heard passing overhead on their way to Liege or Antwerp. By the low trajectory of the missiles, we knew that the launch site could be no more than three miles from our location. In some cases they passed no more than fifty feet overhead.

When a naval unit is detached from the main base of operations it is necessary to send all official correspondence to and from said base by "Guard Mail." As the name implies, one man, or a group of men, accompany the correspondence to and/or from its destination. In November, I was lucky enough to be chosen to ride "shot gun" with the Guard Mail to the newly established headquarters in Paris, France.

While in Paris, Lt. Hardy (who was responsible for the Guard Mail), myself and a ship store petty officer (who had accompanied us from Limburg) attended a concert of the Glenn Miller Air Force Orchestra. The Band had been sent over from England as a morale booster. As I sat in the theater with my eyes closed and listened to the strains of "In The Mood, Tuxedo Junction, String of Pearls" and the other Miller classics, my thoughts returned to home. The war was nothing but a bad dream. When I opened my eyes and snapped back to reality, a cold shiver came over me. I realized that I had survived Normandy, but the battle of the Rhineland was yet to come. I looked around at the faces near me and wondered if the same thought might be in their minds. Glenn Miller was not present during this concert. We later learned that Cap-

tain Miller was missing in action on a flight from England to France.

At the end of the concert, Lt. Hardy and the petty officer went on their individual ways, and I checked into an inexpensive Paris hotel for the night. The following morning I saw as much of Paris as time allowed and, as instructed, we met Lt. Hardy at Naval Headquarters at 1600 hours (4 p.m.) that afternoon.

Unbeknownst to us, the "Parris Barracks Navy" expected us to stay in the naval quarters and report to the Officer of the Deck if we left those quarters. Having been a unit who had slept on the floors of brothels, bistros, and on the bare ground, we paid little heed to these orders. In consequence, we caught hell the next day. As we entered headquarters and identified ourselves, a naval commander sitting behind a desk arose and started a tirade about men who disobeyed orders and how they had Portsmouth Naval Prison for the likes of us.

Lt. Hardy looked at us, shook his head and, with a smile, said: "By all means, commander, throw us in the Bastille. It will be a hell of a lot safer than where we are going."

This only enraged the commander more. He broke naval etiquette by screaming at Lt. Hardy in front of the enlisted men: "When you address me, Lieutenant, you will call me sir, and what in the hell are you doing in those uniforms and carrying those weapons?"

A side door flew open and a four-striper (naval captain) walked in the room, brusquely saying: "What the hell is going on in here? You can hear your shouting all over the area."

The commander briefly described the situation to the captain. The captain turned to Mr. Hardy and asked: "To what unit are your men attached, and why the masquerade?"

Lt. Hardy answered, "Com-Task-Group 122.5"

The captain asked where this unit was stationed.

Lt. Hardy replied: "I'm not at liberty to say."

The captain turned red and said: "By God, I'll find out," and left the room. With this, the commander summoned two SPs to watch over us and told us to wait in the hall. After about ten minutes a yeoman came out, whispered to the SPs, and they departed. We waited another ten minutes and , when nothing happened, Lt. Hardy said:

"It's quite obvious that these are Ninety-Day-Wonders just off the boat. It will take them 'til hell freezes over to make up their minds on what to do about our situation. Let's get the Guard Mail and get the hell out of here."

We walked boldly to the Mail Room, signed for the documents, and walked out of the front of the building. With every step we expected to hear a command of, "Halt," but nothing happened. We became more giddy with every step and, by the time we reached our vehicle, we were laughing out loud. Lt. Hardy jumped behind the wheel of the truck, jammed it in gear, and off we flew down the road. I would like to believe we got away with something but, in all probability, the captain gave orders to the effect of, "Ignore them and they will go away." That is why the SPs had not disarmed us. We never again mentioned, nor had any repercussions from, this incident.

Shortly after returning to Limburg, our unit was split up and sent to various places in Belgium for training with the Army. Prior to Christmas, we once again joined up as a complete unit in Aachen, Germany.

In Aachen we were bivouacked in the *Haus Hofchen*—the chateau of Hans Cadenbach—a high ranking German officer and friend of Hermann Goering.

The weather was bitterly cold, and there was no fire wood to burn, so we did the next best thing—we started burning furniture. Two days later, a German woman accompanied by Army officers came by with a paper which authorized her to move out the furnishings. But, alas, all the furniture had been burned. We were told that we had destroyed a lot of priceless antiques. Our attitude was "so what?" The krauts were lucky we hadn't blown up the damned chateau. We later found out, much to our chagrin, that we had missed discovering a well-stocked wine cellar beneath the chateau.

When the Germans launched the Ardennes Offensive (the Battle of the Bulge), we were under the German guns and forced to make a hasty retreat. Our XO, Lt. Sydney Wright, accompanied by several of our men, drove his jeep past a group of surprised German soldiers. The Germans had wits enough to hide their weapons and our people thought they were POWs. Later they discovered, to their amazement, that this group was the vanguard of the German offensive. Why they had not fired upon our people remains a mystery.

The First and Ninth Armies were racing east to stop the *Panzers*, and our unit—along with a small contingent of Belgian Home Guards—was left to hold the fort in our area. We were instructed that, if necessary,

our boats were to be dumped across the roadways in an effort to slow the enemy's advance.

We had all suffered enemy fire on the beaches of Normandy and expected to suffer further fire when the time came to cross the Rhine. We had not expected to become infantry soldiers, but we mentally braced ourselves and dug in with the intent of hanging on as long as possible. However, the High Command determined that our boats and personnel were too important to the Allied plans to be jeopardized at this stage of the battle. We received orders to retreat and disperse into Belgium. Our unit scattered to various sections of Belgium and did not reorganize until Christmas Day in Waremme, Belgium.

During this time the Germans, under the command of Lieutenant Colonel Otto Skorzeny, had donned American uniforms and had infiltrated the American lines. Our Army had set up road blocks and adopted various counter measures to capture these troops. One of these measures was to verify the names on Army dog tags with company personnel lists (where possible) and, if any discrepancy was found, the person was to be immediately placed in custody and, if he/they resisted, they were to be shot. This was a situation the Navy had not considered. As previously stated, the only portion of our Navy gear we had not left behind us in England were our dog tags and foul weather gear. The naval dog tag was as different from the Army dog tag as a battleship is from a tank. The only thing similar is the person's name, blood type, and serial number. Here we were in the middle of a counter-offensive wearing Army uniforms with the wrong dog tags around our necks. If we had run into a roadblock and had not known the password of the day, or some axiom (ex. Who had the best run average in the game of baseball?), or some event only Americans were supposed to know, we would have been shot on the spot.

When not travelling, our boats were covered, camouflaged, and parked on their trailers in some obscure location. Generally, this was a back road. On one occasion, while in the Ardennes, we had hidden our boats at the intersecting "Y" of two dirt roads. At the matrix of the "Y" the infantry had set up a "Quad-Fifty" machinegun half-track which could be swung into position to cover both roads. Knowing they would be stationed there for an indefinite time, they had "dug-in" in a covered guard post. This post was large enough to accommodate four bunks and a fifty-five gallon barrel used for a stove.

One fog-enshrouded, teeth-chatteringly cold night,

while on guard duty, Simmons and I accepted the hospitality of the infantry soldiers and entered their trench bivouac to get warm. There was room for only four persons so, while two of the soldiers were manning the half-track, the two of us would take their place. The soldiers had rigged their stove to use gasoline and diesel oil as a fuel. This they had commandeered from knocked-out German tanks and trucks. At this road block six tanks and four half-tracks had been knocked-out, so they had an ample amount of fuel.

Navy foul weather gear was made up of coveralls with an inner lining of cotton, a middle layer of oil cloth, and an outer layer of canvas. The Navy had designed these garments to be both warm and waterproof. I had backed up to the stove to warm my back side and, because of the thickness of my foul weather gear, I had not realized how near to the stove I had become. I noticed that the soldier I was talking with had a smirk on his face and saw him nudge his buddy. About this time I smelled something burning and turned to Simmons and said as much. Simmons burst out laughing and, at the same time, I realized that it was the seat of my pants that was on fire. With a hoot and a holler, I raced out of the revetment and scooted on my butt through the snow to put out the fire, while all the time I could hear the uproarious laughter behind me. For the remaining winter I went around showing off the oilcloth of my pants through a burned-out hole in the outer canvas. One of the "green" (newly arrived) Army replacement officers asked me what had happened to my pants and I told him that a bear almost got me while on guard duty in the woods. He walked off with a skeptical look—not knowing whether or not to believe what I had told him.

In January, we once again moved forward. Our unit was ordered to stand by in the town of Andenne, Belgium, where many of our personnel had been prior to the "Bulge." Friendships had been made with the townfolk and, since the town was secure, we decided to celebrate a late Christmas where we did a lot of drinking, singing, women chasing, and general relaxing. In fact, the war was all but forgotten until the middle of February when the cold hand of reality beckoned us once more. Many of the men had become involved with the local women, and our departure became a scene from a tragic movie—women chasing after the trucks crying, and men throwing chewing gum and candy from the trucks to little children falling behind. Some of the men were sniffling, and some just sat quietly with their own thoughts.

The LCVP was constructed for the purpose of transporting troops and small vehicles in an assault wave to an invasion beachhead. To allow the craft easy access onto, and away from, a beach, it was necessary that these boats be designed with a minimum of keel. This made the boat difficult to handle in a heavy surf and/or current. However, in the hands of a veteran coxswain, this difficulty in handling was overcome. This was demonstrated on the Rhine River during construction of the Victor Bridge—the longest tactical bridge ever constructed under combat conditions.

An LCVP was the first naval craft to ever operate on the Rhine River. Whether by chance or planning, it was manned by the same crew who lead the unit into the harbor at Le Havre. This boat was swung by a crane from the back of an Army trailer and dropped ignobly into the river on March 8th, 1945.

The Army combat engineers were starting to erect a floating bridge upstream from the Ludendorff Bridge (Remagen). This was to become the longest tactical bridge in the world, and was aptly named the "Victor Bridge." They requested the assistance of our boats to tow pontoons into place across the river.

My first duty on the river was to lash a floating bridge pontoon section to the starboard side of the LCVP, and proceeded to cross to the east bank of the river. The pontoon extended about ten feet in front of the bow and in back of the stern; this made the boat handling precarious. The river current was running at flood stage of about twelve knots and, when we pulled away from the river bank, it was immediately apparent that this lash-up would not work. About fifty feet from the west bank the current caught the extended bow of the pontoon and started pushing both pontoon and LCVP down the river. Realizing that the boat, crew, pontoon, and Army personnel riding the pontoon were in jeopardy of being easy targets for German artillery, or being smashed against the remnant of a destroyed bridge structure lying half-submerged in the river downstream, I ordered that the stern line to the pontoon be doubled up and bow line be cut. Then, by increasing the boat to full power, we had the pontoon in tow—heading upstream.

While performing these antics, the Germans lobbed numerous shells in our direction. It was not feasible to tow these pontoons into position because doing so would leave the boat upstream of the bridge with no way of getting back down the river short of portaging the boat around the bridge. The Army engineers calculated that if an additional pontoon were added, and the bow of the LCVP was placed in the center, then the boat would be pushing the pontoon like a large wing. When I was asked if I could control the boat in this fashion, I merely shrugged.

The boat pushed off from the river bank with about twenty-five feet of the pontoon extending out from each side of the boat's bow. By giving the boat the full power of its 225 horsepower engine, and turning the helm slightly to port, I found that I could make slow progress upstream and also control the pontoons in the current. Using this method, the bridge was constructed amidst sporadic artillery fire.

Under the force of the current, the completed bridge was threatened to be carried away. Once again, the Navy took the situation in hand—two LCVPs were assigned to put their blunt noses against the bulge in the bridge and pushed at a speed of twelve knots upstream against the twelve-knot downstream current.

To keep the force of the water against the pontoon from ripping the bridge from its moorings, it was necessary to secure the span. To accomplish this, the Army had contructed large cages that they intended to fill with rocks. These cage anchors would then be attached to the one-inch wire cable that had been strung through eyes on each pontoon and secured to the bank on each side of the river. These rock anchor cages would then be dropped into the river upstream of the bridge at various intervals across the river.

While the naval boats held the bridge against the current, the Army engineers pulled a pontoon onto the river bank, placed an empty cage made of rebar and chicken wire on each end of the pontoon, and proceeded to fill these cages with rocks. This was when the trouble started. The weight of the rocks mired the pontoon into the river bank mud. An effort to pull it off was made by the small Army assault boats but, when this proved futile, an Army truck was used to push the pontoon into deeper water. Once free of the mud, the Army small boats (equipped with nothing but small outboard motors) took the anchor cage-laden pontoon into tow and started out into the river. It was obvious that these small boats would not be able to hold the pontoon against the current, and this was when the "Keystone Operation" started.

One of the Army engineers, in his haste to save the anchor-laden pontoon from crashing into the bridge, made the decision to dump one of the cages. In his moment of haste, he forgot a lesson he should have learned in childhood—if one end of a teeter-totter is vacated, the other end comes crashing down.

When the men riding the pontoon levered and pushed the one cage off the end of the pontoon, the weight on the other end immediately capsized the pontoon—throwing men and equipment into the river. The current carried the men downstream at a fast pace; some of them were able to grasp onto a pontoon as they passed under the bridge, but four were carried down river. One of the LCVPs broke off from holding the bridge in place and took up the pursuit of these men. Two of the men were picked up, but the other two were lost. The radioman of the pursuing LCVP sent a message to our boats working down river to be on the lookout for men.

During these operations, the Germans did their best with bomb and shell to get the Navy out of there before the bridge was secure. While we were placing the anchors, a German FW 190 (fighter/bomber aircraft) strafed the bridge—hitting five or six men. Boat #3 was in the middle of the bridge holding it against the current. The crew immediately swung its fifty caliber guns (which the Army had changed from the normally mounted thirty caliber) into action. The plane was in a dive, and the gunners ripped the plane open and it immediately exploded. The remains of the plane crashed within twenty feet of the bridge and, for a short time, we thought it was going to hit the bridge. Three of the men on the bridge who had been hit during the strafing fell into the river and were swept away. The other wounded were rushed to the aid station by the medics.

At the end of the first day on the river, we bivouacked in a German house on the edge of the river. The basement of this house had been taken over by an Army communication unit and set up as an advance telephone station. The Germans who had evacuated this home had left behind (in the basement) a player-piano and a number of player-piano rolls. Most of these were German songs unfamiliar to GIs but, searching through the rolls, we found *O' Tannenbaum*. A signal corp sergeant put this roll on the piano and started pumping away, and the strains of music came forth. At the same time, the Germans across the river decided to start shelling a road about two-hundred yards behind the house. As the shells (sounding much like a small locomotive) flew overhead, the American artillery added to the tumult by starting their own barrage in answer to the German guns. Along with the maelstrom of noise above, the strains of *O' Tannenbaum*, accompanied by the singing of eight men, drifted from the basement of this quaking building.

We remained in the basement throughout the night and, at daylight, we ventured forth to discover that the barn, out-buildings, and the left wing of the house had been destroyed. Turning to Simmons (my motor mac'), I asked: "Was that building in one piece when we entered the basement?"

His answer was: "I don't want to think about it!"

After two days, the engineers had their bridge secure, and the Navy LCVPs assigned to assist in the bridge construction were portaged up river above the last pontoon bridge in the First Army sector to be used for troop transportation and depth charge duty. During the transporting of troops across the river, one infantry soldier remarked: "I got off one of these damn boats at Normandy, walked half-way across Europe and, when I got here, one of these damn things was waiting for me. How did you get here?"

Simmons answered: "We had the Air Force drop us in." The GI looked at him with a you're-full-of-crap stare, smiled and squatted below the gunwhale in preparation for the trip across the river.

When crossing the river, fully loaded with troops, it was necessary to point the bow of your boat into the current and proceed across the river at an oblique angle. This was a slow process, and it exposed you as an easy target for the enemy. When fired upon, your only option was to turn your boat downstream, give it full power and, with the additional speed gained by the current, outrun the redirecting of artillery fire. In many cases, you unloaded the soldiers in your boat many yards downstream from their main body. To help eliminate this situation, the Army artillery spotters would lay down a barrage from whence the enemy fire came. In one instance, the artillery stitched a seam across

With the crew's headquarters on the German barge *Mannheim*, in background, U.S. Navy men who were aboard the first LCVP (Landing Craft, Vehicle, Personnel) to cross the Rhine in historic military venture, work on guns after strafing run by German FW 190. Left to right, the men are: John C. Alger, S1/C, 20, of Boonville, N.Y.; Theodore M. Stratton, Coxswain, 19, Long Beach, Calif.; Gordon T. Simmons, F1/C, 19, Turlock, Calif., and Roy L. Stull, 20, Bergoo, W.V., March 1945.

the side of a hill that completely eliminated any further action from that area. This allowed our boats, operating in that area, to transport in excess of 6,000 troops across the river.

Early on, the Navy was aware that the Germans—like our own Navy—had men trained in underwater demolition. It was also realized that these men would be used to destroy any and all bridges that the Allies threw up across the Rhine. So, with the help of the Army demolition experts, a method was devised to create a depth charge that could be launched from the stern of a Navy LCVP. The method chosen was to place forty one-quarter-pound explosive demolition blocks into a gunny sack with a water-proof fuse attached to the top block in the sack. By igniting this fuse and pushing it from the stern of the boat, a spectacular underwater explosion occurred that nothing swimming in the immediate area could survive. Two boats were assigned "depth charge patrol," and each boat would be loaded with approximately one hundred of these depth charges. They would proceed, alternately, upriver in a zig-zag pattern—dropping a charge every ten yards. The Navy has no exact knowledge of how many of these German "Gamma Swimmers" were killed outright, because their bodies would have gone downstream with the current. On the other hand, four of them were forced to the surface and captured while emerging from the water above the Ludendorff Bridge.

These naval depth charge patrols were under artillery and air attacks, and it takes little imagination to realize the apprehension the crews were under when they were caught in the middle of the river during an ME 262 (Germany's first jet fighter/bomber) strafing run. If one tracer bullet were to have hit one of those charges, the boat and crew would have been vaporized, and anything on the bank of the river—in the near vicinity—would have been destroyed.

Just above the Victor Bridge, there was a large ferry boat tied to a dock. The Army was afraid that a German "Gamma Team" might slip in at night and cut the mooring lines loose—allowing this large boat to come downriver with enough force to carry the bridge away. We carried an Army demolition team across the river to the east bank (along with five bags consisting of fifty pounds of TNT) and tied up alongside the ferry boat. As the men climbed aboard the ferry, the team leader told us to keep the engine running and be prepared to "Get the hell" out of there. What seemed like an hour but, in fact, was only a few minutes, the team came running down the main deck of the ferry

and jumped into the well deck of our boat. The leader was shouting as he jumped "Go, go, go!" Giving full power to the boat, I headed for the center of the river. With five blasts that went off almost simultaneously, pieces of the ferry superstructure were flung high in the air and came raining down like shrapnel. The ferry slowly heaved over at a forty-five degree angle as it settled to the bottom. The demolition team leader started checking his men and found that one man had suffered a "Million Dollar Wound" when a piece of flying debris had struck, and sunk deeply into, his shoulder muscle. We rushed this man to an aid station on the west bank and returned to our duties.

Since moving up river, our bivouac had been in a deserted house on the west bank at the town of Brohl. This site was chosen because of a small boat dock that had remained undamaged.

Early on the morning of March 10, my boat was assigned the task of taking two officers (who we later found out were from the Office of Strategic Services—the forerunner of the CIA) upriver to what remained of the town of Koblenz. On this date nobody was sure whether or not the Germans had evacuated the town. The town had been bombed and shelled into rubble but, to our knowledge, we were about to be the first to find out whether the enemy was still there.

One of the major obstacles in getting upriver to Koblenz was the bombed-out railroad bridge at Kaltenengers. The bridge, when destroyed, had collapsed into the river in a manner as to be a hazard in navigating a boat around a fallen structure. On the west side of the river, the beam structure of the main roadway had fallen into the river from a standing tower at a forty-five degree angle. The boat's bow ramp would clear this structure by inches if the boat was held close to the tower. The remaining structure in the river was acting as a dam and funneling the water through this opening in a cascade. After reconnoitering this passage twice, I told the OSS Army colonel that I could handle the boat with the current directed on the bow going upstream but, coming back downstream would be like riding a giant surfboard through the cascade. If I were to miscalculate, and the bow ramp was to catch the bridge structure, the water would come over the stern and we would sink like a rock. The answer from the colonel was: "I have the greatest respect for the Navy's abilities. Let's get on with it coxswain!"

It took ten minutes with the boat at full power to traverse the ten feet through the cascade into quieter water—it was like a salmon swimming upstream. Above the bridge the river remained swift, but the power of the boat overcame this problem and we continued until meeting the confluence of the Moselle and the Rhine rivers at Koblenz.

The city had been destroyed by bomb and shell, and appeared to be completely deserted. Tying the boat up to a concrete retaining wall below the statue of Count von Hindenburg (so we were informed), we took stock on what we were doing. The colonel told us that we would be entering the town to find the German headquarters which contained documents needed by the Allies. I told Al (my gunner's mate who was also an excellent boat handler) to remain with the boat, while Simmons and I were to accompany the colonel. Stull (my radioman) was to go with the other officer. In the event we did not return, Al was to take the boat back down the river and report our demise.

We armed ourselved with the weapons from the boat which consisted of one Thompson machine gun, an M1 rifle, a carbine, and three .45 pistols—including the two the officers were carrying. We also had three clips of ammunition for the Thompson, one bandolier for the M1, four clips for the carbine, and two clips each for the 45s. We gave Stull the Thompson, Simmons took the M1, and I took the carbine. We left the remaining .45 with Al.

Not a soul, nor any kind of movement, was detected as we walked up the street. The open walls and rubble of destroyed buildings was all that greeted our eyes. Curtains fluttered through broken windows, and bombed-out vehicles smoldered in the street. I remarked to the colonel that I thought the Army had occupied this town and, if so, "Where were they and all the civilians?" He just shrugged. Up the main street, about two blocks, we saw a German banner hanging from a flag staff, and the colonel indicated that was the building we were looking for. We sidled up the side of the street and entered the building through the rubble. Inside were a group of empty prison cells and a lot of debris scattered around the floor. The colonel warned us to keep back from the door. Picking up a brick from the rubble, he threw it at the door as hard as he could. In many cases, the Germans would "booby trap" a door so that the first one through it was "mince meat." By jarring it with a brick, it was hoped that if it was booby trapped it would be set off. This was a very dumb move. If the Germans had placed a large charge, and the brick had set it off, we would have been buried under the rubble. Fortunately, in this case no trap was discovered.

While the colonel was investigating the back room, I told Simmons that I intended to get the banner from the front of the building. Climbing the inside stairway to the second floor, scanning continuously for any trip wires that may have been placed by retreating Germans, I entered a room which gave access through a window to the flag staff. To my surprise, the rope was still on the flag so all I had to do was pull it in. Checking the rope carefully to assure that it was not a trap, I slowly pulled the banner in the window. While doing this, I heard some rifle fire, but did not realize that I was being sniped at until Simmons unloaded his M1 into a church steeple up the road. Making a hasty retreat into the building, we almost ran into the colonel coming out of the back room. He was unaware of what we had been doing and, as he started out the front, I warned him that there had been shooting up the street and it would be better if we went out the back of the building. Half way back to the boat, we ran into Stull and the other officer.

The colonel and the captain walked a short distance, to be out of ear shot, and conversed for a couple of minutes. I asked Stull what was up and he told me that they had found a winery intact. This, to an Army unit, was like finding the Rosetta Stone. The colonel asked me if we had a flashlight in the boat. I told him we had two battle lamps in the boat, and I sent Stull after them. When he returned, we followed the captain to a bombed-out building and, in the middle of the rubble, was a staircase leading down into a dark cellar. We turned on the battle lamps and proceeded to descend the stairs. I told Stull to remain at the top with the Thompson. We came to the first level and, in the beam of the light, you could see row stacked upon row of champagne as far as the light beam would go. We later found out that had we gone deeper into the lower basements of this winery, we would have discovered German civilians and soldiers taking refuge amongst the giant wine casks.

The colonel immediately ordered us to start carrying as much as possible back to the boat. I called Simmons off to the side and told him to hide as many bottles as possible under the bilge boards. Knowing how officers think, I knew that upon our return we would get none of the champagne. We were able to carry one hundred and sixty-seven bottles of wine to the boat before a tank started down the street. Not wishing to determine whose tank it was, I fired up the boat and we made a hasty retreat down the river.

Running with the current down river increased our boat speed to about eighteen knots. We knew that at this speed we would not get caught in the river after dark. The Army had set up seventy-five-millimeter howitzers on the banks of the river so as to be able to sink any barge, boat or object that came down the river. This was necessary to eliminate any damage that might occur by an errant barge or object striking a floating bridge. The only identification that we carried on our boats was an American flag and the Corps of Engineer's flag flown from the same staff at the stern of the boat. The Army claimed that they were unable to see these banners at night even though the artillerymen had giant klieg lights to identify objects entering this zone—their initial reaction was to shoot first and identify the remains. In consequence, we tried to be out of the river at night in areas not first identified to the Army.

Approaching the fallen bridge at Kaltenengers, I slowed the boat down by throwing it full astern for a few seconds, and then placing it in neutral and allowing the boat to coast with the current and, finally, giving it more power astern. Using this alternating method, I was able to line the boat up for a one-shot try through the cascade. When I had it aligned, I told everybody to hang on to something and pray. Giving the boat full power, we shot forward. The eight ton, thirty-six foot landing craft plunged through the cascade—riding the crest like a surfboard equipped with a giant engine. Reaching calm water, we all looked back and wondered how we ever cleared the fallen structure.

In our haste to leave Koblenz, we had set the wine in the well deck in a haphazard manner and, during our antics in shooting the cascade, four or five bottles had exploded after hitting the steel ramp. The well deck of the boat swelled with the sweet smell of vintage Moselle wine. The colonel looked at me and laughed. Turning, he uncorked a bottle and passed it around.

Arriving back at our bivouac area, the colonel commandeered a weapons carrier and loaded the wine in the back. He turned and thanked me and the crew and started to leave. I stopped him and asked, "Colonel, were there really any papers in that headquarters, or were we really looking for that wine cellar?"

He looked at me and said, "Sailor, that is a military secret." He then patted my arm, reached into the back of the truck, handed me three bottles of wine, boarded the truck and drove away.

After he had gone, we raised the bilge boards and retrieved twenty-five bottles of vintage Moselle wine

that we had so unobtrusively stowed away. That evening we found out that Koblenz was where the First and Third Armies intersected and, as yet, the Army had not occupied the town. In effect, the search for those "German documents" had unknowingly led us behind the German lines. The OSS officers may have been privy to this fact, but withheld this information from my crew.

In honor of this "derring-do," we dubbed ourselves "Updike's Raiders" and had one hell of a party. Thank God our officers were doing whatever officers do and paid little attention to us!

During a war, there is always the stench of death in the air and you become immune to its odor. However, at times it can become overbearing. On one date in late March, Simmons and I—having a little time off—decided that we would see part of the Rhine countryside. We swiped an Army weapons carrier and drove into Bonn, Germany. Most of the buildings had been destroyed. The stench of death was reeking in the air, and Simmons made the remark that the bombing and shelling must have killed everybody in town. We entered one deserted building which we were told was the Bonn Medical University. We opened the door to a basement, and the odor was so strong it almost made you vomit. Inside this basement were bodies of men and women stacked head to toe. We made a hasty retreat out of this hell—gasping for fresh air. We had seen men killed, and death was not new to us, but death in this magnitude was overwhelming. Having no knowledge of the "Holocaust" at this time, we wondered why any university would need that many bodies for medical experiments. We had been directed by the Army to report any atrocities, or what might appear to be an atrocity, to our officers. As directed, we reported what we had seen this day and were told that it had been previously reported and that we should not involve ourselves.

We continued operations on the river until one morning in early May when Updike entered our quarters and said "Any of you men want to go home?" In our close-knit unit a certain amount of insubordination was tolerated, so one of the men snapped "Why don't you quit your joking and get the hell out of here?" Normally, this would have brought the roof of Naval Justice down upon the man but, in this case, Updike only rolled his eyes and shook his head. "Well," Updike replied, "the trucks are waiting and I'm leaving with or without you!" One of the men rushed to what had been a window that overlooked the road and hollered, "He ain't kidding, there are trucks waiting."

As we gathered what little gear we had, one of the men asked Updike what would be done with our boats. Updike answered, "We don't care what the Army does with them—let's get out of here." With that remark, we stormed out the door, boarded the trucks and headed for Le Havre and home.

Upon our arrival back at Dartmouth, we were instructed to get back into our naval uniforms and "ash can" our old Army attire. When we went to the armory in which we had stored our naval gear, we found to our amazement that all of our gear had been stripped of our personal belongings, and the seabags with what remained of our uniforms had been stacked in a corner of the armory. When Captain Wenker questioned the Commanding Officer of the base as to what had transpired during our absence, he was told that our gear had gotten mixed with the gear of men lost during Exercise Tiger (the Slapton Sands debacle), and crews who had not returned from Normandy. In fact, we had been listed as "Missing in Action" and, regrettably, our families had been so notified. We were told to immediately send a letter home that would assure our loved ones that we were still alive. Meanwhile, the Navy Department would take immediate action to inform those at home of their error. The Navy, in all its blundering glory, merely informed our families that we were on a classified assignment, and they were unable to disclose any further information. Ironically, this notification arrived home the same time we did.

The personal belongings that had been removed from our gear were never returned.

The war in Europe ended the day we boarded the *Queen Mary* for our trip home.

After a leave, I was reassigned to the U.S. Cruiser *Santa Fe* for temporary duty. Upon this ship's arrival at Pearl Harbor, I was relieved of duty and flown by C54 to the island of Okinawa where I operated a landing craft until VJ Day.

I was regular Navy and not subject to going home as were most of the reserves. I was reassigned to the task force which was to operate in Korean waters. I was attached to the Port Director in Inchon, Korea, where I operated a sixty-foot Navy crash boat in the Yellow Sea from September 1945 until May 1946. The Navy ceased operation on this date, and I was sent to Tsingtao, China, for reassignment. Because my enlistment was coming to an end, I was assigned duty on the first ship returning to the U.S. This ship was the Fleet Tug Boat *USS Cree*. After twenty days crossing the

North Pacific, we arrived at Bremerton Navy Yard. From there, I went to San Pedro, where I was discharged on August 15, 1946.

My first duty on being discharged was to join the "52 Twenty Club." This club was formed by veterans who had no intention of immediately getting a job. Each veteran was entitled to twenty dollars a week for fifty-two weeks while they were seeking employment. To assure the employment office found you no job, you registered as a Beach Jumper, Deep Sea Diver, or some other obscure trade for which there was no call. This allowed you time to spend your mustering-out pay playing volley ball on the beach and chasing girls.

All good things had to end, so I went to work as a mechanic at North American Aviation. Over a period of twenty-two "off and on" years, I worked up to such positions as Project Staff Engineer on the Paraglider Project, Engineer Flight Test on the Hound Dog Missile, and my final position, before the demise of the Apollo Project, was transporting the Saturn SII (second stage of the Saturn Five) from Seal Beach, California, to Cape Kennedy through the Panama Canal. During this sojourn, I had married and was the father of three children.

Upon the successful completion of the Apollo Moon landing, the company put us out to pasture.

After the normal pangs of unemployment, I found a job as an inspector in the oil business. I worked at this trade in Puerto Rico, Iran, Dubai and Alaska. Prior to my retirement from a major oil company in 1985, I was Quality Assurance Director on the Kuparuk River Project on the North Slope of Alaska. My function on this project was to assure that all vendors and contractors under contract to ARCO supplied and constructed materials that met and/or exceeded design specifications. Because we had many vendors in foreign lands, it was necessary for me to travel the World extensively.

Since my retirement, I have worked as a quality assurance consultant for various oil companies throughout the United States. I now have four grandchildren—two of them are in college, and two young ladies aspire to go to college upon graduation from high school. My wife of forty-seven years and I live in Atascocito, Texas, and are now enjoying our retirement.

Captain Walter Karig sums it up in this book *Battle Report* with "The punishment those youngsters took during those first days at the Remagen Bridge belongs in the history book." I think it would have been better said, "The punishment these younsters took from Normandy until the end of the war belongs in the history book." The Navy crews that operated on the Rhine had also taken assault troops into Normandy. Some of them landed in North Africa, Sicily and Normandy, and most of them were unable to vote or buy a beer—legally—in the U.S.

Upon my return to the United States, at the end of the war in Europe, I was asked by the police at Seal Beach, California, to remove myself from a public tavern because I was in violation of a state law which prohibited anyone under twenty-one years of age from drinking alcoholic beverages. One of the police officers remarked, "You young punks are not even dry behind the ears!" Three days after this occurrence, I was on my way to Okinawa aboard a C54 with eight other young "punks" to take a small part in the war with Japan.

The last sight many enemy beach defenders would ever see!

# Part II
# The Large Slow Targets
# (LSTs)

# LST
## Landing Ship, Tank
### (Specifications for the LST-1 Class)

| | |
|---|---|
| Length: | 328' |
| Beam: | 50' |
| Draft: | 14'4" aft, 8' forward (seagoing) |
| | 9'6" aft, 3'1" forward (landing) |
| | 7'5" aft, 1'6" forward (light) |
| Displacement: | 4,080 tons (full load) |
| | 2,160 tons (landing) |
| Crew: | 7 officers, 109 men (2 davit) |
| | 9 officers, 125 men (6 davit) |
| Armor: | 15 pound STS splinter protection. |
| Propulsion: | Two 900 horsepower diesels; twin screw. |
| Speed: | 10.8 knots |
| Endurance: | 6,000 miles radius at 9 knots |
| Number Built During the War (All Types): | 1,058 |
| Description: | Oceangoing ship designed to land tanks, other vehicles, cargo and personnel directly onto a beach. |

Beachhead established, LST moves in. While manufacturers and labor leaders watched, the Army and Navy joined to stage a large-scale invasion maneuver at Cove Point on Chesapeake Bay near the Amphibious Training Base at Solomons, MD, Jan. 13, 1944. Here the huge LST (landing ship-tank) has beached and is ready to unload its cargo. The Army has set up an anti-aircraft gun in the foreground. The visit to the "invasion center" was the first of several trips planned to acquaint manufacturers and labor leaders with the use of landing craft they make. The move is part of the accelerated landing craft program.

Several M-3 tanks parked on the vehicle deck of an early LST, 29 November 1942.

This is the stern of LST 49. Note the anchor, gun tubs, and the small boat on the rear davits.

A small boat suspended above the aft portside of LST 49.

This photograph of several LSTs at Pearl Harbor clearly shows how the doors could be opened, and the ramps lowered to the waterline, for transfer of personnel and material to other craft.

"Two Workhorses of the Navy" — LSTs in the Mediterranean.

Coast Guard lands troops on beach near Hollandia, New Guinea.

LSTs approaching Lingayan, January 1945.

En route to Cape Gloucester, December 1943.

Photograph taken aboard
an LST loaded down with
trucks on the upper deck.

LST en route to Hollandia, 22 April, 1944.

# Carey Surratt, MoMM 2/C

*My father had been in World War I. He told me in some detail about what the Meuse-Argonne of 1918 was like—the trench warfare, the cooties in the trenches, the miserable conditions, running into machinegun fire, and stuff like that, and I knew then that I didn't particularly want to go in the Army. I would have probably ended up getting drafted and going into the Army and I just didn't see me as cannon fodder so, if I had to go in the service, I decided to go in the Navy.*

I was born in Dennison, Ohio, on the 17th of July, 1926. I attended school there and, when the war started, I had no idea what I wanted to do, or where I wanted to go.

My buddy and I went to Canton, Ohio, to the Navy recruiting office, where we enlisted on 15 March 1944. I didn't have my birth certificate at the time (I was only seventeen), so my mother had to take me back the next day to give proof that I was seventeen. They told me that I would be leaving on the 22nd of March for Cleveland, Ohio. I went to Cleveland, where I took my physical examination, and from there I went right on to Great Lakes, Illinois.

We went into Camp Greenbay, and that's where I took my five weeks of boot training. I was in Company 632, and I think we were the first five-week boot company to go through Great Lakes, Illinois. As I remember, it was a lot of marching (to and from the mess hall, and out on the drill field). They taught us some things like parts of a ship—what was aft, what was forward, so on and so forth, how to go aboard a ship, and how to make our bunks and take care of our clothes, etc. We had to prove we could swim, went through our physical training exercises, had to wear our gas masks and were exposed to different kinds of gas.

Carey Surratt

I graduated from boot camp around the 28th of April, 1944, and went home on "Boot Leave" for seven or nine days. My parents were glad to see me, and we never thought too much about my going off to war until I left again to go back. After I left, it was quite a while before they heard from me; as a matter of fact, it was forty-five days before they got that first letter. On the 10th of May, 1944, we went to Norfolk, Virginia (there were 1,667 of us on three different troop trains),

and we arrived at five-thirty in the morning. We got off with our seabags, and went right up the gang plank on this big Army transport—the *U.S.A.T. Imperial*. Once on board, they assigned the working parties, and I ended up being assigned to clean up the hospital. This was my first experience at mopping floors.

We sailed on the 13th of May, at about two o'clock in the afternoon. We proceeded down the coast to the Panama Canal, arriving there on the 19th of May. While there, we took on some three-inch ammunition for the gun on the ship, picked up a bunch of supplies and, on the 20th of April, at about three o'clock, we exited the Panama Canal and went out to open sea. It was twenty-one days before we saw any land—I began to think there wasn't any land out there. We ended up arriving in Noumea, New Caledonia, on June 12th, where we dropped anchor, took on a hundred-thousand gallons of fuel oil and, if I remember correctly, they did some work on the main engines. We left there on the 15th of June, and arrived in Milne Bay, New Guinea. Now, you've just got to picture all of us guys—there were 1,600 of us—arriving there with clean white hats, our shoes shined, and when we departed the ship we had to wade through ankle-deep mud to get to the bivouac area. Of course, being the tropics, it rained a lot there and everything was muddy—it was just a sea of mud. We didn't have the luxury of a stone road, it was just ruts and mud.

While I was there, I was assigned to the 118th Seabees, where they put me to work building pallets to store supplies. I just nailed these together and, as soon as I finished one, they just kept on ripping up pieces and I'd go to the next one. I'd do this for about eight hours a day—nothing excessive—and, when I got off duty, I'd go back to the bivouac area, eat and, if I wanted to go down to the post office to mail a letter (it was just a little place down the muddy road), I'd get stamps and mail it.

On the 3rd of August, I was put on draft and separated from this buddy of mine. He had stayed with me all the way through boot camp, all the way overseas, and now we were separated. The Master-at-Arms one morning came around and told me to pack my bags sea-going fashion—I was shipping out. I asked "What about this buddy of mine?" and he said "No, he stays." So, anyway, I sailed out of Milne Bay, New Guinea, on a refrigeration ship—the *USS Mizar*, on the 3rd of August, 1944. This ship would carry fresh meat and fresh vegetables to wherever our guys needed supplies.

On August the 5th, 1944, I stopped off in Finschhafen, New Guinea. I got off there and was housed in an area where the 60th Seabees had been. There wasn't anything to do except just remain in the area, so I went over to the Red Cross for entertainment. I'd listen to the latest records that came over from the States, and two of those songs were Tommy Dorsey's "Boogie Woogie" and Doris Day singing "Sentimental Journey." Those two songs have stuck in my mind as having heard them for the first time, right there in Finschhafen. On August the 10th, I left on LST 452.

The 452 was the flagship of our flotilla. I went to an island called Biak on her, and returned to Mafin Bay where we stayed for a while. She also made the landing in Sansapor, New Guinea—the last landing made on the island of New Guinea. I was just on there as a passenger—I didn't think anything about it—but I had no general quarters station or anything. In September, I finally caught up with my ship—LST 459—in Hollandia, New Guinea. Now, Hollandia was our new operating base, our home base, and I went aboard the 459 as a Seaman 2nd Class, and was immediately assigned to the deck force. The first run we made, after my arrival, was a supply run back to Sansapor.

As a member of the deck force, the duty was just a lot of chipping paint and removing rust spots on the deck. If you were at sea, you could take care of rust spots on the deck—if you didn't have a lot of vehicles on topside. If you were in port, naturally you

En route to Cape Sansapor, July 1944.

wouldn't have vehicles on board, and you would chip away at the rust with a chipping hammer, knock the rust flakes off the deck—down to the bare metal, then you'd coat it with red lead and go back over it with Navy gray paint. That was a continuing thing. Salt water spray would come up over the top of the ship, so it was constantly rusting. You might have ten or fifteen guys out there—all in a bunch—taking care of a whole section of the deck—just chipping away and painting, chipping away and painting. The old chipping hammer had a sharp edge on it, and you'd bang away at the rust scale, pop it loose, and keep at it until it was all cleaned up, then wire brush it and paint it over. It was just hours and hours spent doing this. When we were in port, I went over the side on what they called a "Bosun's Chair" to chip and paint. You might also handle lines when your ship is tied up against somebody else, or tying up at a dock, or something like that. You had fenders that you'd drop over the side, and the fenders were nothing more than rubber tires that would take the impact from the side of the ship to keep from hitting the dock, and so forth. It was a never-ending job.

While I was in the deck force, we had to clean some water tanks. I think we converted some salt water tanks (called ballast tanks) over to fresh water, so we could take on more fresh water. Anyway, when we did that, we had to take this hatch off, go inside the tank and scrape it, wire brush it, and then paint it. The fumes in there were just unbelievable. You could only stay in there for just a few minutes, and then you'd have to go back out because you'd been exposed to these toxic fumes. Today, they wouldn't even let you do that without a mask on. You'd almost pass out when you went in—you couldn't stay in there very long. After a while, we'd stick our heads back out, get some fresh air, go back in there later and do the same thing over again—in and out, in and out, in and out, until we got the thing completed.

We were bringing supplies aboard late one day, and carrying them directly to the storeroom. Among the supplies were some fresh eggs—something we rarely received. The officers ordered all twenty-six cases be taken to **their** storage area. We knew, from past experience, that the ship's crew would not get any of the eggs, so all twenty-six cases were thrown over the side and broken. Attempts to retrieve them failed, and all hell broke loose. However, the next time we got fresh eggs.

In addition to my regular duties, I was also assigned

to a gun crew. My general quarters station was Second Loader on a 40-millimeter gun on the portside of the bridge. Being the Second Loader, I had to take the ammunition out of the container, lay it out, and pass it on to the First Loader who dropped them in the gun. As the gun fired off the last round, it'd kick the clip out automatically. Once you start firing, you had all these clips laid out, and you wanted to have easy access to them, and not have to reach down in the container where they were stored. They had "stops" on the gun where you could only shoot at a certain angle—you couldn't shoot across the ship or anything like that—it would only go so far, then so far back.

Deck mounted 40-millimeter anti-aircraft gun aboard LST 49.

On the 15th of September, we went up to Moratai in the Halmahera Islands. There, the cruisers and destroyers went in and just "unloaded" on the beach—shelled it, and shelled it, and shelled it, and then we finally hit the beach to unload. The first wave of assault troops hit the beach, and they didn't run into any opposition, per se, so they just pressed right on inland. We ended up unloading and withdrawing from the beach, but our flagship—LST 452—got stuck, and we had to help pull her off. I don't know what had happened to the 452, but she was stuck and needed us

least a hundred yards out behind you; then you go ahead and slide in on the beach. After you're unloaded, you get ready to pull off the beach. The first thing you do is pump all that water out of your tanks—lightening the ship. The second thing you do is take up on your stern anchor. Then you run the engines "full speed astern" and try to waltz yourself off the beach (rocking from side to side by running first one engine, and then the other). As you're backing off you take up on your cable, so it doesn't get into your prop or anything like that. You don't back so fast that you overrun your cable, you just cut your speed back down and drift out. Once you get your anchor up, you house it and join the other ships for return.

Anytime you hit the beach fully loaded, you can expect to be there for eight hours, and that's the bad thing about it. On a landing craft like that, you're at the mercy of being in there until you're fully loaded, and any shelling that takes place—it's directed at you; machinegun fire, artillery, whatever, you're a sitting duck! On top of that, a lot of times you have to wait until high tide so you can back off.

When you get onto the beach, you open your bow doors and drop your ramp. Then you'd try to get some kind of a bulldozer off that could build a jetty from the beach to the ship's ramp. The bulldozer (a D7, D8 or D9) would be brought from the ship to the beach on a smaller craft, then go in and keep shovelling a lot of dirt out toward the ship. Once he had enough dirt and coral out there, we'd raise the ramp and lower it on top of the jetty. This way, when you'd unload, the vehicles could drive right off the ship. We also carried pontoons on the sides that we could

to get her off. We had a big eight-inch hawser on board, so we used that line to pull her off. Her engines were running "full speed astern," and our engines were going "full speed astern," and she was taking up on her stern anchor. We had to work at it, but we finally got her off the beach with the help of a tug.

When you hit the beach like that, normally you have your ballast tanks filled so she sets lower in the water. Just before you hit the beach, you drop your stern anchor—paying the cable out—so the anchor's at

Two LSTs on the beach. Notice the stern anchor line trailing behind the nearest LST.

deploy out in front of the ship and, when they were tied together, we could drive across them to the beach.

Vehicles carried aboard the LST were all lashed down. There were provisions in the deck for fastening the vehicles with turnbuckles so they wouldn't move while underway. Those vehicles stored on the top deck were lowered to the tank deck on an elevator and, once they reached the bottom, they'd be driven off—right on down the ramp. I wasn't directly involved in that; the Chief Boatswain's Mate was responsible for the winches, the elevator, and taking all of the vehicles down and off the ramp.

From Moratai, we went to Sansapor, New Guinea, loaded up with supplies, and went back to Moratai. Then, from Moratai, we went back down to our home base at Hollandia. Hollandia was secured; it had destroyers and destroyer escorts doing picket duty out there just running back and forth to keep enemy submarines from getting in.

On the 20th of October, 1944, the largest invasion fleet in the Southwest Pacific invaded Leyte Island in the Philippines. Sailing toward Leyte, and not knowing what to expect, we arrived safely. We were attacked really early that morning by Japanese "Betty" bombers—the first Jap planes I had seen. Somebody shot one down, the other escaped because it was too high for our anti-aircraft fire, and we went on to hit the beach while our guys shelled it on the way in. When we went in, we had 452 on our left, 171 was right next to her, and the 181 was right next to her—now we're only talking just a stone's throw apart (maybe 10–15 yards apart). Anyway, on the way in, 452 got hit something like eleven times by mortars, and all of the trucks up on top of her deck were just burning and putting off all of this black smoke. The 171 and the 181 got hit on the way in too, but our ship didn't get hit. All the landing craft bottomed out at least 200 yards from the actual beach.

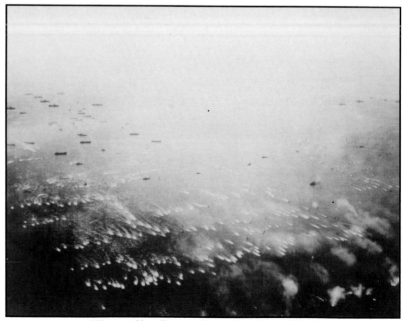

Waves of landing craft streak to Leyte Beach.

Finally, it got so hot from enemy shelling that we had to withdraw. We withdrew and dropped anchor, unloading on an LCT. We had tank destroyers on board whose primary mission was to take Hill 522. We couldn't get the tank destroyers off in time because we had to unload them one at a time; the LCT had to put its ramp up on top of our ramp, drive the tank destroyer into the LCT, then they had to ferry it into the beach, drop off the tank destroyer and return for another load. We had to unload the whole ship that way! It was time-consuming and we were there three or four days completing this whole operation.

During this time, we had a surgical team on board. This surgical team was a team of doctors and medics that were able to perform surgery on board the ship (we had an operating room on there) and their mission was to take care of the casualties we evacuated from the island. Our ship took out sixty-seven casualties from that initial landing. I carried a guy who got shot through the chest and, every time he breathed, he whistled. Another guy got shot in the face, and the whole side of his face was blown away. As you're carrying these guys you have a tendency to bounce the stretcher as you walk. Every time you'd bounce the stretcher, you'd have guys looking up at you and, quietly whispering, "Take it easy, take it easy." You're walking as soft as you can, but these guys were shot, or had shrapnel all over them.

A wounded Marine is carried to a waiting LCVP for evacuation.

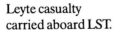

Leyte casualty carried aboard LST.

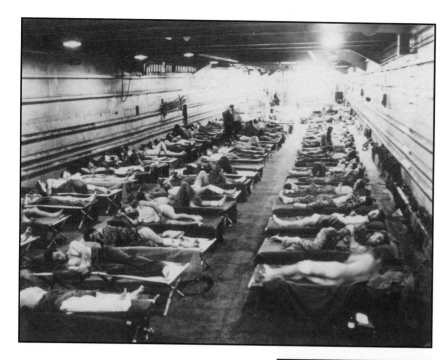

Tank deck of LST being
used to transport wounded.

The scars of battle
temporarily repaired.

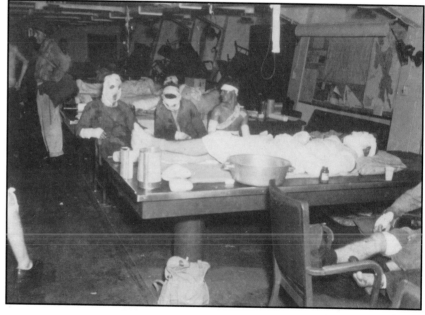

We were only out about a hundred miles from Leyte Gulf, when a sea battle took place. The Japanese and the American Fleet were at it, and we could hear all this radio contact from PT Boats and destroyers making torpedo runs. A hundred miles, and a hundred miles is not very much when you consider the Battle Wagons (Battle Ships), could shoot twenty miles. Our top speed was only nine knots, and we were in a convoy when we left Leyte. If the Japanese had broken through, they would have had a field day with us. It didn't happen that way, so we were able to keep going and, eight days later, we got back to Hollandia, New Guinea. We unloaded our patients—didn't lose a

one and, on the 10th of November, we made a return trip to Leyte.

During this re-supply run, we were escorted by destroyer escorts. There were about fifty ships in this convoy and, on the morning of the 10th we went on general quarters at about 5 a.m. When we arrived in Leyte Gulf, the Japanese were bombing the area. One of our LSTs on our right flank saw a Jap plane, hit him with a short burst, and down he came—crashing in flames between two of our ships. Just about this time, the Japanese were starting to introduce something that would later on become their thing for war—suicide planes. Anyway, we sailed in to the beach and there were about five liberty ships that had been there for some time and had undergone continuous attacks by planes—they had been subjected to fifty-five continuous general quarters.

There were P-38s flying all over the place—they were operating off the airstrip at Leyte. We hit the beach and started to unload at about 11 o'clock. A couple of Jap airplanes swept in and started strafing one of the liberty ships that was loaded down with troops, and crash dived into Number 5 hatch on that ship. It was just unbelievable—the tragedy. At that time, they estimated that 150—300 guys got killed just on that one ship alone. They sent out an urgent request for any help they could get, and our small boats with medics and doctors went over there to help those people that were wounded. There were so many dead on board, that they said they stacked them up just like cordwood.

We took on a lot of casualties, ate supper, and continued to unload. We had just pulled off the beach next to LST 66, and had swung around behind her when a plane came down out of the sun, bombed the 66, and went across our deck and on out to portside. He got out there about four or five hundred yards when our 20 millimeters just tore him all up—when he hit the water there were just pieces everywhere. We were all sort of relaxed just before this happened, and I was sitting in front of the wheelhouse when that Jap went by. He looked down, and I can still see him smiling. He was so low that I could have stood on a step ladder and shook hands with him. When the Jap planes returned, our three-inch on the fantail fired several rounds and, of course, that was just more noise than anything. P-38s were chasing planes all over the place, came in over top of us and, when the Jap planes headed in toward us, the P-38s peeled off because they were afraid we might shoot them down. When the P-38s broke away, this was when the Jap planes started diving into liberty ships and everything else. One of our 40-millimeters hit a plane, and it was knocked off course from diving into another ship—it crashed between a liberty ship and us. Our ships shot down about fifteen planes in about forty-five minutes; everywhere you looked it seemed like there were planes. As we were leaving for Hollandia, just before dark, two suicide planes dove into a liberty ship.

Some of the casualties we were carrying died, and we buried them at sea. We were scheduled to make the landing at Mindoro Island on December 15th, 1944. Last minute changes were made that sent us to Luzon.

From Hollandia, we went on down to Wakde, New Guinea, on December 18th to load up for the Luzon operation. They didn't tell us where we were going, they just said that we'd be sailing through enemy waters for seventy-two hours, that we could expect plane raids, submarine attacks, torpedo boat attacks, and that there'd be land on our starboard side all the way. Of course, we all started guessing where we'd be going—but we had no idea. On December 24th we had Christmas, had a Christmas Play, and so forth, and sailed on the 26th. Outside of Leyte, three convoys came together and headed for Lingayen Gulf—unbeknownst to us, that was where we were headed.

Jap bomb scores a near-miss on LST at Cape Gloucester.

As we passed by Leyte, our convoy got attacked by submarines. The subs fired a couple of torpedoes at the ships, and one torpedo went right underneath an LST. The LST broke formation—he tried to back down to avoid the torpedo and, of course, they chewed him out for breaking formation. You could actually see the torpedo go right underneath the vessel and pass out the other side. Fortunately, the torpedo was set too deep for the depth of the ship but, had it hit, it would have broken her right in half.

We had been told there would be no friendly planes flying below three thousand feet and, just as we were passing Mindoro, we were attacked by a Jap plane. I just happened to be looking back at the time, and here he came. Our guns followed him, and he was coming in just about at water level and, as our 20-millimeters shot him down, we raked the whole side of another ship. Of course, we heard about that, but I don't think there were any casualties. When you're in a situation like that, you don't give any thought to where you're shooting—you just want to knock that plane down. You also have to remember that there were seventeen-year-old kids there on the guns, and that's what happens.

Just outside of Manila Bay, a Jap destroyer tried to sneak into our convoy. He was picked up on radar, and a couple of destroyers went out to meet him. We could see the exchange of gunfire taking place on the surface and, pretty soon, we could see a big flame go up where he had been hit. You know, at night like that, it could have been easy for him to slip in amongst us had it not been for radar. I found out later that radar wasn't really all that good for, when they tried fire control by radar, I saw a plane in one area, and they were shooting nearly ninety degrees away. In this case, the radar had worked and, after three direct hits, it was reported that the Jap destroyer was sunk.

On January 9th, we arrived at Lingayen Gulf. The battle wagons, cruisers and destroyers had been bombarding this beach for several days and, when we went in, several Jap planes tried to get through, but they were shot down. After unloading on the beach, we withdrew that night to a convoy when Jap "bogies" (aircraft) attacked. The anti-aircraft fire was so thick it seemed you could almost walk across the sky on the tracers.

During this time, we had an incident where a destroyer backed up into our bow doors. Of course, because of the sound of the collision, we thought that we got hit by the enemy, so everybody ran up topside only to find out that somebody had accidentally backed into us.

When we got clearance to leave, all the ships started coming out piece-meal, and LST 700 was out on our right flank. Our general quarters had been relaxed to standby, and the First Loader took his goggles off and handed them to me. I had no sooner put the goggles on, when here came a Jap suicide plane nosed straight down for the 700. I hollered "Here he comes," and we tracked it all the way down 'til he hit LST 700. She stopped dead in the water because the plane hit the deck and its bomb went down through the ship and into the engine room where it exploded. We kept going, but a destroyer escort dropped back to stay with her. There were planes all over the place, and the Navy pilots were radioing to stop shooting at them (we were shooting at every plane up there) and they wanted us to quit shooting because they were trying to help us.

We ended up leaving Lingayen Gulf, and headed back south—leaving the 700 there with a destroyer escort. Later on I think they beached her because they thought she was going to sink. The commander of LST 700 was our former executive officer, and when he had left our ship he was reassigned as commander of the 700. After some time had passed, we got back down to Samar and found the 700 anchored there—she had apparently been towed in.

We got word that we could get some repair parts from her, so the Chief Motor Machinist's Mate and several other guys and I went down into the engine room of the 700 to get some fuel pumps, and stuff like that. I went down in that engine room, and it looked like somebody had taken a paper bag of razor blades and shaken it up—that's how the cuts in the steel bulkhead looked from the explosion. The gashes went through the engine covers and rocker arm covers—sliced up just as if it had been cut with a knife through wallboard. There had been two or three guys killed in the engine room, and it was my understanding that the bodies weren't removed for twenty-four days, or something like that—the evidence was there...

Sometime back, before the landings in Moratai, I transferred from the deck force to what we called the "Black Gang" (Engine Room personnel). At the time of the transfer I was a Seaman 2nd Class and, with the transfer, I was switched to Fireman 2nd Class. The executive officer I spoke about (the one who later commanded the 700) was the one I asked for the transfer; I told him that there were some openings down in the black gang. He approved it, and I was made a Fireman 2nd Class.

The first thirty days after the transfer, I was pulling scullery duty (washing all the metal trays, silverware and bowls for the rest of the crew). I'd get inspected by the Chief Pharmacist's Mate, who'd inspect all of my work—making sure all the grease got off the trays, and so forth, so we wouldn't get sick. I'd also have to take all the garbage up topside, and throw it overboard at night. We couldn't drop the garbage during the day 'cause the enemy might see the debris and follow us. At night, you don't have any running lights on the ship, you've got a black-out curtain when you go from the inside to the outside—there's no light visible, the only thing you could see was the phosphorous in your wake. In other words, if you're following another ship, that's the only thing you could see.

After I got out of the scullery, I went down and worked in the engine room, stood watches in the engine room—two hours down, and two hours up, then it was up to you to wake up your relief. You'd wake him up in time to get dressed, get down to relieve you so that you could hit the sack and get some sleep. We had watches that ran from midnight to four o'clock in the morning, four o'clock in the morning to eight o'clock in the morning, etc. Once you'd stand a watch, then you'd move up to the next one. Say, for example, I had the eight to twelve tonight then, maybe, tomorrow night I'd have the four to eight. What it does is eliminate the fixed watch.

While you were on watch in the engine room, you'd always take readings—you had a clipboard with a form on it describing the readings you had to take every thirty minutes. For example, you'd write down the saltwater temperature in, and the saltwater temperature out; oil pressure in, and oil pressure out; read the individual cylinders on the engine and make sure they were operating properly. You had to walk around and take readings from each individual gauge.

The diesel smell was always there, and the engines were noisy with a high-pitched squeal. You had two twelve-cylinder engines running and the whining was just something you had to get used to. While we were at sea, we had a light where we could acknowledge the bridge. If the bridge wanted to increase the engine speed by five or ten rpms, they'd push a button and the light in the engine room would go on. If it blinked once, we'd increase by 5 rpms. If it blinked twice, we'd increase by 10 rpms. We also had enunciators that would register requested speeds of the engine, like "full speed ahead." Full speed was something like 300 rpms, and flank speed was almost all you could get. Standard was somewhere around 278 rpms. We used to run about standard speed all the time.

When we were operating in the New Guinea area, along the equator, I'd sit in the hatch in my shorts because of the heat. Once they blinked the light, I'd increase the speed, then go back down and sit in my chair in the hatch. I could look up through the hatch at the moon and watch it race across the sky. I'd also look at the guy roughly fifty feet away from me—across the engine room—and, because of the noise level, we got to where we could read lips. In rough water (like we had up in the South China Sea), if the propellers came out of the water, and you're not standing right next to the engine, the engine would shut down when the over-speed trip kicked out. To keep the engines from shutting down, we'd hold the over-speed trip in, and when the prop would clear the water there'd be this high-pitched whine and, when it hit the water again, she'd give a lunging effect.

In addition to your routine duties, there were times when you had to take your bedding up and hang it over the rail for the day to air it out, take your mattress up and air it out, and you might have to do your laundry or have somebody do it. When everybody was up, your bunk was folded up and hooked into place against the wall. When you're at sea, and lying in the bunk, you're rolling from one side to the other. It had a little rail to keep you from rolling out and, once you got used to it, you'd lay there and go to sleep without thinking anything about it. I've seen guys get flipped out of their bunks when the seas got that rough—you'd ride up on a swell and the ship would come sliding down, bounce and give a flipping effect.

When we'd get ready for an inspection, it seemed like it was easier just to paint over something rather than wash it. You'd end up polishing the deck plates, and what that amounted to was cleaning them real well—making sure they shine. You'd pump the bilges and make sure the bilges didn't have any oil or anything in them. When the commander came down to inspect you, you didn't want anything he could gig you for. We painted the inside surfaces white (and we had plenty of white paint), so we just painted up a storm—it was easier than cleaning everything all the time.

When you'd go into port, sometimes you might have to overhaul the engines. You might have to put new sleeves in the main engines, so you'd pull the old sleeves with the chain hoist, pull the heads off, pull the liners out, disconnect the connecting rods, pull the connecting rods out, put new piston rings in, put new

Part of ships company's after crews quarters—portside, looking aft.

liners in, grind the valves—reface them, do all the maintenance right there in port. A lot of maintenance can be done on board ship. These were big two-cycle diesel engines, that had eight-inch journals on the crankshafts. They had air blowers to pull the air in, and injectors that would inject the fuel in at something like 18,000 pounds per square inch.

We sailed from Samar, our new advanced base, to load up in Mindoro, in the Philippine Islands. We made the landing at Mindanao in March, 1945. While we were there in Mindoro, I happened to look across and see this kid I went to high school with. He was in the Marine Corps, and we had loaded up the Marine Air Wing known as the "Wake Island Avengers." Now, these guys were going to go in (once the air strips were secured), and get everything ready for when the pilots arrived with their planes. During that landing, we hit the beach, and I spent the whole day rolling six drums of gasoline around from one side of the ship to the other. Of course, I was not the only one involved. The

Japanese mortars were trying to zero us in, and they kept exploding on one side of the ship, and we would roll the drums to the other side. Then they'd land on the other side, and we would roll the drums back again. They never seemed to be able to zero us in where they could actually dump it in right on top of us. You really can't explain that—it just happens!

After that, we returned to Mindoro, where the ship's crew loaded the ship for a return run to Mindanao. We loaded the tank deck full of supplies—cases of fruit, canned vegetables, all kinds of stuff like that—case after case. The tank deck was roughly ten feet high and a hundred feet long. We returned to Mindanao, dropped off the supplies and headed for landings on the Islands of Jolo and Tawi Tawi in the Zulu Archipelago. We were the only LST in these two operations. During this operation, a mine sweeper got in a minefield and lost the bow of the vessel. We sent a small boat into the minefield to rescue the crew.

94

Head in troop compartment.

We returned to base and joined twenty-four other LSTs to sail to Cairns, Australia, where we loaded up with Australian troops and equipment to make the invasion of Borneo. On our return back through the Coral Sea, the water was extremely rough and we lost our pontoons. We also broke a crankshaft in our starboard main engine. We sailed on one engine to Milne Bay, New Guinea, where we beached and dropped off our load.

Australian troops disembark from LST on Borneo beach.

We departed Milne Bay, and sailed to Manus Islands for repairs. While there, we took gunnery practice by shooting at drones and live towed targets. We received a new complete starboard main engine. They cut a hole in our tank deck, pulled the old engine, inserted the new one, and welded everything back.

We left the Admiralty Islands and returned to Samar, in the Philippines—our home base. We laid at anchor and waited for further assignments.

It is now November, 1945, the war's over and we now have an assignment to make a run to Okinawa. We took a load of mail, some relief troops and, once we got out into the South China Sea, we hit a typhoon. The kids got sick, the mail got wet, and we were tossed around like a cork. There was a liberty ship off to our right (starboard side) and, as they were going up on a swell, the liberty ship would be way up above us. Then, as we would go up, it would go down. It was just up and down, up and down. As we would go up on a swell, the swell would roll out from underneath us, and we would drop. The water just poured into our tank deck. We had acquired a jeep some way—had that jeep shackled to the tank deck—and the water was so rough, it broke the shackles. The jeep was slammed from one side of the tank deck to the other—back and forth—until it was destroyed—bent the wheels and everything else. During that typhoon, the water was so rough that when I went out on the upper deck, I sat down on the rail (holding it with my left hand) and I could grab a handful of water with my right.

We arrived in Buckner Bay—the guys were sick—and we saw an LST approximately 150 yards up on the beach. Sitting there high and dry, the typhoon had pushed it so far up on the beach, that there would have been no way to get it back out to the water.

We finally returned to Samar, where we got orders to go over to Subic Bay, in the Philippines. When we got there, we went into drydock—the purpose being to scrape the barnacles off the bottom of the ship. We also did some engine work, repacked the tubes in our shaft alleys, and put some new propellers on to replace the ones damaged by coral reefs. The big scrapers we used to remove the barnacles were twenty-four to thirty-six inches across. The ship's crew had to go down and help scrape the barnacles off, then they painted it.

When we got out of drydock, we got ready to go back to the States. The war had already ended, and the guys that had enough points to go back stayed on the ship. We ended up with a skeleton crew to bring the ship back to the States. We left Manila on the 10th of December, 1945, and, on the way to Pearl Harbor, we broke down off of Guam; a water line had ruptured, so we had to weld it. Finally we ended up pulling into Pearl Harbor (after twenty-four days) and we took an LCT aboard and sailed for Long Beach, California. When we arrived in Long Beach, we put a list on the ship (filled all the ballast tanks on one side) and slid the LCT off into the water. After we were there for awhile, we ended up going down through the Panama Canal. When we got to Colon, we tied up at the dock and got liberty. There were various things to avoid, like the different houses, and stuff like that, some of the bars were off-limits, but we just went in there, walked along the streets, and visited various bars. We never ran into any trouble there at all. When we left there, we towed an LST up to the mouth of the Mississippi River.

At the mouth of the Mississippi, the ship's captain turned the ship over to a pilot. The pilot brought the ship on up the river—about a hundred miles or so—to a quarantine area just south of New Orleans. There we unloaded all of our ammunition and, after doing so, we were able to go on up the river, drop anchor and take liberty. I had been gone for almost two years, and I had written my mother and dad to tell them that I would be in New Orleans. They came down and I got to see them—it worked out fine because my dad was a railroader and they were able to come down on the train. After a time, they went back home, and we ended up taking the ship back down the river and over to Galveston, Texas, where we de-commissioned the ship. I had to finalize all of the engine room logs before I could depart.

LST 459 was de-commissioned on the 12th of April, 1946, and struck from the Navy List on 19 June, 1946. She was sold to the New Orleans Ship Wrecking Company on 31 October, 1947, and subsequently scrapped. She earned six battle stars for World War II service, and was credited with shooting down four Japanese planes.

After I went through the de-commissioning exercise, I ended up going into the Naval Receiving Station there where they cut orders on me and gave me a thirty-day leave. When I reached my hometown, I didn't really want to get off the train—I didn't want to leave my buddies. I wanted to be home, but I didn't want to leave them—we had been together for so long—lived together. When I got up to get off the train, I said "so long" to these guys and said I'd see them later and, of course, I just never thought to get addresses. A friend of my dad saw me get off the train, and he walked up to me and looked at me, and said, "Boy, your folks are gonna be glad to see you!" He loaded me in his vehicle and took me on home. After my thirty-day leave, I reported to Chicago where I was discharged on the 23rd of May, 1946.

When Mr. Surratt re-entered civilian life, he "played a little baseball" for a county team in his hometown while drawing twenty dollars a week for fifty-two weeks. Later, he went to work on the Pennsylvania Railroad as a brakeman and attended diesel school on the GI Bill of Rights. From there, he began a thirty-five-and-a-half year career with the Army Corps of Engineers; repairing surveying instruments and, later, with the Department of Defense (DoD), he travelled worldwide, training cadres of military personnel on new equipment entering the military supply system. His duties included training assignments to Vietnam in the application and use of sensors to monitor infiltration. He also conducted schools to train personnel in the installation of sensors in military arms rooms.

Mr. Surratt is currently a member of the United States LST Association. The purpose of the Association is to reunite former officers and crew members who served aboard these vessels during, and after, World War II. The Association has grown to exceed ten thousand former crew members. He regularly attends national reunions of the Association where he meets with former shipmates he served with over fifty years ago.

He currently resides in St. Charles, Missouri, with his wife, Nancy.

# J.A. Brinkman, F 1/C

*When we finally got to Great Lakes in January, 1946, all of our luggage from the train was out there, so we picked it up and they put us in this big, warm barracks. Someone there wanted me to enlist in the Navy Reserve, but I laughed saying "Just sew that 'lame duck' on my shirt—I'm going home." I took the North Shore train (an electric commuter train that ran between Milwaukee and Chicago) and got off at Sixth and National, where I walked one block north to Pierce. Carrying my ditty bag and sea chest, I arrived home and hugged my wife, at which point mv daughter began to scream—this strange guy's got her mother!*

I was born in Ahmeek, Michigan, in 1920. I moved to Milwaukee when I was three years old, and lived most of my young life on Sixth and Pierce. First, I went to Holy Trinity—a Catholic school—because my father was a janitor there. When he quit that job, I went to Vieall Grade School on Fourth and National. Later, I went to Bay View High School and, since my block was the farthest block from the school, I had to take a streetcar down to First Street, then take another one all the way out to the school. Most of the time I couldn't afford the streetcars, so I would go down to Second and Greenfield and wait for the people that got off to give me a transfer. If I didn't get a transfer (ninety-nine percent of the time I did), I'd have to walk those miles and miles to the school.

I come from a very large family, I was number twelve in a family of fourteen children. I had a lot of older brothers and sisters, and two younger sisters. Things were tough. We lived on the county, and my father never really had a lucrative job. He was a janitor for the Catholic School, but he really was a very learned man. When we were still in Michigan, he was a mine inspector—an elected position that paid very well. One day he made the mistake of shutting down one of the Holtman/Hancock mines and, when it came time for the new election, he was not re-elected. He was pretty badly hurt about that, and that's when we moved to Milwaukee. He was later vindicated because, not even one year later, they re-opened the same mine and it collapsed. When the cave-in occurred, quite a number of miners lost their lives. He had been right all along—the mine was not safe, but that didn't bring his job back. He always said that when you go through a mine and hammer a timber, if the sound is hard because the timber is taking weight, then that mine's not safe. Timbers are only in there to be an indication of loose rock—not for load-bearing purposes.

My mother had four sons in the service at one time: my brother Slim, my brother Burt, my brother Bob, and myself. Slim, Burt and Bob were in the Army, and I was the only one in the Navy. I was drafted into the Navy in late '43. When I went down to be drafted (there was probably a hundred of us there for induction), the guy in charge asked if any of us would be interested in joining the Navy. I stepped forward 'cause I'd rather be in the Navy than in a muddy trench. At least you get decent food. Maybe about two dozen of us stepped forward, and they shipped me down to Great Lakes.

I had a good tenor voice (I'd sung in the chorus in Milwaukee, and the chorus for Allen Bradley), so the Choir Master asked me if I wanted to sing in the Great Lakes Choir. I said "Sure" so, when I got through boot camp, he asked me if I wanted to go to school there and stay in the choir? I agreed, so I was enrolled in the Motor Mac' School—Diesel School. I did very well in Diesel School for, out of about a hundred guys, I was in the top ten. After this, they said they had an opening in Advanced Diesel School, so I stayed on and, in the meantime, I was also an amateur golden gloves boxer for the Navy there at Great Lakes.

I ended up being among the top three men of this class, and they shipped me out to Detroit to the Ford Plant for another advanced diesel school. With this transfer, I was promoted to Fireman 1st Class. I was lucky to be in Detroit, because my eldest sister (the first born) lived nearby in Grosse Point. My wife joined me there—along with my new daughter—and that was the last time I saw my little girl until I got out in '46.

Upon graduation, I was in the top four of the class, so they sent me down to an additional advanced school in Gulfport, Mississippi. While in Gulfport, I was also boxing. Because I was boxing, I would have my weekends off because I was either boxing or had free time. My wife left the baby at home with Grandma, and she came down to visit me in Biloxi.

When I graduated and left Biloxi, they sent me to Brooklyn Navy Yard where I picked up my ship—LST 49. The 49 had just returned from the ETO (European Theater of Operations), and when it pulled in,

Fireman 1st Class J.A. Brinkman on the 20 millimeter anti-aircraft gun aboard LST 49.

Now, my wife came to visit me in New York, too; she stayed on 46th or 47th Street—right there on Times Square. Again, I was fighting in the ring, so I had time off to see her. I remember one fight I had in New York. We went to another base, and I was fighting a colored guy in one of these three-round fights. I don't know what the hell happened, but he hit me before I even knew it, and I fought all three rounds and never came to until I was taking a shower after the bout. I had to ask my manager what had happened, and he told me "You lost." He said that I had put up a good fight, but I don't remember a damn thing—the other boxer hit me up the side of my head and put me on "queer street"—and I stayed there for all three rounds—just fighting by instinct. I won the majority of my fights—I was pretty good—and I picked up some gold medals along the way. I only weighed a hundred and forty-three pounds, so I fought as a welterweight but, with the food that the Navy fed me, I actually grew about three or four inches in height!

Just before we left (we were ready to ship out of Brooklyn Navy Yard) they marched up about twelve sailors under Marine guard and put them aboard our ship. These were guys that had gone AWOL. Just off Cape Hatteras, we broke our main shaft drive (fortu-

Posed shot of a 20-millimeter, no magazine loaded. The man in the seated position is resting on a belt, and he can traverse the weapon by "walking" left or right on the foot plate on the mount.

most of the crew got off. All the while, they were rejuvenating the ship—they took the single 40s off the fore and aft, put on dual 40s, and put on two additional 20-millimeters—one on each side.

I was in the "Black Gang"; I tended the two large power diesels that ran the ship, and the four six-cylinder engines that ran the generators. I would have to check and grease the drive lines and bearings. Also, if they had to have something repaired, they would come to me, but most of the small boat men did their own repairs. During my spare time, I'd take pictures and develop them. My General Quarters duty was to operate the 20-millimeter on the starboard side—middle gun.

I don't recall exactly when we left, but I know I was there for Christmas in New York in '44. Right after Christmas, they shipped us up to New Haven, Connecticut, to pick up pontoons for the ship. From New Haven, we went back down to Brooklyn where they put an LCI on our deck.

20-millimeter in action.

Deck-mounted 20-millimeter
anti-aircraft gun aboard LST 49.

nately, I wasn't on duty when this happened), and we had to put in at Norfolk for repair. When we pulled in at Norfolk, all but two of those guys disappeared again – they didn't want to go – period – that was it!

Once we were repaired, they shipped us on down to Panama where we went through the canal. When we got over to Coco Solo on the opposite end of the canal, we got liberty. Coco Solo was nothing but a great big prostitution operation. They had a square block there of little one-room businesses, and each room had a black broad in it. It was really a sight to see – all shapes and sizes. Coco Solo was really a wide open town. One of the guys got into a bad case of "rot gut" there and, hell, he was bleeding – his tongue was bleeding, his whole body was wracked up, and they finally took him off the ship on a stretcher. I don't think he ever lived, hell, he was squirting blood out of both ends. Nobody ever found out what happened to him.

We waited there for a flotilla (a group of ships with a destroyer escort) of about seven or eight ships, and then we went to Pearl Harbor. At Pearl, we joined up with another flotilla and went to Saipan. While off the

coast of Guam, we ran into a typhoon just before we invaded Okinawa.

After having gone in on the first wave in the invasion of Okinawa, we were sitting empty off shore, when a Kamikaze came after us. We were sitting with two other ships (LST 48 and 50) in something like a "V" formation; our ship was at the head, and the 48 and 50 were across from each other. The Kamikaze was headed right for our fantail and, as he passed over, he was so low that I could have practically reached up and punched one of his tires. He had seen that we were empty, so there was no sense hitting an empty ship. As he passed over us, however, the 48 and 50 were so set on hitting him, and he was so low over the water, that they were shooting each other up. The Kamikaze turned around and headed back into the beach where he hit an LST that was loaded down with lumber. That ship burned so bad that it was just a big ball of fire. Being in the "Black Gang," I had to go in with a small boat and man the water pumps – we pumped water on that ship for twelve hours.

An LST engulfed in flames.

Our captain, instead of following the other ships, took a short cut. He was a funny duck. He'd walk around in tennis shoes with no socks, cut-off dungarees, and a dirty tee-shirt. He was the captain of our ship, but his rank was lieutenant. Anyway, he cut across and didn't go out the way we were supposed to go out, and we hit a reef and were high and dry.

We were sitting ducks for four days, waiting for a tug to come and pull us off. When we hit the reef, we split our fresh water tank and fuel oil mixed in with our water. Then, of course, when we made coffee with half-water and half-fuel oil, we got diarrhea pretty bad. The whole ship had it, Holy Christ, you had to stand in line to go to the head, and before you got there you had to go take a shower because you'd soiled yourself anyway.

In the meantime, we opened the bow doors, lowered the ramp, and got off the ship for awhile. A couple of the guys weren't wearing any shoes, and ended up cutting their feet all to hell on the coral. They didn't even know it until they got back aboard ship, because the cuts were like razor cuts and they didn't notice it until they saw all the blood. I put on tennis shoes and, while I was out there, I picked up a starfish—a beautiful, absolutely gorgeous starfish—I had six of them. I brought them aboard ship, and I put them in an extra locker I had "commandeered." I put these starfish in the lowest of my three lockers, and left them there. About a week later, the guys would be walking through and say, "Hey, Brinkman, did you take a bath?—this room stinks!" I didn't smell it—my smeller's not that good anyway—and finally I found out what the hell it was. Those starfish had rotted and, goddam, it was just terrible. When I finally opened up that locker, and saw what the hell it was, it was nothing but a mass of decaying jelly. I didn't know that what you had to do with a starfish was put it out in the sun and let it dry out. I hadn't done that, so I had a hell of a job cleaning that mess up.

After getting off the reef, we limped over to Eniwetok, where we went into drydock and they welded up our hull. From there, we went on to Pearl, where we were designated to pick up tanks and troops for the invasion of Japan. We were in Pearl Harbor when the war ended, and the next morning those of us who had liberty went into Honolulu.

Later, instead of loading us with war materiel, they turned our ship into a mail carrier. They constructed mail sorting stations on our tank deck, and loaded our deck down with mail. That only took a couple of weeks, and then we were shipped out again. Along the way, we stopped off at Eniwetok, Guam, and then we headed over to China where we went up to Shanghai. We docked at Shanghai, where we unloaded a good portion of the mail for the soldiers and Marines stationed there.

Once we shoved off, we had to pass back down through a river we had mined during the war. We put out a big beam on the front to deflect the mines, and we had to watch like crazy for them before the ship hit

Time-lapsed photograph of the celebration on VJ night. The streaks are flares fired into the air at Pearl Harbor.

This is what remained of our ship's flag after the typhoon.

them. We came awful close on one occasion when the guy that was on watch made a mistake and said "Mine on starboard, mine on starboard!" What he meant to say was "Turn to starboard"—to avoid hitting the mine on the port side. Well, they turned the other direction, and just missed the mine. We actually exploded a lot of mines in the Yellow Sea, where we would see them floating and blow them up.

While we were in Okinawa, we were hit by another typhoon, and this was the worst. We picked up and went out to sea, and we were only gone two or three hours, when it hit us. Some of the other ships lost their steering in the storm, and a destroyer came within fifteen feet of our fantail. LST 50 lost her bow doors and, when she came back, all she had left was the ramp. LST 48 also lost her bow doors, but she went down

with all hands—we never saw it again. While the storm raged, you could put your hand against the bulkhead and feel it come in and out six inches—you wouldn't have believed it, but the ship flexed that much! You would sink down into a trough, and you couldn't see anything but water and the sky above. Then you'd go up to the top of a wave and see other ships all around you. The worst part was being aboard that ship and not knowing what was happening with the weather. The kamikazes had been bad, but the typhoon was worse.

We had been on the eastern shore of Okinawa, and the storm drove all these ships that couldn't get out, up on the beach. Hell, they were a hundred feet from the water! There were LSTs, LCIs, liberty ships, everything, high and dry on the beach after that typhoon—I'll bet that some of them are still there. That was a real bad one. It wiped out the post office on the island, and we had to go ashore and pick up all the packages and mail that was left behind—it just blew the post office right off the face of the earth. It wasn't like a tornado that picks something up, carries it away and drops it, it just flattened everything—the trees, the buildings, everything.

I had acquired a lot of points, and I wanted off. We had been there since about the end of November and, on about the 18th of December, I got a call from the Captain that a passing liberty ship had room for ten additional men. We were actually operating over-strength at the time so, since we didn't need any re-placements, the Captain said that ten of the eighteen guys who had enough points could leave with the lib-erty ship. He said that the numbers we drew would be the order in which we would be transferred off of the ship. Well, we drew numbers, and I drew number nine. After that, he told us that we had to be ready to go in forty-five minutes.

Prior to this, I had gone ashore in Okinawa and picked up a sword at one of the tombs (it was a bad thing to do, but I did it anyway). It was a beautiful sword. It had a gold and silver handle with what looked like rubies and other jewels. It was a gorgeous sword, and not rusted or anything. When I got it back to the ship, I found that my sea chest was too short for the sword, so I cut a small hole in the side of the chest, and this left about four inches of the sword hanging out. Needless to say, when I got my sea chest back, my sword was gone—someone aboard the ship had stolen it. I hope the SOB that's got it appreciates it! It didn't belong to me, really, it belonged to that grave, so I felt that God was treating me like the crook that I was.

I took a lot of pictures and developed them onboard the ship but, because of the few moments we had to pack up and get over to the liberty ship, and the re-striction of how much we could carry, I left behind my photograph enlarger, my chemicals, my tanks, and prac-tically everything else. I left a lot of my laundry, and a lot of money that guys owed me, but I was just happy to get off of that ship.

Once onboard the liberty ship, we were assigned duties for the rest of the trip. Since my name started with a "B," and I was only a Fireman 1st, I wasn't on that lousy liberty ship a day when they put me in the galley—I was a "pearl diver"—I washed dishes on that lousy ship for four days. That darn ship took a "hun-dred years" to get home—it seemed like an eternity.

When we pulled into San Francisco, under the Golden Gate, nobody met us—there was nothing—I thought someone would be there to welcome us home. We had spent Christmas aboard that liberty ship, and not even the Red Cross was there to give us a candy bar. I didn't have any money to take a train or plane home, so I ended up waiting for a "Cattle Car" to get there. You look every day on the billet, and you even-tually see your name. When you see your name, you get your stuff all packed, and then you go to the train station and get on a Cattle Car.

They called them Cattle Cars, but what they were were open cars with a head at each end with bunks in-between that folded down. They were two bunks high, and about forty feet long. They would say that break-fast was at seven, and it's four cars down. They'd call you and you'd get up and stand in line, wash your face and take a leak, and walk down four cars to the chow car. They'd do the same thing again at noon, and in the evening.

All along the trip back to Great Lakes, we were constantly pulling over to the side and shutting down while some express would come through and shake the hell out of us. It took us something like four days to go from San Francisco to Great Lakes, and it was dirty—you couldn't take a bath, all you had was a com-mode and a sink where you could wash up. You had forty other guys in that same car.

When Mr. Brinkman returned home, he resumed his pre-war employment with his father-in-law who, while he had been away, started up Steriline Dairy Equipment—a company that manufactured pasteuriz-ing, holding, and refrigerated tanks for the dairy in-dustry. In 1956, he switched jobs to begin a lucrative career with General Truck (a dealership for General Motors and Kenworth) as a truck salesman, remain-ing with that company until his retirement in 1986.

# George W. Leach, MoMM 2/C

*On December the 7th, 1941, the day the Japanese bombed Pearl Harbor, my father and I were together down at Kingston, on the campus of the University of Rhode Island. He had bought this three-tenement home, figuring to send his six kids to the University. Well, I had gone out to the car to get some tools—Dad was in the house—and I had to turn the radio on and catch this news. I went running in the house and said, "Dad, you've got to come out and listen to this!" The poor man broke down and cried. He just knew that he had three sons who were going to be in the service, and it ended up that all three of us went in the Navy.*

The Leach brothers. Left to right: Jim Leach was a radioman stationed in the South Pacific on the island of New Caledonia; George Leach, and John Leach (also an amphibious sailor). Both Jim and John were drafted out of high school, and remained in the Navy until the end of the war.

I was born on July 25th, 1923, in Providence, Rhode Island. I grew up in Greenville, and lived there all of my life—except for the time I spent in the service. I graduated from the East Greenwich Academy, and went into the Navy in December, 1942. I would have gone in earlier, but I had to have a football injury (torn cartilage in the left knee) surgically corrected before they would let me in. The reason I went in the Navy was because I had hay fever so bad that, if I was stuck in a fox hole, I'd give all our secrets away. At the

time, the Navy was pretty well filled-up, so you had to go in six years—or nothing—so I joined for six years. I went to Boot Camp for thirteen weeks and, at that time, I think deep back in their minds they were thinking of this Amphibious Force, but they weren't telling anybody. I think our thirteen-week Boot training was the first one of that length.

At the end of the training, they called us in for something like an aptitude test. Supposedly you had a choice, but I don't think we really did. They asked us what we were interested in. Well, at that time, diesel was the big thing. They thought that they were going to develop diesel where they were going to be powering cars, so I thought my future might be in diesel. I could have gone for aviation mechanic, but I picked the diesel and I was sent down to Richmond, Virginia, to train for diesel mechanic. While we were there, we worked on large, slow-acting diesels—I mean cylinders so large that you could climb in. These diesels were really slow rpm, but geared high for output. Then they broke us down in groups to train on these little Gray Marine diesels, which we later ended up having a lot to do with in the LCVPs. We began the training in the last of February, and graduated on the 22nd of April, 1943. From there, we went down to Little Creek, Virginia, where they trained many, many people for the Amphibious Force. Of course, being a Northerner, I wasn't used to the heat—as a matter of fact, I ruined the pigmentation on the skin on my nose for life, having burnt it so many times.

They got us up bright and early, and it was a rigorous training but, I'll tell you, it came in handy. When we got to England, later on, they taught us a lot of tricks that saved a lot of lives and those people that hadn't paid attention lost their boats—some of them even lost their lives because they didn't do the smart thing. As an example, in a small boat in a high sea, when you start taking in water, they told us to shut off the sea suction and pump right out of your bilges, to cool your engines. Well, many people did it, but a few didn't. As a result, when we went in to hit the beach at Normandy, some of them were swamped. Quite a few swamped, to be honest with you.

We trained on the LCP(R), and then they came out with the LCVP, which could carry a jeep as well as personnel. I preferred the LCVP by far, it was more sea-worthy, but both boats had the same power plant—the Gray Marine diesel. The Gray Marine was a darn good engine; it required maintenance—in fact, when we eventually got on the LST, there were six of the small boats, and I was assigned to maintain the engines on all six of them. Each boat had their own engineer, but then one guy had to be over the rest to make sure they did it—and did it right. Once I got aboard the LST I was a motor machinist's mate but, prior to that, I was a fireman.

We always ran the small boats to the tops—we weren't satisfied unless we were going top speed. I would say that we all periodically pulled the covers and checked the gaps on the valves to make sure that things didn't change from operation to operation. Of course, we were always cleaning the bilges because if we wanted to cool the engine with the bilge water, it was very important that you kept your bilges clean so that you didn't suck something up into the pump. A great percentage of your fuel oil in a Gray Marine diesel is used as a coolant as well as a fuel. In other words, better than sixty or seventy percent of the fuel bypasses and goes right back to your tank. As a result, if you didn't keep your eye on it, you could put all of your fuel back in one tank and flood yourself or, since there is a tank on either side, put a hell of a list on your boat. So you had to be on the ball to make sure that you were putting the fuel that was bypassing back equally into the two tanks. Also, all of your linkage for the throttle had to be maintained. Later on, I had mine fall apart one night when we were shuttling a group of officers. The cotter pin had fallen out of a pin connecting two of the steering arms, and there was no way we would have been able to find it down there in the bilges. In the end, I found myself laying down underneath of the coxswain all night holding that pin in place.

From Little Creek, they shipped us out as a unit to Pier 92 in New York, where there were thousands and thousands of sailors waiting for shipment overseas. We were there a little over a week (getting to run around the city of New York) and, on the 22nd of July, 1943, we headed for England aboard a liberty ship. Of course, they didn't tell us where we were going, and all the way across the ship had to zig-zag. Along the way, somebody zigged when we zagged, and we had a collision at sea that damaged our stern—right where I was sleeping. When they rang General Quarters, we came up out of the after living quarters and I saw this big ship heading right at us. I was one scared person! Of course, it didn't sink us, but it really scared us. Both of the ships returned to Brooklyn for repairs, and we didn't leave again until the 31st of July. Because we were separated from our original convoy, we left this time in a very small convoy with no escorts. The first time out there were about thirty-five or forty of us, and we had destroyers and destroyer escorts all around us. The next time, we were all on our own, and we were pretty scared.

On the trip over they carried three of our small boats up on top. Every time we'd have a big rain storm, we had to drain them, but the boats were weather-proofed with shipping grease. After we left Ireland, we went up around the northern part of the United Kingdom and came down the English Channel into East

Hamm. From East Hamm, we had to truck these LCVPs over land and, every time we came to a bridge, we had to stop, get out, and drop the ramp on the boat so we could clear the bridge over head.

One of the incidents I'll never forget happened in a restaurant over there in England. I had to go to the bathroom and, over there, the tanks for the commodes were way up high. So I was sitting on the darn stool and reached up for the chain to flush it but, when I pulled the chain, the whole darn thing came down across my shoulders and I was soaked. The water was all rusty, and we had on good clothes. You see, the Navy would never allow us to wear our dungarees in public—we had to wear our "whites" or "blues." All the time we were trucking those LCVPs across England, we had to wear blues, and I was a mess. That porcelain tank sure hurt, but I didn't get injured—only embarrassed.

From there we went down to a little town called Instow, a hamlet in Appledore. Before the war, Instow was **the** resort in England—that's where everybody in England went that had some money to enjoy their summer vacations. They put us up in a hotel there and, as you know, in England they had one bathroom for the whole floor. Well, they had eight of us to one room, and there must have been three hundred of us in that darn place. We were stacked up like kindling wood on bunk beds, and I think that some of those rooms had as many as a dozen fellows in them. We came up with a buddy system for taking showers—the first guy in (say one- or two-o'clock in the morning), he'd finish and come back and tap the guy bunking next to him to take his turn. That was how we'd get a chance to take our showers. We'd have a good time at night—"chewing the fat"—and guys'd be talking about their girlfriends back home.

We had a very unusual set-up inasmuch as every six small boat crews had an officer, but we never did. Our officer was coming down the supposedly roughest water in the world—the Bristol Channel—and he was on an LCT (they say) when they capsized—he never made it. Consequently, we could never go to an officer if we had a gripe like getting a promotion, or something of that nature. It was like going to the Chaplain—you'd go to an officer with your problems and see if he could help you. Everybody around us was getting promotions that we thought we should be getting as well. Well, we had one man—his name was Durbin—and he was a real B.S.'er from Rhinelander, Wisconsin. Durbin was a coxswain and a lot older than

the rest of us—ten or twelve years older—and he had been around. He kind of acted as our leader, so we always went to him with our problems.

One night we were talking, and somebody brought up the name of Diana Durbin—the movie star—so we said to Durbin, "I suppose you're gonna tell us now that you're related to her!" He said, "You bet your ass I am—that's my cousin!" We didn't believe him, so he wrote her a letter and she wrote back "Dear Buster," (we never knew that was his nickname) "Oh, did we used to have fun as kids!" She sent him all of these pictures, and we had to believe the guy.

Another time, we were laying there one night and he says, "Jeez, my wife's having a baby tonight!" We all said, "What the hell..., are you crazy?", and he said, "Wait and see." He was right, he had a premonition, and sure as heck he gets a letter about a week later that said she had her baby exactly when he said it.

We used to play jokes on each other, and there was one guy that always wanted to sleep naked. He slept like a log, so we picked his cot up one night while he was sleeping, carried him outside and put him right there at the bus queue. The next morning, all these English people were lined up there waiting for the bus, and he was laying there bare-assed naked. When he woke up, he tried to wear that damned cot!

The tides at Appledore were as much as thirty feet, or better. Many times, what they would do, we would leave the boats in a little channel, drop the anchor and, when the tides went out the boats would be sitting high and dry. In the mornings, sometimes around two- or three-o'clock, they'd take us out while there was still no water, and we'd climb in the boats and just lay on the deck until the water came up. Once we could move, we'd light the engines up and go off to pick up our soldiers.

Our training consisted of forming different lines (the "vee" formation or line abreast), and rendezvous—waiting for the time they would want us to hit a specific beach—and then we'd go in and hit the beach to drop the soldiers off. When we finished, we'd head back out, take the boats where they wanted them, drop anchor and wait for the DUKW to come pick us up.

We lost quite a few people one day, and they "buried" it, of course. That particular day, we didn't have our full ranking lieutenant—we only had a Lieutenant, J.G. The Army had a captain who out-ranked us, and they were in the third wave, while I was in the fourth wave. Now I'm gonna tell you, the seas were higher than the length of the boat: we'd be pointing right straight up in the air, and the water'd be coming over the top and, the next thing you'd know, we'd be coming right straight down. We were some scared people! We were afraid to make a right turn—come to starboard—because then we'd be laying in a trough. Well, the Army Captain put out the order to hit the beach, so they had to follow his command and turn right. There were two LCMs with Sherman tanks aboard, and they flipped—losing the soldiers and sailors. I believe one of the LCVPs also capsized. Outranked, or not, the Lieutenant cancelled the exercise on the spot and told us to return to base. Still, the water was so rough that we were all afraid to come about and head for shore. Instead, we just kept going and going until we hit shore way up the Bristol Channel—everybody was going everywhere to save their own lives. We went up there to get out of the weather, and called back to base to let them know we were alive.

Just about ten days after that incident, a guy who lived in Detroit got a letter from his wife relating to the incident—not even knowing it was us—about these high seas that we went out in.

We had started our training in September and continued through to the following March. Now, I don't know if the Army or Navy will own up to it, but we had what we were told was the best unit over there. Well, they came and got us, put us in trucks, and shipped us to an LCVP training base where we put on a demonstration for the Admiral. We did so well that they once again put us in trucks and sent us off to another station where we put on yet another demonstration.

On March the 27th, we went to Dartmouth by truck, and were assigned to various LSTs—I was assigned to LST 230. Once onboard, I was assigned to the "Black Gang" in the main engine room. When you start out, you're nothing but an oiler, and you record engine temperatures, oil pressure, and things of that nature. Very shortly after that, I moved up to Motor Machinist 2nd Class, and it wasn't long before I was in charge of the watch. You generally had three people: one guy on the "bells" (the announcers for changing speeds), another guy walking around checking that everything's running alright, and the third guy would check pressures and temperatures. This last fella also had to go way back in the stern and check the refrigeration systems, and I liked that because they had to give you a key and I'd eat some ice cream while I was

back there. One day I got caught red-handed; I was sitting there eating ice cream when the Chief Cook came in and asked "What the hell are you doing there?"

"Do you want some?" I replied.

"I can get all I want," he said, "I don't have to steal it!" Later, he said he never forgot that—"Do **I** want some?" There was never any punishment for it, though—I got along with everybody.

We were the very first LST to cross the Channel—the only thing ahead of us were the minesweepers. Our Captain, evidently, was a mustang—he spent his first fourteen years in the Navy before he made Seaman 1st Class. From then, he just moved right on up through the ranks. He loved his sailors—he was part of us. Well, we were assigned to be the first LST, and we had a big Rhino barge loaded with Seabees way out behind us on the anchor line. When we hit the storm on the 5th of June, they had to turn all of us back. Now, when you're out on fifteen-hundred fathoms of anchor line, and you've got to turn, those Seabees were no longer behind the minesweepers or the LST, they were out on their own. There were magnetic mines all over that channel, and the Seabees were screaming and hollering at us, but there was nothing that we could do. Afterwards, we thought that we could have pulled them in closer before the turn with the stern capstan but, instead, we made this wide, sweeping turn and, as it turned out, everything was all right and we all made it back to England without incident. Those guys sure were scared, and I sure couldn't blame them.

The amphibious attack on Normandy was the most exciting day of my life. The Germans had that damned cannon that was outdistancing the range of our battleship's guns. As a result, our ships dropped us off at sea in our small boats some twenty to thirty miles from shore, because they had no protection for us, and they couldn't take a chance on losing a battleship, or a PA, or a KA. They dropped us off sometime between one and two o'clock in the morning, and we rendezvoused until about five-thirty. We then went over to our assigned PA to pick up the Army personnel.

In my own opinion, I thought the earth was going to break. Out to sea, we could feel the vibration of the earth from the shelling and bombing on shore. You can go to all of the Fourth of July fireworks you want, and watch the explosions in the sky, and nothing would resemble that day. I was only twenty years old, and every now and then you'd see a big ship and, the next

*USS Augusta* lies off "Invasion Coast." Steaming in almost within rifle range of the French coast, the U.S. Navy cruiser *USS Augusta* looms mammoth in size comparison to the tiny landing craft speeding toward shore.

thing you know, you'd see it sinking. Most of the time it was the magnetic mines that were drifting around us that caused the losses, and it was something you just couldn't believe. Ships were going down only a half-mile away, and all you could do was just think how lucky you were.

Our small boat crew took Army mortar units in to the beach, and a lot of the small boat people out there turned chicken and didn't report in when they dropped off their first load. Well, what they ended up having to do was to put more than they had planned on each LCVP that showed up for another run. Because of that, a lot of the small boats swamped. That's why I say that this training we had at Little Creek really paid off for me—I remembered to shut the sea suction off and pump the bilges to keep my boat afloat. I remember shouting to the guys beside me to shut off the sea suction, but there was so much excitement that they must not have heard me. Two of the LCVPs beside us sank.

As soon as we hit the beach, the officer in our boat—a "Ninety Day Wonder"—ran ashore with the soldiers. I was screaming at him to come back, and I ended up tackling the son-of-a-gun; he was actually shaking with fright. When we went back out, our officer was so scared that he made us pull alongside of a PA that had an Admiral's flag flying. He said, "Let me off right here—that's the safest place in the world!" After five or six days, I told the crew that we should go and pick him up. We went back to the PA, and I asked them to look and see if they had this ensign onboard. They went all through the log book and found that he had never logged in. Now, these officers weren't trained as well as us in the small boats because they had been shipped over there and were then told that they were going to be in the "Amphibs." But, still, they were officers, and they knew their job. Anyway, we never again saw our ensign who had transferred over to the admiral's PA. As a matter of fact, about a month later, he called our ship and wanted us to come pick him up. Our captain said, "No way, I don't want him on the ship!" So the PA's small boat pulled alongside our LST, and the "Old Man" had us throw his gear over to him and said, "Don't ever come back." This officer was a traitor in our books! Later on, this son-of-a-gun tried to get our small boat crew court-martialled for leaving him on the PA!

A number of LSTs – including ours – were used as hospital ships to perform emergency medical treatment for casualties. I actually saw this young Army lieutenant get his arm amputated without any anesthetic; his arm had been all ripped and torn by shrapnel and, because there were so many casualties, they had used up the anesthetic before they got to him. He was hooting and hollering, but they had three soldiers pin him down while they took off what was left of his arm. It took about ten or fifteen minutes to get that arm cut off.

We initially had two officers assigned to us. The night that we were given our sealed orders regarding the invasion, one of our officers kind of threw a fit, and they had to take him ashore to the hospital in Dartmouth. They put two sailors on him for twenty-four-hour guard duty, where each stood twelve-hour duty to make sure nothing was going to happen. Being on a small boat, after we made our invasion, our job was to stay behind and lead the bigger ships in because we knew which areas had been cleared of obstacles. The fellows on the ship, however, said that when they got back to Dartmouth, the officer was standing there on the dock with the two guards waiting to get back onboard. It caused us a lot of trouble, but we used to call him "D-Day."

The small boat people were left behind for almost a week to fend for themselves – beg, borrow or steal food – while the LST went back to England. A lot of the ships didn't want to feed us but, occasionally, we'd pull up alongside one and they'd throw over a Jacob's ladder and let us come on board to eat. Other times you'd get aboard and get in line for chow and, since everybody knew their ship's company, they'd ask "Who the hell are you?" We'd tell them that we were sent there for chow, so we usually got to eat. It really wasn't surprising that they would spot us because, by this time, we were pretty grimy. Since our ship was gone, we didn't have access to a shower or shave (like the ship's company we mingled with), so we stood out. At night we'd try to find an LST where we could stay and, if that didn't work, we'd just tie up to their stern and sleep on the well deck of our boat.

After we thought that we had more or less secured the beach, we were called out to a destroyer escort. We pulled alongside, and three newspaper people (a photographer and two writers) got on board our boat. Before leaving, an officer said that they were with the *New York Times*, and that we were to treat these people like admirals. We had to take them ashore, but they didn't realize that, even though we were amphibious, this was a boat – it's not meant to go all the way up on shore. Well, over there, for every foot the tide drops, it goes out a hundred feet. At the time, I was the coxswain of the boat, so I hit the beach, dropped the ramp, and they said, "Hey, do you think we're getting off in that water? Not us. They told you to drop us off on dry land!" So I backed it off, found another place without any sandbars, and I hit the damn beach as hard as we could hit it to get them closer. Well, there was still water up to about our knees, and they refused to get off. It so happened that I had two of the biggest sailors in the fleet aboard (they both weighed about two-fifty, or so, and ended up as the two top heavyweight boxers) so I told the guys "Give them a piggy-back." It should have embarrassed the reporters into going ashore on their own, but my guys ended up actually carrying them in. In the meantime, while we were putting up with this silliness, the damned tide went out. We were previously told that we had to get our boats in and out as soon as possible, because there were ships out there that had to use the beach for unloading. Since I was stuck there, I told this Army captain what had happened and, just about this time, a couple of German aircraft broke through our defense barrier and strafed the boat. I dove under the LCVP and a shell came down through the top and lodged in the hull – just above where I was laying. Anyway, the captain got a bulldozer, and they pushed us out to sea backwards – bending the rudder and propeller shaft. We limped out to an LST, and they sent me to a repair ship where I worked all night fixing the boat. About the 10th, we saw our LST and just headed for it.

From Normandy we went on down to Italy, where we trained and shuttled troops and supplies. On one of the occasions where we got to go ashore, some buddies and I went in to Leghorn, Italy, and three of us met these truck drivers carrying gas up to the front lines. We hitched a ride with them – despite the bombing in the area – and went to the Leaning Tower of Pisa. The driver of our truck said "You guys are crazy, we're going up here because we have to. I'm going because the guy in back of me is keeping an eye on me, and the guy behind him is keeping an eye on him; otherwise,

I'd be cutting off and heading back." Of course, we were young and crazy, and full of excitement, so we insisted that we wanted to go. Finally we got up to where it was pretty hot—you could hear the bombs—and the driver said "Lookit, get off here and go over to the Leaning Tower of Pisa, that's more interesting than riding with us. I'll pick you up on the way back." Using good sense, we got off, saw the Tower, and caught a ride back on his return run.

When our ship first pulled into Leghorn, there were ships sunk everywhere in the harbor. Some of them were sunk purposely so that the Germans couldn't use the port, and some were sunk by aircraft bombs. We had picked up an Italian pilot to guide us in, but we needed an interpreter. Well, one of the lowest-ranked kids we had onboard, a little Italian boy named Gallo from Providence, Rhode Island, could talk fluent Italian. So they announced over the PA system, "Do we have anybody aboard who can speak Italian?" The little guy shouted, "Me, me, me!" That was the biggest thrill of his life; he had to interpret the Italian pilot's words to our captain as to how to direct the ship. As a result, they gave him some kind of citation, and it made us all feel good and happy for the kid.

In the invasion of Southern France, once again, our ship was among the first ones in. There was nowhere near the amount of enemy defensive fire that we had encountered at Normandy, but one of our sister ships—LST 282—was hit and destroyed. There were three of us that always travelled together: the 47, the 282, and the 230. All the small boat crewmen knew each other; we had all trained together, no matter whether you were a signalman, a bow hookman, a coxswain or a machinist. As a result, anything happened to any one of us, and we were all concerned. All in all (except for the loss of the 282), after hitting Normandy, the attack on Southern France was dull; we expected far more than what actually happened.

After Southern France, we went down to Bizerte, North Africa. At that time, they were thinking of sending a couple of LSTs around back of "The Boot" (Italy) to invade the Germans in the Balkans. As it turned out, instead of using two of the new ships just in from the States, the ships kept back for this purpose were the 47 and 230. In the meantime, we did a lot of transporting between Italy and Africa, often carrying a lot of German prisoners. During this time, we saw a lot of Italy, and raised some hell. We were in Naples; went up to Leghorn, and hit the Islands—Corsica, Salerno—just transporting people around.

On one of our trips between Italy and North Africa, we hit a hurricane. Generally, it was a three-day trip, but the storm caused us to sail for ten days to get to our destination. A couple of the LSTs split—I don't think anyone sank—but everybody, and anybody, that could weld was put to work welding them back up so the things wouldn't split wide open. They used angle iron, channel iron, flat bar—you name it—to temporarily hold those ships together. We were lucky. We had a bunch of soldiers onboard at the time, and I swear that it was their prayers that kept us going.

We did a lot of small boat training just outside of Bizerte, North Africa. Liberty in Bizerte wasn't much to get excited about, but it's time off the LST. One afternoon, as we passed through the starboard section of the LST to go on liberty, we noticed several bunks had no mattress covers on them. We kind of laughed and joked about it thinking someone had either stolen them or the bunk owner himself was selling them to the black market (a mattress cover or white sheet was worth twenty dollars!) Well, an hour or so later, as we walked around town, I noticed a male native wearing a white sheet with the name "W.M. Philips" stenciled on the bottom of it. We all had a good laugh and wondered why he didn't remove his name. Sometime later, as we walked the streets, we saw Philips with a couple of his mates. When we told him what we'd seen, man, he took off running up one street and down the other—hoping to find the native before an SP or a ship's officer noticed it. No one else of authority saw it, so he didn't get into trouble, but it sure was good for a laugh.

On the 28th of December, we headed back to the United States and, on the 17th of January, 1945, we landed in Norfolk, Virginia. We tied up starboard side to the dock, secured the main propulsion engines, then everyone headed for the coffee pot. About a half-hour later, we were notified by the dock master that we had to move the LST to tie up portside to the dock in the same slip. In the meantime, many of the officers' wives had come aboard. Seeing as how we had already secured the main engines, it was decided to move the ship by using the forward and aft capstan and large hawsers. I was assigned to #3 station (starboard side) with a boatswain's mate and another seaman. All of the wives came out on deck to watch the activities when our boatswain yelled "Get that asshole out!" As luck would have it, one of the officers' wives was standing near a loop in the line, but she didn't understand that a loop in the line was known as an "asshole" in Navy language. She covered her face and ran into the officers' quarters crying—thinking she had been called a bad name. After securing the ship portside, there was an announcement over the PA system for the crew assigned to #3 station (starboard side) to report to the Captain's wardroom. The Captain, in the presence of the officer and his wife, the ship's executive officer, and we three peons, started to speak in a loud and stern voice. He turned and looked at the boatswain's mate and said "Who called who an asshole?" The boatswain's mate was a shy sort of person and just couldn't get the words out of his mouth, so I spoke up and said "Captain, we were paying out our line on the starboard side as we were moving the ship to port when the boatswain noticed a loop, or an 'asshole', in the line that could get caught in the ship's chock as it passed through." The captain readily understood the Navy terminology and you could see that he wanted to laugh, but he held his composure and dismissed us.

From there they sent us around to Boston where they changed us from a winter ship to a summer ship; they put a lot of big blowers in to keep us relatively cool at our next destination—the South Pacific.

While we were going down the east coast, we got a call to pull into an area right near Annapolis, Maryland, to take on equipment. They loaded us down with pontoons, welded Rhino barges on our sides, and these were going to be used to build a dock in the Philippines for mail delivery. Now, you're not going to believe it, but it was the damnedest town I've ever seen in my life. They claimed that nine out of every ten men in that area had gone in the service, and the women were waiting there when we arrived. I was actually **attacked** once by a group of them, and they even got aboard the ship when the watch officer left to make his report.

This was where we really found out what our new "Old Man" was all about. We hadn't been paid (of course there was no need for taking your pay anyway while we were at sea) and, after being in Norfolk and Boston, the "Old Man" wouldn't let us get paid—he said we'd only blow our money. While we were loading the pontoons, and everything, the Paymaster came alongside and wanted to know if the Captain was onboard. It just so happened that I was on the stern end and, when the Captain was asked if the crew wanted to get paid, he took his billfold out, looked through it and said "No, we've got plenty."

Well, the guys wanted to get some money, somehow. Most of the guys on that ship were mid-

westerners—Colorado, Montana, Utah, and so on, but there were three of us who came from the east. These other guys asked us if we could go ashore and get some money. The captain wouldn't give us a pass but, when I had been leading ships in to the beach over there in Normandy, I had picked up the ship's seal from a minesweeper that had sunk. I talked one of the clerks into typing up a pass for me to go back home, and stamped the damn thing with "my" official seal. On the train north, the MPs and SPs were going through the train checking everybody, and I happened to run into one of our guys who was heading up to New Hampshire. When I asked him what he was using for a pass, he replied that he had written one out in long hand; I got as far away from him as possible, for the MPs sure wouldn't be fooled by that, and I didn't want to be around when he got caught. Then I ran into the other guy, and he was going to New York. I asked him the same question, and found out that his pass was only a little better—he had typed up the document, but it had no seal. Nevertheless, we all made it to our homes without getting caught.

When I arrived home, I found out that my mother had gone down to Florida, and my father was working out on Martha's Vineyard as a civil engineer for the government. The only thing I could do was go see my girlfriend—she was a nurse in training—and ask her for some money. She and the other girls who trained with her at the hospital were only getting fifty-cents-a-day, but she went around and was able to collect something like thirty-five or forty dollars. I went on back to New York, and was sitting there in Grand Central Station waiting for the train to come, when I saw one of the guys sitting there in a corner on the floor. He hadn't been able to get any money at all (he couldn't find anyone), and didn't even have the money needed to catch the train back down to Maryland. I paid for his ticket back and, when we got there, we found that the third fella had been able to pick up fifty bucks, or so.

We hung around that town in Maryland for another week, or two, and then headed out and went down through the Panama Canal. Because of being delayed by picking up the pontoons and Rhino barges, we ended up going all the way out to Hawaii unescorted. It took us twenty days, but the water was like glass—it was beautiful.

Right north of Midway (an area still occupied by the Japs) we had a collision at sea. Prior to this, our Quartermaster picked up on the radar that we were on a collision course with another ship coming in from the port side. At the time, the other ship was seventeen miles away. Well, we had that new Captain on board, and he just kept going—hearing the Quartermaster call out "Fifteen miles—collision course, Twelve miles—collision course," and we still hit the other ship. The collision ripped the bow door and anchor off of our ship, and rolled us over—knocking many of the guys to the deck. No one was hurt, but there sure was a lot of investigation going on—we had radar, and the other ship—a liberty ship—didn't. Well, we made it into Guam, where the ship got repaired and the "Old Man" got court-martialled.

This Captain had replaced the other one who was transferred home with the ships that had left us behind in Bizerte. Once, while still in the Mediterranean, the new Captain wanted to get a "feel for the wheel," so he took us out to sea when the waves were pretty high. In fact, while riding in our small boats on one side of the LST, we could look under the ship as she raised up on the waves and see the guys on the other side in their small boats. At some point, he called us alongside to pick us up. We told him that because of the rough seas we couldn't do it, but he ordered us to do it anyway. The first craft that went alongside got hooked up on the stern of their boat. Now, you always try to hook up the bow first—if you're moving—but they couldn't get the bow hooked up and the davit cable ripped the securing post right out of the stern of the boat. We finally convinced the Captain to take the ship inside the breakwater, and they were able to pick us up without any further mishap. As we went on in to the dock area, we went "full ahead," and he drove us up on the beach so far that they couldn't get us off the beach for almost a month. They ended up having to get sea-going tugs from Oran to pull us off the beach. Naturally, the Captain later claimed that he had ordered "full astern." Some of us made the mistake of laughing and, the Captain, having seen them snickering up on the bow, turned to the sailor on the helm and said, "You see those guys? Well, they're laughing at me, and I'm gonna have the last laugh because I'm gonna break everyone of them!" That sonofabitch, he started doing it, too! He didn't do it that day but, sooner or later, he started breaking everybody for one thing or another. This captain—a full lieutenant—came from Cleveland Heights and he was a rich fella that thought he was a lot better than the rest of us, but it was a great day when he left. On that particular day, he made us all go and dig out our dress blues—even though we were down in the hot South Pacific. He made

us all stand at Quarters, while he patted himself on the back, then he had us line up on the sides of the ship—saluting him—while he circled our LST in a small boat, filming the whole event on his little home movie camera. I would have loved to have been a fly on the wall in his house when he showed that movie, for every one of us were giving him the finger as he passed by!

I think I'm alive today because of President Truman's decision to drop the A-Bombs. On the 29th of July, we left Okinawa, loaded down, and were within weeks of the invasion of Japan. Just prior to the bombing, however, we had the Army troops aboard, and an LCT topside, when a typhoon came up. It hit us when we had the biggest assembly of United States ships ever in one port. Most of us went out to sea and rode it out, but one destroyer tried to ride it out at anchor and ended up on shore. We were all scared like hell (there were ships all around us), and we thought we were going to hit one another trying to get out of there. This typhoon was far worse than the hurricane we ran into in the Mediterranean. During the course of the typhoon, we must have had a thousand bells (ship's bells) trying to keep the ship's nose into the sea. These "bells" were speed changes—ahead on one, stern on the other—trying to keep the bow always facing into the sea. (Author's note: During this hurricane, one ship's anemometer [wind speed indicator] blew away as it was recording 187 mph.)

We heard about the surrender while we were in Leyte at 8:25 in the morning, on the 15th of September. So we left Leyte, and went to Batangas Bay and unloaded. On September the 6th, we left Batangas—loaded with Army Engineers—and went into Tokyo Bay on the 15th, where we dropped anchor at 3:45 in the afternoon.

The women in Japan were beautiful. They were bashful, but the men would run and hide when they saw us. There were no problems with them at all—they were just timid. On other islands, however, some of the Japanese continued to resist. Once, while we were in Okinawa, one of the officers on a ship pulled into the beach right beside us was shot and killed by a Japanese sniper up in the hills. That kind of shook us all because we had pulled liberty the day before—you know, liberty, we went ashore and drank two cans of beer—so that was a real shock to the crews on both of the LSTs.

As soon as we got in Japan, they started calling the guys back to the States for discharge. You had to have "points" in those days, and anybody who had forty-four points was allowed to go home. As I said, we arrived on the fifteenth, and on the nineteenth eleven guys headed for the States. In the meantime, we were just shuttling troops from one island to another—some were engineers, others might be infantry—we were just switching them around.

When we were in the southern part of Japan, it was so hot that the Captain said, "Look, I'm gonna make a drastic change—I'm gonna let you wear your 'whites' to go ashore." I think we were in Kobe at the time, and when we went into town we got the hell beat out of us by the Army. You see, the Army had been there for some months, and they all had their girl friends. Well, we went on liberty to one of the big dance halls (the dance halls all seemed to be called the "Grand Cherry") and we stood out—we were all in whites—and, Jesus, the girls were all asking us to dance! Of course, we were all dancing and having a good time but, boy, when we went outside, the Army guys beat the living hell out of us. You couldn't get up without getting knocked right back down again. There must have been about a hundred and fifty of them, and ten or twelve of us. Well, they called the MPs with dogs. They got us out of there with one of us to each jeep with a dog, because they were still knocking the hell out of us in the jeeps. When we got back to the ship we were a mess—just terrible. The other guys in the crew saw us and, the next night, they went out in full force for a little retribution. Now, this was unusual, because the Army and the Navy got along good—it was usually the Marines against the Army, or the Marines against the Navy. Anyway, when the guys came back (and some of these guys were really big people), they were all laughing and smiling, saying "We whupped the living s--t out of them." That was the end of liberty in that port.

Later, we turned several LSTs (ours included) over to the Japanese. On January 15th, 1946, we arrived in Saipan with a group of LSTs and started stripping them down prior to their delivery to the Japanese. By this time, our ship was manned by a skeleton crew. They broke us down into the leaders of the different trades: say four or five of the deck hands, the coxswains, boatswains and the same thing with the Quartermaster and radioman, just to familiarize the Japanese with the operation of the ship. I'll tell you, the Japanese were very, very smart. We picked up a crew of about eighteen or twenty Japs, and they were top-notch. These guys had me in the bilges following every single line. If

it was an oil line, they wanted to know where it came from, where it went, and whether it was a discharge line or a suction line. In fact, I learned a lot about this ship because we had tended to take a lot of it for granted. Like an automobile, you know that the gas comes from the tank to the pump to the carburetor and that's it. Not those guys—they wanted to know every single thing about the ship, and they had us in the bilges like you wouldn't believe. After we reviewed all of the systems, we went out to sea for two days and showed them how to operate the ship. On our return, we went back out with them and watched while they operated.

After we turned our ship over to the Japanese, I went to another LST—the 648. We started operating in and around Japan like a ferry boat and, as a result, I managed to hit every one of the Japanese home islands. It was just a matter of transporting troops from one end to the other. One time we had a problem with the engine room where we took on a lot of water and all of the electrical systems had to be cleaned. We went into a Japanese shipyard and they had to strip and rewind the motors. It was quite a procedure, and I was amazed that, despite the fact that they were kind of backward, they knew what they were doing. As a matter of fact, I can recall that they ran out of insulation. Well, they used the shoestrings from everybody on the ship (since the shoestrings were hollow) and put them on the wires to insulate them. But it did the job, and we got back to home port.

Before they did the A-Bomb testing at Eniwetok, we were the little ship that took all of the natives, dogs, pigs, cats, outhouses, chicken houses—everything—off that island to another island before the blast. If you'll recall, later, the natives weren't happy and had to be moved again and we were the ship that did it. Our ship was a little AG (auxiliary cargo), and our job was to feed, medicate, and generally take care of the natives. If they became more ill than we could handle, we usually took them to a hospital at Kwajalein. We got along pretty well with them, but we had two real problems: first, because of the language barrier, we couldn't understand them and they couldn't understand us. Second, if you got two beers in them they went absolutely crazy.

One night we went ashore at Kwajalein for a little party. Well, the natives we had aboard the ship somehow managed to get some beer and, in a karate-type fight, one native managed to break another native's neck. The guy's neck they broke was my oiler. Once we got out to sea I was looking for my boy "Lomak" (that was the name we gave him, because it was the closest we could come to pronouncing his real name), and one of the natives said "Ooh, he bad!" I ran down and got ahold of the "chancre mechanic" (corpsman), told him about the injury, and we returned to port with the conscious, but paralyzed, native. Well, they took him into the hospital, but he wouldn't do nothing without me–I had to be there when they drilled the two holes in his head to put the traction tongs on him. Well, now we had to go to court, and what the hell jurisdiction did we have to punish a native of the islands? "Lomak" eventually died and, as the trial later revealed, the guy that broke his neck was the son of a Texan who had skipped the United States because he had committed a murder! The guy was eventually judged guilty and hanged there on the island.

During my time out there, we transported anthropologists to all the different islands to study the races. I suppose it was interesting, but it was also boring as hell. Also, we learned that there was this venereal disease that this country could not cure. What they did, they had something like three soldiers and one sailor that had caught it, and there was nothing we could do in this country in the way of curing them. So they built a weather station–a real nice building–and these guys were going to be there for the rest of their lives. We had to bring food, and you'd take the food to a gate, and you weren't allowed to talk to them or nothing. After you left, they'd go pick it up. Boy, I'll tell you, did that ever scare the hell out of anybody and everybody who was there to see this! I always thought, "Jeez, what the hell do their parents think?"

I was scheduled for discharge in November, 1948, so, after my second leave home, I pulled SP duty in California until my release. As an SP, our biggest problem was the civilians rolling the sailors. On top of that, we couldn't touch a civilian–we were expected to only follow them and get the local police.

Our preparation for SP duty involved no training, really, at all–it was just to use common sense. They vaguely reviewed regulations but, as far as specific training, you just carried a .45 with nothing in it–no ammunition. Of course you had the billy club–something to play with while you walked the streets–spinning it. You had to be a 2nd Class or higher to be picked for SP duty. As far as I can remember, I never saw anybody lower than a 2nd Class rank and, most of the time, they used right arm; in other words, boatswain mates, quartermasters, and the like–specialties in which a sailor wore his rating symbol on his right arm. Left arm ranks were always something I thought that you could use when you got out of the service. These rates were for machinists, radiomen, welders, or sheet metal workers.

On one particular night, we had witnessed this guy flashing a thousand dollars or more, and he was becoming inebriated. We kept telling him that he was going to get into trouble, but he wasn't listening. Well, we were riding the paddy wagon, standing in the rear, and watching when we saw these two civilians dragging this guy down an alley. I told the guy with me–his name was Lyons–"The hell with this," so we stopped the paddy wagon and grabbed the two civilians. Of course, they started putting up a battle, but we had our billy clubs and we took care of them. When we took them in to the police station, man did they get mad at us–they ran us up one side and down the other. I pulled out over a thousand dollars and said "This is what that son-of-a-bitch took from one of our men!" He said, "We don't give a damn, you're not civilian police–you're SPs." "Suppose it was your brother," I replied, "What would you do?" Well, that was one case where we could see it happening–going to happen–the guy was stupid. He was happy just to be back in the States, and he was drinking.

On another occasion, two drunk sailors on a motorcycle got into an accident on Bank Street. We ran out there just in time to see this woman run into a nearby bar, get two shots, and pour it into them. When the police got there, others said, "Oh, they're drinking!" I said, "No, this woman poured some liquor into them," and it cleared them. I'd never seen anything like it–I wouldn't have thought that fast. She was protecting her Navy.

Some of the sailors we dealt with were belligerent as hell, especially if they had been drinking too much and, if you had to go for one of them, they wanted to show off. All we'd do is call for more help; there was no sense getting into a fight because even if you may have been right, you always ended up at a damn courts-martial and someone might say you used excessive force.

We dealt with numbers–we'd always call backup. I don't really recall getting into fisticuffs. A lot of times I felt we were doing the guy a favor, because you knew they were going to get in more trouble. Most of the time it was because they had been thrown out of a bar–the liquor was the worst thing that was around them.

After getting his discharge in California, Mr. Leach returned home to Rhode Island and trained for awhile to become a printer. After a short period of time, however, he learned that Electric Boat had immediate openings for diesel mechanics in the production of submarines, so he applied for the job. (He was there to see the keel laid for the first atomic submarine, and its christening by Mamie Eisenhower.) His career with Electric Boat lasted until his retirement thirty-seven years later.

# Jerry Chappelle, MoMM 1/C

*We were told that if an LST made only one trip to the beach and unloaded, then it paid for itself.*

I was born here in Eureka, California, in 1925. I grew up in the same town, went to school here, and graduated from high school in '42.

I had intended to go into the Navy because, in those years, money was very scarce and my chances of going to college were a little bit less than nothing. My twin brother, Tom, and I both figured that we could get into the Navy, and that would be a place where we could both learn a trade that would serve us after we got out. My original intention was to stay in—I was a regular Navy sailor—but I wanted to get submarine service. It seemed, however, that everybody that was any good in Engineering School ended up on the LSTs because they needed those more than they did the subs.

There were several reasons why I joined the Navy, but first of all, I never had any desire to be a ground-pounder in either the Army or the Marine Corps. We had naval ships come up here because I lived on a bay that's navigable. We had tin cans (destroyers) and other ships that came in and, as a kid, I'd been aboard them and it always looked to me like the sailors had a whole lot better life than what the Army guys did (there wasn't any question about it—they do). You might be in the same position of getting your butt shot off just as anybody else, but at least you had a dry place to sleep at night and, as a general rule, you'd have at least half-way decent chow during the day. Another reason was that the Navy had a lot better chance of your getting into a service school to learn something—which I did. I ended up in Iowa State College of Agriculture and Engineering for a three- or four-month stint, and then went on to the General Motors Plant up in Detroit, Michigan, and then on to my assignment. I learned a lot in the Navy that stood me very, very well for many years because I worked all of my life in something that was associated with engineering—first in the trucking business, and then with a machinery company where I ended up as a manager of a branch here in Eureka.

My brother and I were sworn into the Navy at the Federal Building in San Francisco in either late January or early February, 1943. We had to ride a bus from Eureka to San Francisco, and we got into San Francisco sometime around six in the morning. We had meal tickets for some place fairly close to the Federal Building where we went in and got some breakfast.

After that we went over to the Federal Building where we had to stand around and get run through the line buck-ass naked for several hours to get our physicals and all of that baloney. Finally, we were sworn in.

It was kind of funny, but while we were standing there naked down in the basement of the Federal Building on Golden Gate Avenue (just off of Van Ness), they were examining the WAVES at the same time. They had these lines painted on the floor for us to follow and, some way or another, and I don't remember whether it was the guys that got off the line or the gals, but we ran into each other and there was a whole bunch of screeches and screaming. Everybody managed to get back into their own place, but we got the hell bawled out of us by some Chief, so it must have been the guys that got off of the right line. As I remember this meeting of the sexes, there was just a handful of girls, but there were several hundred of us—the guys were standing there grinning and the girls were standing there screaming.

From San Francisco they put us on a train to Farragutt, Idaho. That was the only place I have found that was any closer to Lower Slobovia (from the Li'l Abner cartoon strip), and the only place I found that was any worse was Hokkaido, Japan. We got into Farragutt; it was in the morning and barely over twenty degrees above zero. In all the time that I was there (six to eight weeks—whatever boot camp was at that time), the snow never left the ground and, at night time, it was generally in the range of about twenty degrees below. I can't remember it ever getting above freezing—it was slushy and lousy; actually, it was a hell of a place to put a boot camp—I can't imagine one that was any worse. It was bad for illness; they had scarlet fever and meningitis running rampant, and it killed a lot of people, including two men from this town (I knew both of them), one of them ended up dead, and the other fellow ended up in bad shape—his total time in the Navy was boot camp and then he got "medicaled out."

Anyway, from there we went to Iowa State. We had Navy people training us, but most of them had been civilians that were basically uniformed educators. We had one instructor—a first class specialist (a special rating for this type of duty)—and, although I can't remember his name, I recall that he was a bald-headed big guy. He was really good, and our machine shop instructor was really good as well. The service schools there were tough because it was a case of either you keep up or you drop out—one of the two. Every week we would have a test and, if you didn't make the grade on one, you had the next week to pick up that test with a passing grade plus get enough points to cover what you didn't get on the one before, or you were history. The student's rates were changed from a Seaman 2nd to a Fireman 3rd because, at that time, there was no 3rd Class Petty Officers in the Black Gang, so we had one single red stripe on our left sleeve. You were under the gun quite a bit; you had to keep your nose totally clean and the slightest infraction and you were gone—they didn't play around. I'm guessing, but the attrition rate for those students who didn't make it through the course was probably about 20%. The Navy was pretty tight about who they sent to schools—especially engineering and other technical fields, you pretty much had to have some idea of what you were doing and, of course, you started to really learn once you got on board ship.

Detroit, Michigan, was a great deal easier—it wasn't anywhere near as tough, and we got a lot more liberty. Detroit was a great liberty town and we were studying over at the Van Dyke Plant of the Gray Marine Engine Company. This was actually training for small boats. At that particular school we trained on the Gray Marine which used the GM 671 Prime Mover and, at that company, they put the marine accessories on it (the salt to fresh water heat exchangers, and all that sort of thing, and then they hung a twin disk clutch and reverse gear on the back end of it). They got the engines from General Motors and just converted them to marine units. That was the engine they used in the LCVP and a myriad of other vessels. The 671 was a great engine. During the summers of '41 and '42 I had worked for a trucking outfit and, at that time, Cummins' Engine Company dominated the trucking industry to a great extent, and General Motors didn't seem very much. After the war, however, there were lots of General Motors engines in trucks and, for many years, GM engines were one of the standard engines for over-the-road highway usage. On the engines we worked on, if you put it on battle setting with the Ninety injectors, you got 225 horsepower out of that particular engine when it was full-bore ahead (they got less when in direct connection in trucks). They were very dependable, extremely good engines. The only real

problems with them had nothing to do with the engines; the sea filters were always picking up some kind of garbage when you got in close to the beach. We didn't have to work on those engines very much at all and, to the best of my knowledge, they very seldom conked out. When we were in Southern France we were a mother ship for quite a while, and we worked on a lot of those engines, but it was mostly just a case of changing the injectors and things like that.

From Detroit, we went to Little Creek, Virginia, for two or three weeks. Then we were reassigned to Solomans, Maryland, where we did some additional training. We went out on LCIs and LSTs a couple of times and, for a period of three or four days, we were over fighting a peat fire on the other side of the bay (that was pretty miserable). Then the time came one day when they had us all lined up and they just started assigning crews and the Skipper would walk up and some yeoman would call out the names and they'd alphabetically pick five of us for assignment to the LSTs. My brother and I were assigned to LST 47 even though it wasn't finished yet, but it was well along.

At Solomans, as I remember, there was no liberty. At Little Creek, we had a few evenings off, and there was a good friend of mine from Eureka that was in the Blower Repair Shop in Little Creek, so my brother and I went over and visited him and his wife and kids a couple of times, 'cause he lived very close to the base. In Solomans there wasn't any place to go. You could go over to the base canteen, or whatever they called it, get a couple of 3.2 beers, and that was about it. I was pretty much working details (like fighting that stupid fire) or the usual drilling and, of course, we had training classes that went on all of the time.

From the Solomans we were put on a train and headed for Pittsburgh, Pennsylvania, which, as I remember, took a couple of days. When we got there we were quartered in an old barracks in Coraopolis, Pennsylvania. We had meal tickets for all of our meals, and I distinctly remember that these tickets were for Augie's Cafeteria, and it kind of lived up to its name—it was a genuine "greasy spoon." Pittsburgh was a great liberty town, and we got liberty just about every night.

We picked up the 47 on October the 24th of 1943. She was brand new and, of course, wasn't yet commissioned. It couldn't be commissioned because going down the rivers (the Ohio and, eventually, the Mississippi) the mast had to lay down on the top deck in order to pass beneath the bridges, so we couldn't really fly a flag. As I remember, it took about two weeks to get to New Orleans. Along the way, we always tied up or anchored at night. There was a Coast Guard crew that took us down to New Orleans, and that was where you learned your job the most. After about two weeks, when we arrived in New Orleans, those guys departed and, from there on, you better remember what they had taught you or you'd be out of luck. We stopped at Baton Rouge to pick up provisions and a full load of fuel, and the ship was commissioned at Algiers. The mast was raised, the radar was hooked up, we went through the commissioning ceremony and then on to the shakedown cruise. Our shakedown cruise was out in the Gulf and to the upper edges of the Caribbean. It was a standard shakedown; gunnery practice, drills, refueling at sea, collision training, and the like, throughout the days and then we'd anchor at night at Panama City, Florida. We didn't have any engine problems, but there were minor things that caused us to go back into the Navy Base at Algiers (across the river from New Orleans) to get some repairs done that we couldn't handle ourselves.

We did have some trouble, and it was usually the steering gear—this was one of the weaknesses of the LSTs—it was hydraulic to electric, and it gave all kinds of fits. I think every LST afloat had it—one time or another they had their steering gear go out, and sometimes with the utmost rapidity.

After the shakedown cruise was over, we went to New York City. On the way we ran into a hell of a storm off the coast of Cape Hatteras that nearly tore us apart. The LST was designed and built to bend, and this storm proved it for we had about a three-foot bend from fore to aft. Had it not bent like it did, it would have busted in half.

After about a week in the Navy Yard in New York, we went to Boston and spent some time in the yard up there while they made some modifications. Of course we didn't know it at the time, but we were about ready to leave for Europe. We went from Boston to New York Harbor, and then over to Bayonne, New Jersey to an Army ammunition depot. They put wood all over the entire tank deck; they laid stringers down, put stringers up the bulkheads for about five or six feet, laid boards all over that and sunk the heads of the nails and filled the nail holes with putty or plastic wood so that our tank deck was solid wood. Then they proceeded to load five hundred tons of demolition explosives on board. They also loaded an LCT on our top deck (we carried one of those every time we went on a long trip—we carried one halfway around the Pacific

for several months). With the LCT on the top deck, and the explosives on the tank deck, we went to a fuel depot and fueled our own tanks and all of the ballast tanks with the exception of two that I used to trim the ship—that was my job, I was what they called the Oil King.

The Oil King was a job I learned from a Coast Guard water tender while we were going down the Mississippi. That particular job made the engineer that got it responsible for anything liquid onboard ship: the ballast system, the oil, the transfer of fuel, the fresh water system—all of that. You carried a certain amount of ballast all of the time (depending upon what you've got for cargo), because it keeps the bow of the ship down. Loaded, we only drew about four-and-one-half feet forward, and about twelve-and-one-half feet aft. The main thing is that you're trimming, all the time, everyday, first thing in the morning as a rule, and sometimes twice a day. You have to trim from port to starboard because the ship will develop a list even if you use so much as a foot of water out of the fresh water tanks—which were all the way aft. Say, for example, you take on a portside list and it's down several degrees. Well, you'd pull water out of the portside trim tank and put it in the starboard trim tank. We had two Gardner-Denver vertical split case pumps (rated, I believe, at 50 horsepower), so they were capable of pumping something like 1,500 gallons a minute. Everything under the tank deck (with the exception of the main engine room, the generator engine room, and a void compartment clear up in the bow) was compartmentalized into tanks for the ship's fuel, cargo fuel, or ballast water. Then there were three tanks up forward that, when we were normally running, were not full; they were called beaching tanks. When we went into a beach, those tanks were loaded full and, when you wanted to get off the beach, the first thing that happened was those tanks were pumped out and, although they weren't very big tanks, it would raise the bow somewhat.

For every compartment onboard the ship there was a ballast or fuel tank below it in the very bottom of the hull. I can't remember exactly how many tanks there were running from just aft of the bow to some short distance forward of the stern, but there were three rows of tanks athwart the ship: The port wing tanks, big center tanks, and then starboard wing tanks. The generator engine room and the main engine room occupied the center compartment, and they had a ship's fuel tank forward of them, with a ballast or fuel tank on either side. Immediately aft of the main engine room were the lube oil tanks and, aft of these were fresh water tanks with the shaft alleys running on either side of the center tanks.

The upper deck carried the officer's staterooms, the officer's wardroom, the Old Man's quarters, the officer's head, the ship's office, the galley, the galley storeroom, and all of that. The deck above that was called the boat deck. That's where the davits for the small boats were located, the chartroom, the bridge, the radio room, and the degaussing room. Above the wheel house is a tower-like structure that is known as the flying bridge. The ship was conned from up there; they had speaking tubes that ran down to the wheel house beneath it, gyro-compass repeater, phones, and everything that was necessary to conn the ship. Every LST made had a different looking flying bridge because that was up to the Skipper as to how he wanted it, but they all built flying bridges which were elevated up about another deck in height. The lower bridge was very seldom used because they were so low you couldn't see over the elevated bow of the ship. The flying bridge was totally exposed to the elements—some of them made a canvas cover, but I don't remember that ours ever had such a cover.

After filling her up at the fuel depot, we had one tank that didn't have anything in it, so they plugged the surface vents and filled her up with aviation gas. As we were backing out into the river at Bayonne, the pilot somehow ran us up onto a mud bank and knocked three of the blades off of the portside screw. They pulled us into the Brooklyn Navy Yard, and I was always told that before any ship went into a yard you were defueled and your ammunition was taken off—the

whole thing—but, apparently, our convoy date was too close. We went in during the middle of the afternoon, and they had fire watch all over that place. We had ruined the screw and the tail shaft was bent, so they cut a hole in the after end of the ship and snaked our spare tail shaft out. They stuck the new tail shaft and propellor in, and we were out the next morning. From there, we went on back up to Boston.

We left Boston and went to Halifax, Nova Scotia. Leaving Halifax in late February, '44, it took us about two plus weeks to get across the Atlantic because we were in about a three-and-a-half knot convoy. There were some old British coal burning merchant vessels, and three-and-a-half knots was their best speed—the speed of the convoys was the same speed as the slowest guy in the line. When we went across the North Atlantic to Europe, I was the sight setter on a gun crew—the three-inch fifty naval rifle on the stern. There were anti-aircraft guns scattered all over the ship. There were three 40-millimeters and two 20-millimeters on the bow, two 20s just forward of the deck house, a couple of more 40s on the boat deck, and the three-inch fifty on the stern which was later changed over to a twin-mount 40.

Condition One was general quarters, and Condition One Mike was beaching. When we went into beaching condition, my station was up in the forward ballast control room where I controlled those three beaching tanks. We had a diesel-driven auxiliary fire pump up in the same compartment (that was one of the things they put on in either New York or Boston). I'd go up there, get down, and just stay in that compartment until we were secured. I had a sound-powered phone so I was in communication with all the rest

Auxiliary (Generator) Engine Room—forward view from the starboard side. The engines were three Superior GBD8 driving DC generators.

of the ship, so I would know what to do and when. All of the ballast tanks (except the three beaching tanks) were controlled from the generator engine room—what they called the auxiliary engine room.

Our first port of call was Milford Haven, Wales. We came in through the channel between Ireland and Scotland, down the Irish Sea, and into Milford Haven. We put in there, got behind the sub nets in calm water, and got a good night's sleep for once. We shut down everything (except the generators) and didn't have to worry about any U-boats picking on us there. We were there just overnight, and headed for Falmouth, England, the next day. From Falmouth we went up to Scotland—a place called Rosaneith on the river Clyde—and then down to Dartmouth, England, where we unloaded the LCT. That was rather a spectacular thing: we'd ballast the ship down to a forty-degree port list, and the LCT was on these great big timber skids that measured two to three feet above the deck. They'd take all of the rails off on the port side and, once they had it all unhinged, they'd fill all of the starboard ballast tanks on the LCT with fire hoses, and then, through some kind of special arrangement, all of the chains on the starboard side were cut loose at the same time and she slides off and hits the water with a big bang and a splash.

Once we arrived in England, we were primarily engaged in training. We'd load up the Army and go out into the channel—go here and there and, of course, all of the ships made numerous feints up and down the channel to train the crews and give the Army guys some training as to what it was going to be like when we had to go do the real thing (and also to confuse the Krauts). We'd just train, train, train, and very seldom were we in port for more than a day at a time. We spent a lot of time in Falmouth, and quite a bit in Dartmouth, Plymouth, Southampton, Torquay—all along the Devonshire and Cornwall coast.

We had liberty quite a bit in Falmouth, and I've wondered all these years if a pub called the Grapes' Inn is still there—it was one of our favorite watering holes. Of course, it had been there for centuries, so I don't know why it wouldn't still be there. We had liberty in Plymouth but, boy, that was a bombed-out place. The English were far more reserved than we are, in some instances, but we ran into everything. We met people that seemed to like us very well (several of us off the ship made very good friends with the people that owned that little Grapes' Inn pub), and then you ran into the other kind that did nothing but squawk

about Americans—that we were "overpaid, over-sexed, and over here!" We made friends with a lot of Limey sailors; they traded us rum from saving up their rum rations for sugar, butter, and stuff like that. It seems that British sailors aboard their own LCTs just didn't get the same amount or quality of food that we received. If those guys got anything for dessert, they had to furnish the stuff and make it themselves. From what I heard, life in the British Navy never progressed much beyond Captain Bligh. The officers lived like kings (if anybody can live that well onboard ship), but the enlisted men kind of lived like dogs. For the most part, the civilian people were pretty good.

Our liberties were up at 2300 (11 p.m.), and the only time I didn't spend the night on board ship was once when several of us missed the liberty boat. It had shoved off just a little early, and we had made it to the dock just in time to see it going out. We spent a miserable night in a Red Cross canteen and, because they didn't have any beds, bunks, or anything, we sort of huddled up together to try and stay warm. In the morning, we caught a small boat out to our ship and I got ten hours extra duty for missing the liberty boat.

We loaded up in Dartmouth, travelled to Southampton and departed for the invasion on June the 4th, 1944. The invasion was supposed to go on the 5th but, about midnight, the Skipper came down and said that it had been postponed for twenty-four hours. A lot of the ships that had left after us went back into port, but we didn't—we just circled around and around out there in the channel until the next night (5–6 June).

I didn't see very much of the invasion because I was either down in the generator room or the hole (forward ballast control room). We had reveille at about 11 o'clock the night of the 5th, went to General Quarters at about 0400 (4 a.m.), and General Quarters Mike at about 0600 (6 a.m.) I wondered what was going on outside but, when the naval bombardment started, that was something! We had three "wagons" (battleships—the *Texas, Nevada* and the *Arkansas*) nearby, and the biggest guns any of those had was the fourteen-inch, and one had twelve-inch guns. Boy, I'll tell you, the Old 47 would rock from side to side something fierce every time those guys cut loose with a salvo. That was real noisy. They would all fire their nine barrels and, when a couple of them would coincide, you'd have eighteen barrels cutting loose at the same time. Those shells sounded like a freight train when they'd come across you. I didn't actually go up there into the forward ballast control room until we were about ready to beach. Before those times, I was down in the generator room with the ballast system.

When we'd go to general quarters, the whole ship was sealed off—the watertight doors are shut, so you don't move around much. There were a lot of people who couldn't understand how we could stand to be three or four decks down in the hull and, if something hit us, the guys haven't got any chance to get out. Most of the time—if something hit us—it wouldn't make any difference anyway. We could get up those escape trunks pretty fast. We could open the watertight doors to get out, and each hatch had either six or eight dogs (securing levers) on it, so you could un-dog the hatch and get out if it was necessary, but you dogged it behind you again. If the engine room got hit and you had to get out, you just had one hatch to un-dog and it was up at the top of the escape trunk into either the troop compartment on the portside or the mess compartment on the starboard side. There was also a little round hatch up on the top of the light hood on the main deck.

The forward ballast control room was only as wide as the ship's center tanks (about 30 feet), and only about six feet from fore to aft. Actually, it was a void space, and there was an escape trunk on one side so you could get into it. You'd go down through a hatch in one of the troop compartments, then through a storage compartment and another hatch into the ballast control room. I was all by myself when down there. I could hear a lot more of what was going on around the ship from this compartment than I could in the engine room and, since the steel on the outside was only three-eighths of an inch thick, you could hear things kind of like rattling around in a tin can.

After we unloaded on the beach, we took a thousand Krauts and one French woman back to England. They had fished this woman out of what, in the Pacific, they would have called a "spider hole." She had been in a hole up on the side of a cliff on Omaha Beach, and she had been shooting at people. We were told that she had been living with some German officer and the MPs picked her up and brought her onboard. She was just basically a hooker. They kept her up in one of the officer's staterooms in officer's country with a guard at the door.

We actually didn't have much contact with the prisoners. I did guard duty because I had what was called a 24-Hour Watch—I didn't stand regular watches, I was basically on duty 24 hours a day. There were a number of us on that, so we got stuck with guard duty

down on the tank deck. It was pretty well suited for prisoners because, if you went to the tank deck, you had to go down a ladder. These ladders had lines attached to them, and all you had to do was pull two bolts at the bottom, loosen the two at the top, and haul the ladders up. Every hatch alongside (the machine shop, the electrician's shop, all of the different store rooms, the carpenters mate's, the shipfitter's shop, and all) was dogged down and locked so that nobody could get off the tank deck. It was pretty secure. We also had about a twenty foot "no-mans land" with a couple of lines stretched across the tank deck. The officers were in the very aft end, and the enlisted people were in everything forward of that.

Of course, we searched them as they came onboard, and anything they had with them that could be used as a weapon was taken from them. They also checked everybody that came aboard to see if they had the SS "lightning" marks tattooed on their arm because you never knew. There were so many of those SS guys that would grab an enlisted man's uniform and put it on before they were captured to avoid detection. I remember hearing that one prisoner had scratched the living daylights out of his upper arm to try to get that tattoo off, but they took him and moved him off—what they did with him, I don't know.

We got to unload on the Mulberry floating harbor just once, and that was great. They were built in England, and the one on Omaha was put up by the Seabees. Instead of having to beach, we just pulled in and pulled the side railings on the top deck and drove the trucks and whatever was on the top deck directly onto a ramp and off onto the Mulberry. At the same time we opened our bow doors, dropped our ramp, and unloaded the tank deck on the Mulberry as well. That Mulberry was great, but a storm came along and wrecked the whole damn thing. The weather was terrible when we started the invasion, but on about our third trip across the channel (enroute to Omaha) a really bad storm came up and tore the Mulberry all apart.

We made somewhere between eight and twelve trips across the channel; most of the trips were to Omaha and Utah Beach, but we did make a couple trips or so to one of the flat beaches (Gold, Juno or Sword).

Around the latter part of July, or the first part of August, we went down through Gibraltar and into the Mediterranean. We first stopped off at one of the islands off Italy, and then on down to either Bizerte or Oran. Those were the two ports in North Africa that we worked out of the most—probably the most out of Bizerte. We kind of dinged around between Africa and a couple of places in Italy where we took on additional people, fuel, water, and so forth.

On the 15th of August we went into a town called St. Raphael on the Riviera on an operation called Anvil/Dragoon. For those of us out in the harbor it was, at times, a little hairier than Normandy, because we didn't have to contend with many enemy aircraft in Normandy. Down there in Southern France, however, they had a goodly amount of air raids—particularly just off the beach. I guess the Army pretty well walked in during the invasion—it wasn't tough at all, but the Germans sent a lot of aircraft over, and they did a lot of bombing.

I suppose anybody's going to have a certain amount of apprehension, but I can't say that I was ever totally scared. I guess that I just had kind of a fatalistic attitude about the whole thing, and that was: if you're going to get hit, you're going to get hit. My only thought was that if we do, I want to get it all at one time, rather than getting all shot up/all messed up. I never was really scared. After making that trip across the Atlantic, sitting on top of a floating bomb, you can get kind of hardened to the whole thing.

After the invasion of Southern France, we made a bunch of trips back and forth from France to Africa. Once the Army secured Marseilles and Toulon we were in both locations for a while, and served as a mother ship in Marseilles. Following that, it was just work horse stuff—back and forth from Africa to France, and that was where we got into a storm just after leaving Africa.

The weather was bad when we left and, by that night, we were hitting one hell of a storm and we started to get some hellacious cracks along the main deck about twenty to thirty feet forward of the boat house. Any of us that knew how to weld were up there welding and trying to patch and hold that thing together. The wind was blowing and the water was coming all over the top of us. To prevent our being washed overboard, they'd string a line or a cable or something, and we'd hook onto that—we'd just tie the line around our waists. The worst part of it was that it was wetter than hell and colder than the devil and, of course, the LST was either rocking from one end to the other, or side to side—I don't think any LST ever did just roll one way—it was a combination of both. Given that it had 320 feet of flat bottom, there was nothing to keep it going straight. Finally, the Old Man said "Enough!"

and, since the winds were coming from the European side, he somehow or other managed to turn the ship to Africa. The old boy had been in the Navy for many, many years (he was a Chief Boatswain's Mate who had got a commission) and he was tough, but he sure was a good seaman. He managed to get that bucket turned around and headed back to Africa without getting us caught in a trough and swamped. I don't know how the devil he did it, but he did it. We headed back to Africa—got the sea behind us—and went into a Navy yard at Bizerte where we got patched up.

On or about the 29th of December, 1944, we shoved off for the States. The trip back across the Atlantic wasn't bad at all—it didn't take near as long as the trip to Europe because we didn't zig-zag, the convoy was small and, because it was basically an LST convoy, we managed about eight knots.

We first put in at Norfolk for a day or two while the yard removed the two forward small boat davits (of our previous total of six).

From Norfolk we went to Boston where they installed evaporators in the largest of the fresh water tanks. These evaporators converted salt water to fresh water and, with them, we could make two thousand gallons of fresh water a day. Even though we originally could carry a hundred and twenty-five thousand gallons of fresh water, if we had two or three hundred (or more) troops onboard, that water can go awful fast—even as tight as we rationed it. We could take showers onboard, but not often unless we were in port and tied up to where we could have a hose running to a water source for immediate replenishment. A later class of LSTs, the six hundred series, were built with the evaporators and the ship's heating boiler down in that same compartment. They did the same conversion with us, except our boiler remained where it had always been (one deck up from the main engine room, on the starboard side).

They exchanged our single mount 40-millimeter on the bow for a twin, and put a director tower up aft of it between two single barrel mounts that we retained. The director had a Mark V Sperry Gyro sight and, when the gunner moved that sight around by means of a bicycle-like handlebar, the twin 40s followed it. They also exchanged our 3-inch Fifty on the stern for a twin 40 back there, and put fiberglass insulation on the overheads in the living areas to prevent condensation from dripping down later on while we were in the Pacific.

When we first arrived in Boston, we got a thirty-

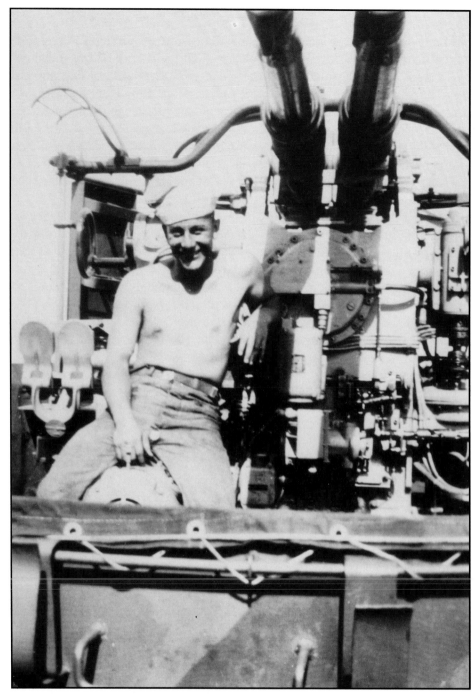

40-millimeter dual-mount anti-aircraft gun.

day leave, so my brother and I went to San Francisco and then on to my mother's home in Santa Rosa. Of course, it took a lot of time travelling, but the thirty days gave us a pretty good leave. We picked up my mother's car in Santa Rosa and went up to Eureka, where we spent about a week. We had a chance to see some of the people we knew and hadn't seen in a long time. While we were in Eureka, we stayed with a lady who had been my seventh and eighth grade school teacher. She lived just across the street from where we had lived, and she was a real nice lady with a big house

and lots of room. There were a lot of people in the town that we didn't know, and a lot of changes because Chicago Bridge and Iron Company had come into town right at the first of the war and were building big floating drydocks for shipment to installations throughout the Pacific.

After we returned to Boston from the thirty-day leave, I went to school for a couple of weeks to learn how to operate the evaporators. In the meantime, our Engineering Officer transferred out, we got a new one, the First Lieutenant left and he was replaced, and there were a lot of personnel changes. We went from Boston, down through the Panama Canal to San Diego, then up to Bremerton, Washington, where they did some more work on the ship and we loaded up and, sometime in the middle of April, we shoved off for Pearl. From Pearl we went to the Marshall Islands, Eniwetok, Guam, Saipan and, from there, to Okinawa.

When we got to Okinawa, the invasion was still going on hot and heavy. We made a number of beachings at Okinawa and Ie Shima, running between there and the Philippines many, many times—Subic Bay, Batangas, Manila, down on Mindanao, a whole bunch of places in the Philippine Islands where we picked up different Army units, and all kinds of equipment. We carried everything from tanks and bulldozers to you name it. We landed those in Okinawa, and that was always a hairy place because it was in aircraft range of Japan and, of course, the worst thing there was the damn kamikazes—there were lots of them up there, and the Japanese were getting pretty desperate about then.

Sometime around August 10th, a rumor got started that the Japs had sued for peace. It was false, but the rumor spread all over the whole harbor of Naha, and these crazy characters started firing everything that they could get their hands on—everything from small arms to 5-inch 38s. They were sending these shells up and, you know, an accepted law of physics states: that which goes up has to come down. The shrapnel was clattering on our top deck like mad, so the Old Man put the ship into General Quarters right then and got underway—circling the harbor until order was restored. In the meantime, a couple of ships rammed each other, and it was a hairy mess. Fortunately, we escaped any injury. There was a lot of crap that had to be cleaned off the top deck and some minor damage, but nobody got hurt. That would have been a hell of a thing: do both sides of the puddle, then get a hunk of shrapnel through your head from your own guys!

We were in Okinawa when the Japanese actually sued for peace, but we were real leery because you never knew what they were going to do—they were so damned fanatical they might have thought that since they missed their chance to die for the Emperor, they're liable to just go off on their own! So everybody was pretty apprehensive, pretty careful. We got underway for the Philippines shortly after that. We were in the Philippines when the Japs came aboard the "Mo" (*USS Missouri*—BB-63, the battleship upon which the

LST 47 on the beach in the Philippines.

surrender was signed) on September 2nd, and signed their names. We went to Japan shortly after that—in early September—and then we went back and forth between the Jap Islands and the Philippines.

I think I went on the beach in Japan no more than three or four times, even though I was actually there—off and on—from September to April. We went to a number of ports (Yokuska, Tokyo, Yokohama), and up to Hokkaido, where it was covered in snow (to get into the buildings you actually had to walk through a tunnel of snow to get through the doors—it was a miserable place). One time I went ashore to visit a couple of Army buddies in a camp outside of Tokyo but, other than that, there wasn't any reason to go ashore there. Any place that served either food or drink was off limits because there were too many reports of guys being poisoned or ambushed. Whatever, I had no desire to go on the beach at all—if anybody wanted to get me back in Japan today, they'd have to drag me kicking and screaming.

After a period of time, the word came down that we were going to turn the ship over to Military Sea Transport. The ship was no longer going to be a commissioned vessel, so everybody started stripping the guns off and stacking the barrels (except the 40-millimeters—they were too heavy to move, so they just took the barrels off). We inventoried all of our gear, the machine shop supplies, and all of that, and then we found out that the ship wasn't going to go over to MSTS at all—it was going to the Japs! I hated that! We had worked so damn hard for better than two years to keep that bucket afloat, running, and able to fight, and now we had to turn it over to the Japs. Why, that just galled the living daylights out of a lot of us. Some guys didn't care—all they wanted to do was go home but, boy, it sure put a bad taste in my mouth!

LST 377 had been in service since the North African campaigns. She was now assigned the job of going around Tokyo Harbor and picking up mostly 20- and 40-millimeter ammunition off of all of the LSTs for shipment back to the States. One day she came alongside, and we found out that she didn't have hardly any Black Gang left at all. I think the highest rated guy they had onboard was a 3rd Class Motor Machinist Mate, and he was a small boat man. My brother talked to somebody on the 377 and wrangled a transfer. You see, he and I were regular Navy and, since all of these guys were getting off on points, we only had seventeen or eighteen men left from the original crew—all the rest of them were new guys. He got off on the 30th of

December, I believe, and found out that there was a hell of a lot of work that had to be done on this other ship. I had done the Oil King's job, the main engine room, and the evaporator room, so they sent a message over asking if I wanted to transfer off. Well, heck yes, I did, and so I left the ship on the 3rd of January, 1946, and went over to the 377. We got some more engineers, started to work to get her in working order to get her back home, and had a darn good Black Gang by the time we finished up. I was a 1st Class Petty Officer then, and we didn't have any chiefs (Chief Petty Officers) at all, so my brother and I had the Black Gang. He had the generator room and small boats, and I had the main engine room and the evaporator room—we had a good Oil King, so nobody had to worry about him. We had a good skipper, and a darn good engineering officer—he said he didn't know anything about engineering, but he was willing to learn, and

Left to right: Jerry Chappelle, T.J. Duke, Jim Gorman, and Tom Chappelle. The leather jacket wasn't Navy issue, but the "Old Man" never said anything.

worked well with all of us. The skipper's name was W. Scott Dukes, and the engineering officer was Joe Shearer.

On the trip back across the Pacific we had a real big catastrophe with the port main engine—it blew up the forward gear train—but we managed to scrounge enough parts on the ship to be able to get it running up to standard speed. It was a miserable several days job to get it back in running order (we were in a horrible sea), but we managed and made it back to the States.

We made port in San Francisco, and this was the first time I had ever arrived at that city on a naval vessel. My brother and I got a couple of days worth of liberty, and then went over to Treasure Island. My hitch had been up for some time, so we were supposed to be discharged at T.I. We were over there for about a week, and the Chief that ran the barracks where we were quartered was supposed to assign everybody to work details. He was a great guy, and he said that he'd be damned if he was going to assign 1st Class P.O.s to work details when they had just got back from the Pacific. Instead, he told us to be there for muster at 0800 (8 a.m.) every morning, and gave us open liberty—we'd come back every morning, and say "Here," and just take off again. After about a week of this—waiting for our discharge—we found out that they had quit discharging people on T.I., so we had to go out to Camp Schumacher over by Pleasanton. We were at Schumacher about three days, and it was miserable—couldn't even get into the galley and eat unless you wanted to stand in a line that was about a thousand sailors long. It was crowded as all get-out because of all of the reserves getting discharged at practically the same time.

When we had stopped off at Pearl Harbor on the way back, a two-and-a-half striper got my brother and I into his office and he wanted us to reenlist because they needed chiefs on minesweepers for operation off Bikini Island for the A-Bomb tests. I said sure, for it was my intention to stay in anyway. I told him I'd re-up, but I wanted thirty days leave in the States first. "I can't do that," he said—he couldn't and we didn't, so that was the end of that.

After my discharge in April of '46, I was on the beach for about two months and then enlisted in the Naval Reserve and stayed in until about '56. We didn't have a drill or pay status up here, so there didn't seem to be much sense in staying in because you couldn't get advanced or anything.

When my brother and I got back, we started out in the trucking business together with a rig of our own. We ran it until late '46, and found out that there just wasn't enough money in it to support both of us. So we flipped a coin to see who was going to go get a job, and that fell to me, so I went to work for a freight transport outfit. Tom was already married, and I got married a little later when I got reassigned to Eureka to handle the big rigs around town. They wanted to send me back on the road again, and I didn't want any more of that—I had a little guy coming up, and he wasn't quite "launched" yet, so I didn't want to leave my wife as she was eight months pregnant. So I quit that and then things were kind of up and down for a year or so. The economy wasn't very good around here, but then in '49 I went to work for a stock hauler for a year and, in '50, I went to work for another fellow who had a brand new Kenworth, and I ended up working for him for almost twenty years. When he went out of business in '67, I went to work for a machinery company here in town, and worked for them for twenty years—I ended up as manager here in Eureka for about the last eight. I retired in '87, and my wife retired in '88—which was great until she got sick about three years ago. She died last year—we had been married for forty-nine years, and twenty-four days.

The LST Association is going to bring LST 391 back to the States. It has been a part of the Greek Navy for quite a long while now, and they kind of gave it to the LST Memorial Association but, of course, we've got to bring it back. The only thing holding it up is that the Association has to get an international arms permit, and this one piece of paper is the last hurdle they have to overcome before sending a crew over to bring her back. The intention is that she's going to be a seaworthy ship capable of travelling to different places and kind of earn her own keep as a memorial ship.

# Herbert W. Stamer, QM 2/C

*The greatest reward I received from my Navy duty was having served with so many great men during the war, and to have been able to continue to maintain a friendship with so many of them afterwards.*

I was born on February 24th, 1924, in Hoboken, New Jersey. My parents were of German and Swedish descent, and had immigrated to the United States in 1911 and 1919. I grew up in New Jersey and, from the age of three, I lived in Lyndhurst, near the Hackensack and Passaic rivers.

Upon my graduation from Lyndhurst High School, my first employment was as a mail clerk for a local bank. Later, I found employment at the Bendix Aviation Plant in Teteboro, N.J., working as a stock clerk in their IBM department, where I soon learned how to work on punch card tabulating equipment.

At the age of eighteen, I enlisted in the U.S. Naval Reserve at the New York City Recruiting Station. On December 13th, 1942, I passed the entrance examination and was given the rank of Seaman 2nd Class. Exactly one month later, I was sent to the newly developed Naval Training Base (Greenbay Area, Company 82) at Great Lakes Training Base, where I received my Boot Training. While there, I sang with the Great Lakes Naval Base Choir, made a knot board for display inside the barracks that had a total of 103 different knots and splices, and taught signalling to the other members of my company.

After completing my basic training, and finishing as number eight in my company of 140 men, I was transferred to Newport Naval Training Center, Newport, Rhode Island, to attend Quartermaster School. There, I learned the many requirements for ship navigation, chart handling, and more signalling. I also learned the important rules of the sea regarding safety procedures, was taught all of the many different ship drills, how to figure sunrise and sunset, and learned a lot about celestial navigation, time and tide reports, and so on.

Upon completion of this phase of my training, I earned the rating of Quartermaster 3rd Class, and was sent to the Amphibious Training Base at Solomons, Maryland. Arriving at the base, there wasn't much to see except for big open fields that were cemented over with large areas for drilling. Parade grounds are an important part of all Navy training grounds; we had to line up and be counted, there were always ceremonies to attend so we wouldn't forget how to salute, and this was where we received instructions for our day's work.

During the rainy days, we appreciated being able to walk on a solid base. Without the concrete below us, we would have been trudging through mud. One of the stories about Solomons is that it is the only place in the world where you can stand up to your neck in mud, and still have dust blown into your face. It was a dirty place for sailors and, worse yet, it meant a lot of washing clothes as they became red from the dust and dirt in the area.

Our barracks were simple wooden framed buildings. They were similar to those we had at other bases. When I travelled through America and saw buildings like them, I would always feel that they were overgrown chicken coops. They were our homes, but they truly were no place like home.

We had a dining hall, and the food was always good. On the walls of the mess hall were signs stating: "Take all you can eat, but eat all that you take." Having just finished eating at home, and seeing how difficult it was for my folks to get good quality food, I did not waste any food. Navy beans were a good part of our diet, and they did taste good. We had fresh bread, fine meats, stews, plenty of potatoes, good salads, and some kind of desserts—either pudding, cake, or fruit. Lemonade, and always a cup of coffee, and no talk about rationing.

On August 25th, 1943, I was assigned to Crew 4193, U.S.A.T.B., Solomons Branch, Washington, D.C. (the abbreviation stood for United States Amphibious Training Base). We were introduced to our Captain, Lieutenant (JG) Joseph Frank Krall. We all called him Joe (except when we were in his presence, then we called him either Captain or Skipper). He was a former Chief Boatswain's Mate who had been given a field commission. He was as tough as nails, and he didn't stand for any nonsense.

The crew was made up of a bunch of men who had never seen a ship, were away from their homes for the first time in their lives, came from big cities such as New York, Philadelphia and, as such, had a lot of "street smarts." As tough a bunch as you'd meet anywhere, but a team so bonded that it was like a real family. I have often thought that if I were going to outfit a pirate ship, these men would be just what I would look for. We became a family and, as in any family, we had our differences, but we were all united in our war efforts.

We learned that we were going to be assigned to a Landing Ship, Tank. This was a new idea, and we had never heard of such ships prior to coming to this base. As a matter of fact, my first memory of the "Amphibs" was when Chief Roberts came in the classroom for Quartermaster training. He said that we would be assigned to a newly formed branch of the Navy. These ships were called landing craft, and we would be expected to take these ships and boats and land our troops on assigned beaches during invasions. We would then be expected to do the best that we could in getting off the beach and return to our regular Navy base or ship. The same as men serving on PT boats, we too would be "expendable."

There weren't enough LSTs around to permit us to go directly aboard one so, for some time, we practiced on a painted mock-up of a deck so we could tell where our battle stations would be located. When General Quarters sounded, we would rush to our designated stations where we would assume a watchful eye over the operation. We also hoped that we were in our correct place on the field so we could escape any Boatswain's Mate's tongue lashing for taking too much time, not being able to tell the difference between the bow and the stern, or for not knowing the port from the starboard side of the ship.

A quartermaster was expected to be a good signalman, as well as being able to assist the officers in navigation. I would climb up the makeshift wooden signal bridge where all of the tools were located (signal flags for semaphore signalling, a flag bag to be used on a makeshift mast with the signal cords hanging from the yardarms, and a small blinker type of light for use in sending morse code messages). Signalling can become very boring after many hours, but it was required training for silent communication with other ships. On the signal lights we had to be able to send and receive at least ten words a minute. We would practice morse code by blinking our eyes, or by slapping our knees when seated (the right knee representing a dot, and the left knee representing a dash). Of course, we remembered to call them the Navy way of dit's and da's. We were amused by the morse code, and we made a little ditty: "Three dits, four dits, two dits, da!, Solomon Islands, rah, rah, rah." You can find the meaning by looking in your own code books.

We had a lot of inspections, and there were so many officers around that had to be saluted; on one occasion, an inspection took two-and-a-half hours. We all had to have good haircuts, and be clean shaven—no facial hair—and the Skipper would remind anyone who was trying to grow a beard that he wasn't old enough for such nonsense and have him cut it off. The haircut was given by one of our shipmates. We had a talented bunch of men, with a lot of varied job experiences, so there was always someone around who could fill a job requirement. There was a shortage of shoe polish at the Ship's Service, but I was one of the lucky few that had enough left for a good shoe shine for when the Admiral made his inspection.

For some reason, I didn't think that brothers would be stationed aboard the same ship, but we had a set of twins named Tom and Jerry Chappelle. They looked so much alike that it was almost impossible to be able to tell them apart. I guess whoever assigned them to the ship couldn't make any identification either and decided not to split them up. They were both motor machinist mates, and part of the Black Gang—which is what those in the engine room were called.

We had liberty and could visit the town of Solomons, Maryland. There was a main street which ran the entire length of the town. There were three restaurants in the town, a movie house, and a hotel. Sailors could get beer there, but there was no hard stuff. It was a typical one-horse town and, if it wasn't for the people walking down the street, and an occasional car, the town could have been classified as a ghost town. There wasn't any U.S.O., or any real entertainment—with the exception of the movie house, which consisted of a large room, straight back chairs, and a stage in front. It reminded one of the old-fashioned plains opera houses, except there was no bar involved.

I was assigned Shore Patrol duty, and was stationed at the Woodburn Restaurant—a place built for defense workers. It was a restaurant, and had tables and booths. There was a large cooler, made of wood, which was used to store the beer bottles. Quarts and ten-ounce bottles were sold for ten or twenty cents a bottle. Near the entrance, there were three "one-armed-bandit" slot machines where you could put in a nickel and pull down the handle with the hope that you might get a dollar back. There was a Wurlitzer juke box with some fairly new songs like: *Begin the Beguine, Pistol Packing Momma*, and several of the Andrews Sisters' songs. All that a sailor could do was eat, drink and talk—no real doings at all.

There were quite a few women in Solomons but,

with the exception of a few old maids, the women were married and showed it. I've never seen a town with the appearance of so many expectant mothers—many of whom appeared to be teenagers.

We finally were able to take a trip on a real LST, and we operated in the Chesapeake Bay area. There always was some fear of motion sickness and, as a child, I really made a mess in my uncle's car from car sickness. The motion of the water in the Chesapeake Bay was different from that of the ocean, but it was enough to make me sick. Sea sickness is not a joke to those who have it, and I know that I wasn't alone, for other men could be seen with their buckets in hand—we quickly learned to check the wind so we didn't spit into the wrong direction in those moments requiring relief. Generally, after about two days or less, I would get over it. There were always some sailors who would try to suggest that a good cure would be to get the cook to give you some raw pork or other greasy food. While that certainly wasn't helpful advice, it was important that bread be eaten to prevent what was called the "dry heaves" (this happens after your stomach has been emptied). One of the men was so sick from motion that he had to be reassigned to shore duty. He couldn't even use an elevator, and he required medical attention.

The time on the cruise went fast, and there was a lot that had to be learned. We learned how to determine the sunrise and sunset, and how to use tide tables. When you are doing celestial navigation, it was important to know how to use those books and tables designed for this. The charts had to be updated on a regular basis, as the tides change the shorelines, the channels, and the location of buoys and markers had to be placed exactly where they were located.

Accurate time is one of the most important parts of any navigation formula, and it was my job to wind all of the ship's clocks on a daily basis. I also had to check with the Greenwich Observatory each day to determine the exact time. We would listen on the short wave radio for those beeps and signals from England, and compare our ship's chronometer with the exact time. We were reasonably happy that our clock was only about 1-3 seconds off on a daily basis. A second is quite a distance, and we concluded that if we were able to be within seven miles of where we thought we were on the open sea, then that was close enough. When we approached a shore, we would know the exact location of any light house or other landmark. This was easy to find out through the use of hydrographic bulletins which had drawings of the shoreline of any place we might be sailing. We did not have radar at this point, so we used the very basic tools available. The transient on the compass located on the wings of the bridge, the sextant for measuring the angles to the stars or sun, and a good chart which properly located all of the buoys and channels.

We had a gyro-compass which we used for all of our directions (I remember that it came from the Walter Kiddee Company, in Belleville, New Jersey). We also had a magnetic compass on the bridge as a back-up system. In order to calibrate the magnetic compass, we had to go through an exercise called "swinging the ship." We would turn the ship in different directions, and then set the magnetic compass by means of moving small magnets located under the main compass. By doing this, we were able to overcome the magnetic influence of the area. We also needed to swing the ship so we could adjust our degaussing system used to neutralize the ship's polarity and make it less attractive to magnetic mines, or being detected by any submarines.

The steering of any ship that was over 300 feet long, and 50 feet wide, wasn't always easy to control. It was necessary for the officers to understand just how long it might take to change from one course to another. It was important that the directions to the wheel house be clear and timely to make changes smooth. Any too fast changes would result in a ragged train in our wake and pull us off course, thus making exact positions difficult to determine. We also had to learn that when two ships are travelling side by side, there is an attraction that can cause the ships to slam into each other. That was not good seamanship, and a good officer would make certain that there were good fenders over the side next to other ships to prevent any scraping actions. The fenders were generally made of hemp rope woven into large basket-like objects about two to three feet thick. In some cases, automobile tires might be used as fenders.

The Skipper asked me to teach the officers (whom he called "ninety day blunders") how to figure sunrise and sunset, and how to do some navigation. He had confidence in me but, at this point, not much confidence in the officers. Joe Krall was a lifetime regular Navy man. As a former Chief Boatswain's Mate, he was used to getting things done his way, and in a hurry. He didn't have much respect for those men who, after just a few months in the service, could become officers before they had earned their sea legs. He really didn't have any officers that he could warm up to. I think that this was an inferiority complex that Joe had because he lacked many social abilities. He knew how to handle a ship, and didn't have a lot of patience when it came to getting things done. He was a taskmaster but, as I had to spend a lot of time with him, I found him to be sensible, pleasant, and eager to teach when he felt his efforts were appreciated.

On this trip, I had to stand the "midwatch" (which was from 00:00 to 04:00) on the signal bridge. Every half hour, I had to check the location of the ship to see that we were where we were supposed to be. It would have been difficult to explain to the Skipper just why we weren't where we were shown on the chart to be. It was rather cool standing out in the night air but, in the Navy, there is always supposed to be a cup of coffee for men on watch. I managed to hear a five-minute news report on the war; it told about the Nazi retreat in Southern Italy, an air raid in France by the British in which one German cruiser had been sunk as well as three other ships, and how a town that was bombed was cut off from gas, water and electricity. It also told of the capture of Leyte—a Jap-held island in the Pacific.

On August 10th, I learned of the surrender of Italy, and was happy to learn that we had one less member of the Axis to worry about. I also learned that one of my old girlfriends (whom I had gone out with before I met Alice) had a brother in the U.S. Army, and he had been killed in action while on a dangerous assignment working with the Rangers. He had just become engaged while he was on furlough.

We completed our training on October 6th, and I was given another ten days leave so I could go home again to my family and to be with Alice. Then the orders read for me to go to Pittsburgh, Pennsylvania, for further duty.

Our crew arrived in Pittsburgh, where we picked up the *USS LST 47*. We left Pittsburgh and went down the Ohio and Mississippi rivers to New Orleans where, on November the 8th, the ship was formally commissioned. In the New Orleans Delta region we practiced ship handling, learned more about making the necessary corrections to charts, and how to use the Hydrographic Manuals that showed all of the navigational information for the regions within which the ship would serve.

My initial service on active duty was in the American Theater (consisting of the Atlantic Ocean) which, at this time, was infested with German submarines.

One of the most exciting moments during my time of service, however, occurred when we were travelling north along the eastern seaboard and ran into a severe storm at sea off the coast of Cape Hatteras, North Carolina. The waves were mountainous, and the weather so terrible, that we arrived at our destination of New York Harbor fully ten days behind schedule.

During the ship's crossing of the Atlantic, we had submarine alerts, and our escort vessels dropped depth charges to help protect the convoy. The most hazardous event, however, occurred when the ship ran into ice and stormy seas off Nova Scotia. We were transporting a tremendous amount of ammunition in the hold of the LST and, during this storm, it broke loose and there was only one way to handle it: all available hands reported to the tank deck and formed a human blanket over the bouncing boxes of 20- and 40-millimeter ammunition. Fortunately, the cases were eventually re-secured without further mishap.

Meanwhile, on the way over to England, I taught the ship's officers how to predict sunrise and sunset, and also how to use the different navigation book.

Herbert Stamer, Marseilles, France, 1944.

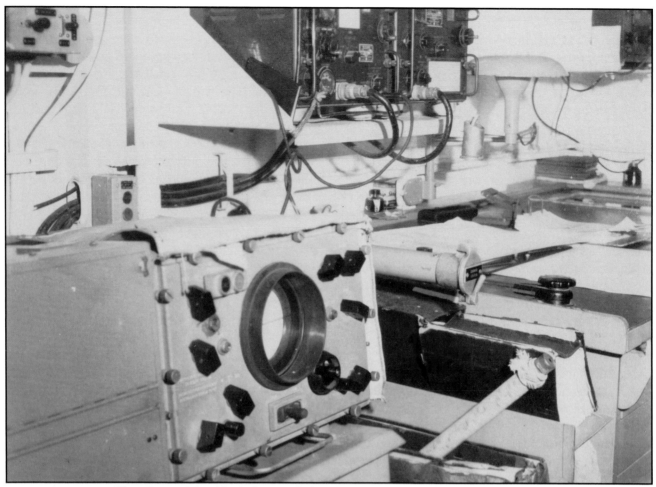

Chart Room. The ship to shore radio is at the top center, and the radar is below it.

We arrived in England in March, 1944. For several months we practiced landings on the shores of England and, on June the 2nd, we proceeded on orders to France. Along the way we had to purposefully delay our trip across the Channel so that the ship would arrive off Utah Beach on June the 6th. The ship arrived at 2:00 a.m. and lowered our small boats at 4:00. In these small boats, our crews delivered forty demolition men onto the beach, where they were among the first Naval personnel to initiate action against the German coastal defenses. Of the forty men who started out, there were only thirteen left three days later, and only a couple of those remaining few escaped injury.

The Invasion of Normandy was certainly one of the most exciting battles of the entire war. It was a time when we saw so many soldiers, and ships, and men being killed by the Germans—the English Channel was red with the blood from those men killed at the beaches. We saw the flying buzz bombs which the Germans sent over to England on or about June 10th, and we saw the British Spitfire airplanes use their wings

to dip under these slow-moving bombs and tip them so that they would crash into the sea and explode. The sight of seeing the thousand allied airplanes going overhead at 2 a.m. on June the 6th, and the many gliders that we saw in tow, was certainly a thankful scene. When the gliders went over, I thought about a grade school friend who served as a glider pilot. He was lost during this battle. In all, the ship made a total of ten landings during Operation Overlord. Afterwards, we were ordered to go to Bizerte, North Africa, and then on to Naples, Italy, where we loaded the ship for the upcoming invasion of Southern France.

On August the 15th, we arrived at San Raphael Bay, and took part in the D-Day Invasion of Southern France. We served in this area—going back and forth between France and Africa many times. We also served in Marseilles Old Port Harbor, where our ship was designated as a mother ship. During the time we were there, our ship's bakers made bread for the soldiers and civilians for about forty days.

On December the 26th, 1944, we began our return trip to Norfolk, Virginia. From there, we sailed up to Boston Harbor, Massachusetts. In Boston, about thirty men from our crew were transferred off the ship, and thirty new men were assigned to take their places. The ship was completely gone over for needed repairs, and then was painted Pacific Green. At the end of March, 1945, LST 47 departed for the Pacific Theater of War.

Later, while stationed aboard an LCT in the Pacific, I visited the city of Lingayen in the Philippines. I had the opportunity to meet the Mayor of the city, and he mentioned that when the Japs held the area they demanded that the Filipinos provide food for their men, or face punishment. On the other hand, when the U.S. came in, the Allied Command had an attitude of "Oh, you poor people. Don't worry, we will feed you and give you a place to live." One side treated the people with threats, the other with compassion!

After the war I returned to Bendix Aviation and worked for a period of time in their Data Processing Department. My career after the war varied; I worked as a manager of an IBM Service Bureau, held several sales positions selling various business products, and retired in September, 1987, from the position of Vice President of the Broome County Chamber of Commerce.

Through the GI Bill of Rights I secured my first home mortgage and was able to get a college education. I graduated from the University of Cincinnati in 1972 with an AS in Industrial Engineering, and a BS in Business Management. Coincidentally, my daughter, JoAnn, graduated the same year (and the same university) with a Teaching degree.

# Part III
# Appendix

# Officers and Crew of LST 47

by Herbert W. Stamer

The **Captain**, called "Skipper," was in charge of the ship's operations, and the highest in command.

The **Executive Officer**, also known as "Exec," was second in command. In the event that anything might cause the Skipper to be away from the ship, or incapacitated, the Exec would assume full responsibility for command of the ship.

The **Deck Officer** was in charge of all of the seamen on board. His crew consisted of the following: **2 Boatswain's Mates, 2 Coxswains, 15 Seamen 1st Class,** and **13 Seamen 2nd Class**. This crew was in charge of keeping the ship maintained and clean. They handled all of the lines and equipment used in securing all equipment and storage used on the ship. They were divided into two groups—one group was assigned the top deck, the other group handled the lower deck. The lower deck also included cleaning of all the crew quarters, latrines, and any recreation areas on the ship. Both crews would work on any materials or details requiring large work crews, such as the storage of munitions or food stores.

The **Engineering Officer** was in charge of all machinists and shipfitters on board. His crew consisted of the following: **2 Chief Motor Machinists, 15 Motor Machinists (both 1st and 2nd Class),** and **8 Firemen (both 1st and 2nd Class)**. This crew was responsible for all work and operations of the ship's main and auxiliary engines, other mechanical equipment such as emergency steering apparatus, anchor winches, and any loading ramps on the ship. There was also a group of men who were responsible for repairs to the ship and correcting electrical problems. This included the ability to use lathes and also welding equipment as required: **2 Shipfitters 2nd Class, 2 Electrician Mates (both 1st and 2nd Class),** and one **Watertender (or Oil King)** who was responsible for all liquids aboard (water treatment plant, ballast and, after the ship entered the Pacific, the ship's evaporator).

The **Gunnery Officer** was in charge of the crew that maintained the ship's guns and ammunition. He had control over all rifles and carbines, as well as the small arms ammunition. His crew consisted of the following: **3 Gunners Mates** and **one Fire Controlman** who was training to become a gunners mate.

The **Ship Doctor** was in charge of the crew that dispensed medical service as required. There was no doctor assigned to the ship on a regular basis, so the work of dispensing medical service was handled by the pharmacist mate. If serious conditions existed, the person requiring a doctor would be transferred to the Flotilla Doctor, or the doctor would come aboard to perform any needed operations. The crew consisted of **2 Pharmacist Mates (1st or 2nd Class)**.

During the Normandy Invasion, additional medical personnel were added: **11 Pharmacist Mates (1st and 2nd Class),** and **6 Hospital Assistants**. This added crew handled the treatment of all wounded men who were picked up during Operation Overlord. They were made up of a specially trained group called "Foxy 29." They were trained in the handling of most surgical procedures, and also had the training to handle any conditions where poison gas might have been used by the Germans.

The **Communications Officer** was in charge of all communications operations. This included the understanding of radio communication, radar operation, degaussing equipment, and handling the equipment needed to translate secret messages using a special coding device. His crew consisted of the following: **2 Quartermasters (both 2nd and 3rd Class)**. LST 47 didn't have a chief quartermaster, so the quartermaster 2nd class was in charge of the men in this division. This consisted of the following: **3 Radiomen 2nd Class, 2 Signalmen 3rd Class,** and one **Signalman Striker.** Later, **one Radarman** was added during the Pacific operation.

The duties of the quartermasters and signalmen were to receive messages from other ships using morse code, semaphore flags, and signal flags suspended from the ship's yardarms. During the crossing of the Atlantic, signal flags were used to designate the assigned course. In the event that the convoy was to initiate an immediate change of course, the Flagship would hoist the command, each ship in the convoy would raise identical flags, the Flagship would quickly lower her flags, and the other ships would lower theirs as well. The signalled command would then be sent to each ship's wheel house, and the new course of the convoy would be made.

If a halyard (the rope used to raise and lower flags) happened to break, it was the quartermaster's duty to climb up the mast (75 feet above the main deck) to the yardarms (which stretched about five feet out) and replace the broken halyard with a new one. This could be very exciting, for it meant hanging out over the main deck without benefit of any safety device. The same was required of a radioman; in the event the radar equipment became inoperative, a person would have to climb to the top of the mast and fix the malfunctioning equipment.

In addition to radar, there was an additional navigational system called LORAN that used radio communication to locate the ship's exact position. This eliminated much of the need to perform any celestial navigation, and greatly simplified the process of determining the ship's exact position.

The **Commissary Officer** was in charge of ordering all food and ship's supplies. His crew also maintained all of the ship's records, and operated the ship's service which sold needed articles such as soap, cigarettes, candy, etc. The crew consisted of the following: **1 Chief Commissary Service** (he made up the menus, handled storage of ship's stores, and assigned needed working parties), **1 Ship Baker, 1 Ship Cook SC 2nd Class, 2 Assistant Cooks SC 3rd Class, 2 Steward Mates StM (both 1st and 2nd Class**—the steward mates were black men who served the officers mess, and did some general cleaning service in the officer's quarters), **2 Storekeepers SK 2nd Class** (they operated the ship's service, and also secured books, cards, movies and phonograph records for keeping up the crew's morale), and **1 Yeoman Y 2nd Class** (he kept all the records of the ship. He prepared the ship muster rolls that listed all of the personnel who would be paid. He maintained the Change Reports which listed the names, ranks, and serial numbers of all persons received or transferred on the ship. He issued all needed liberty cards, and provided identification for men when required. He maintained the logs of all court-martial activities, and also kept the ship's records—called the deck log—that listed all people that visited the ship).

Just prior to the Normandy Invasion, March 27th, 1944, there was a special group added to the ship's crew. These personnel were the small boatmen and their officers. Their duties primarily concerned the operation of the small landing craft which ferried personnel and equipment. The group was comprised of the following personnel: **6 Small Boat Officers** and 6 Small Boat crews. Each crew was made up of **1 Coxswain** (to steer the boat), **1 Motor Machinist Mate** (to keep the boat's engine and equipment operational), and **2 Seamen** (to handle the lines, communicate with other craft, and to man the onboard machineguns while they were in action). After returning to the States from Europe, two of the small boats were removed before the 47 entered the Pacific theater of operations.

The LST 47 was used as a training ship and, during an invasion period, the ship would be transformed from troop carrying to become a hospital ship (with needed cots and a complete operating room located on the tank deck). The "Foxy 29" group of pharmacists and hospital assistants had four groups onboard for training during the two months before the actual invasion.

A demolition crew was taken from New York Harbor to England, and they remained onboard until the actual invasion of France. When the 47 arrived off the Normandy coast, the demolition unit was loaded aboard the small boats and taken to Utah Beach—thus becoming some of the very first Navy personnel to take action on French soil. Their group consisted of the following men: **9 Officers (Ensigns), 1 Warrant Officer, 2 Coxswains** (to handle the rubber rafts to get ashore), **2 Boatswain's Mates, 6 Gunner's Mates,** and **6 Seamen.** There were additional demolition men that were picked up off of the *USS Bayfield* and taken in on the landing at Utah Beach.

Under normal conditions, all men on the ship were required to stand watch in their designated areas. This was normally four hours on duty, and eight hours off. During combat activities, however, it became four hours on, and four hours off. To equalize the duty, there is a period called the Mid-Watch, which was from 1600 (4 p.m.) to 1800 (6 p.m.), and 1800 (6 p.m.) to 2000 (8 p.m.), which made it possible for men to have swing shifts and not always be on the same shift. If this did not happen, then some men would always have to stand watch from midnight until four in the morning, and they would not be able to sleep during the day.

During General Quarters, everyone was required to go to their battle stations, and there were no changes of shift. During Normandy, I can remember being awake for over eighty hours, and almost falling asleep while standing watch.

When ships were in dock, and there was limited need for standing complete watch, the ship's personnel would be granted liberty. This meant that half of the crew could go ashore one day, and the other half could get liberty the following day. This provided much needed recreation for the men.

# Shipboard Drills and Activities

by Herbert W. Stamer

**General Quarters**: The ship's alarm system was activated, and a loud noise was transmitted throughout the ship. When this alarm was rung, all of the ship's personnel had to report to their assigned battle stations as quickly as possible. Every person on board the ship stopped whatever he was doing and ran to the place on the ship that had been assigned to him. These places included all of the gun stations, the after steering station, the small boat areas, the conning tower, the main wheel house, and other areas of importance. Everyone immediately began to search for whatever was the cause for the alarm. Communication, while at General Quarters, was done through radio head sets and microphones.

Under normal conditions, all crew members were required to stand watch in their designated areas. This was normally four hours on duty, and eight hours off. During combat activities, however, it became four hours on, and four hours off. As previously noted, during General Quarters, everyone was required to go to their battle stations, and there were no changes of shift.

**Man Overboard**: If a person happened to fall off the ship and into the water while the ship was underway, an alarm was sounded to indicate a man overboard. The instructions were for the small boat crews assigned for the "man overboard condition" to report immediately and lower their assigned small boat and be prepared to rescue the individual. At the same time, the instructions to the wheel house were to stop all engines and to steer in the direction of the side where the person had gone overboard. The reason for stopping the engines was to prevent any possibility of the man overboard from being sucked into the propeller screws where he would be cut apart. The reason for steering in the direction of the man overboard was to make the distance to the person the shortest possible. There were several life preservers located on the top side of the ship, and there were sailors assigned to throw these preservers towards the man overboard. It generally took about three to five minutes before the man overboard could be reached, and several minutes before he could be returned to the ship. When the person was rescued, it was generally the practice to give that person a shot of rum to help warm up his body. Too much time in the cold water could result in hypothermia and, possibly, death.

**Emergency Steering:** The ship had an area near the stern (under the top deck) that housed a special hand-operated steering system. Normally, the ship's steering was controlled at the ship's wheel house, and special pumps hydraulically enabled the ship's rudders to change position. Occasionally, these pumps would develop leaks or, for other reasons, fail to function properly. When a malfunction occurred, it was necessary to disengage the normal steering devices and connect heavy steel cables to special connections leading to the rudders. Then a cable was used that, through turning, changed the ship's direction. Any subsequent commands to alter course transmitted from the main wheel house were received and acknowledged via a head set and microphone set up.

**Ship's Inspection:** The ship had regular inspections for cleanliness. The Skipper, or an assigned officer, would wear white gloves and check all of the ship's quarters for signs of dirt or dust. In some cases, instead of white gloves, black gloves were used, as dust can appear easier to see. All areas under cabinets were searched to see that there were no articles in places that were not easy to see. In some cases, an officer would place—beforehand—something under a cabinet which should have been located by the cleaning crews. If, during the course of the inspection, these things were recovered by the inspection party, those men responsible for cleaning would be put on report and could lose their liberty privileges.

**Personnel Inspection:** When the ship was in a port where liberty could be granted, the Skipper would have the entire crew (except those on watch duty) assemble on the main deck in full uniform. A complete roll call would be made to ensure that everyone was accounted for. Then the Skipper, or another officer, would inspect all of the men for proper uniforms, cleanliness, and clean shaves. The ship's yeoman would accompany the inspection team and have a note pad to record any individual who did not pass inspection. Chances were, those who failed to pass inspection would be denied their liberty privileges for the day. Usually, only half of the crew could go ashore at one time — the other half could get liberty when the first half returned.

**Exercise Drills:** Many mornings, while in port, the Captain would have the men assemble on the main deck of the ship, and the Boatswain would lead the crew in a series of physical exercises. These exercises included jumping-jacks, sit-ups, push-ups, running-in-place, etc. There were also times when boxing matches were held on the main deck as entertainment for the crew.

**General Maintenance:** As a ship is exposed to the weather, it was necessary to remove any rust from the ship's surface. This meant that chipping irons and steel brushes were used to dig out any rust. The area then required painting with a zinc chromate paint and then, after that had dried, it was painted with the ship's standard colors. Until a person has experienced this duty, it is hard to imagine just how difficult the removal of rust can be.

**Recreation:** There were a number of books and playing cards on board which were donated by the Red Cross and other organizations. Some men brought along their own dice, and it was not uncommon to see men playing "galloping dominoes" on a blanket spread out on the deck. LST 47 was fortunate to have a piano on board, and there was a crew member among us who had played professionally with leading name bands such as Tommy Dorsey. There was also a drummer, a trumpet player and, for a while in the Pacific, a violinist. The ship also had a phonograph, and records were played for the entire crew to hear over the public address system. The ship radiomen would also make it possible for the crew to listen to radio programs such as the "Hit Parade" and other entertaining shows.

**Church Services:** The ship did not have a Chaplain aboard but, when the ship was in port, religious services were available to the crew. In that several religions were represented by the men on the ship, generally a small boat would be lowered, and the men of respective religions would be transported to either a ship or shore location where they could participate in either Mass or Protestant services. LST 47 had only one person on board of Jewish faith, and he generally went to services of Mass with a shipmate.

# LST Beaching Procedures

**1. Twelve Hours Before H-Hour, Final Beaching Preparations Are Begun.**
1) All tank shoring is removed from the tank deck, thus leaving tanks secured by chains alone.
2) Main deck is cleared except for cargo.
3) Ventilation intakes are opened.
4) Exhaust fans within the tank deck are started.
5) Order is issued to "Man the Tanks."
6) Fire watch is stationed on the after platform of the tank deck to guard against backfires from vehicles being started. Tank turret gunners man the ship's permanent carbon dioxide systems on the bulkhead.
7) After all exhaust fans have been running for at least five minutes, and the Officer of the Deck has given his permission, the engines of the tanks may be turned over for testing.
8) The signal for starting the tank engines is given by the Army officer in command.
9) The carbon monoxide indicator is monitored. If the concentration of carbon monoxide becomes dangerous, the alarm sounds, and all engines must be stopped.
10) Traffic control light system is tested.
11) Upon completion of all tests, the order is given to "Cut the Engines."
12) A report is made to the conn that the tanks are secured.
13) Ventilators continue to run until all exhaust has been cleared; then the fan switches are cut, the ventilators secured, and a report of same is made to the conn.

**2. On Nearing Enemy Territory, the Ship Goes to General Quarters.**
1) The Captain and the Gunnery Officer are at the conn.
2) The Executive Officer is in the chartroom.
3) All guns are manned and ready.
4) The Engineering Officer is in charge of both the main and the auxiliary engine rooms.
5) The First Lieutenant has charge of the damage control parties—stationed aft, forward, and in the decontamination room.
6) At least three hours before H-Hour, the order is given to "Trim Ship for Beaching." As the ballast is shifted, the ship changes draft until she reaches beaching trim (9'-10' aft, 3'-5' forward).
7) Upon completion of ballast adjustments, the Engineering Officer reports "Ship at Beaching Trim."
8) The Captain orders "Complete Preparations For Beaching."
9) The third of the three auxiliary diesels is warmed up to assure full supply of electric power for the door, ramp, and winch motors.
10) The Assistant First Lieutenant, and two men of the un-dogging detail, un-dog the bow doors.
11) Meanwhile, the shipfitter, and three men from the un-dogging detail, un-dog the ramp.
12) When the doors are cleared, a report is made to the conn. The report "Door Un-dogged and Free" is relayed to bow and ramp control.
13) The order is now given for all generators to supply power to all beaching machinery.
14) The ventilators are given a final check.
15) The fire watch is again posted.
16) The operation of the door and ramp motor is tested, and reported to the conn.

**3. Thirty Minutes Before Beaching, the Order is Given to Sound the Beaching Alarm.**
1) The ship goes from General Quarters to Condition 1 Mike—Beaching Stations.
2) The First Lieutenant comes forward to take charge of bow door and ramp control.
3) The ventilators are started.
4) The troops man their tanks, and the fire watch stands by as the engines are started and warmed up.

5) The lashing chains securing the tanks are released.
6) The lashing chains are removed on the main deck.
7) Extra gasoline drums are jettisoned.
8) The elevator winch cover is removed, and the clutch engaged for elevator operation.
9) The stern anchor is readied for letting go as soon as the command is given; the wire securing straps are removed, the power is checked, and the winch and its controls are tested to check their operation.

**4. Twenty Minutes Before Beaching, the Order is Given to Prepare to Open Doors and Lower Ramp.**
1) A quartermaster is stationed forward to take soundings with a specially rigged line—marked every foot. The soundings enable the navigator to check chart soundings.
2) When the ship is a half-mile from the beach, the sanitary system is cut off.
3) When the corner ramp dogs are cast free, the leading man signals ramp control by holding his arms over his head.
4) Permission is requested of conn to test the ramp.
5) The motor is started, and the ramp opens slightly. To save time in combat, the motor is un-clutched, and the ramp put on the brake. This way, the ramp can be lowered in twenty seconds.
6) All stations for beaching now report "Manned and Ready."

**5. Just Before Beaching, the Command is Given "Open Bow Doors."**
1) When the doors are parallel to the keel, "Bow Doors Open" is reported to the conn.
2) The command is then given "Lower Ramp," and the ramp is lowered to about six feet above the waterline.
3) Word is passed to "Let Go Stern Anchor" when the ship is about two-and-a-half lengths from the beach. The clutch plate is released and, as soon as the anchor has grounded, the winch is permitted to run free.

**6. As Soon as the Beach has been Hit, the Order is Given to "Drop the Ramp."**
1) The ramp is lowered.
2) The order is given to "Disembark." The traffic light flashes to green, and the tanks move out quickly.
3) The ship must be held at right angles to the beach throughout the unloading; this prevents broaching (swinging parallel to the beach).
4) As the unloading progresses, the ship grows lighter. Ballast must be added forward to keep the bow on the beach; the engines are kept driving forward; the stern anchor is slacked off so the ship can be constantly driven into the sand, but enough tension is maintained on the cable to keep the stern from swinging.
5) When the last tank has disembarked, the report "Tank Deck Clear" is made to conn.
6) The order for unloading the main deck is given.
7) The elevator pins are removed from their sockets—releasing the elevator from its housing.
8) The elevator guides are installed.
9) Vehicles on the main deck are jockeyed into position on the elevator. A guide is stationed where he can watch the elevator and signal directions to the operator.
10) Vehicles are lowered on the elevator from the main deck to the tank deck where, once the elevator comes to a complete stop, they drive directly off the ship through the bow doors.

# Amphibious Service
# Medal of Honor Recipients

**Douglas Albert Munro**
Signalman First Class, U.S. Coast Guard.
September 27, 1942

Nearly five hundred U.S. Marines lay trapped by overwhelming Japanese forces at Point Cruz, Guadalcanal. If not soon evacuated, it was doubtful that any would survive.

Petty Officer Munro commanded twenty-four Higgins boats. His job was to get these boats to the beach and bring the battalion of Marines back to safety. Upon approaching the shore, Munro's small boats came under a withering hail of Japanese machinegun fire. Ignoring the extreme peril to his life, Munro placed his craft directly between the Japanese gunners and the rescuing craft. Just as the evacuation was about to reach a successful conclusion, Munro was killed instantly by enemy fire. His remaining crew, two of them wounded, continued to protect the others until the last small boat had withdrawn.

**John Joseph Parle**
Ensign, U.S. Naval Reserve.
July 9–10, 1943

Just as the Allied amphibious assault on Sicily was about to hit the beaches, a smoke pot aboard an explosives- and ammunition-laden boat accidentally ignited. Should this craft explode, the enemy would be warned, and the entire operation would be in even greater jeopardy.

Knowing full well the personal risk he was taking, Ensign Parle (an Officer-in-Charge of Small Boats) leapt into the craft, extinguished a burning fuse and, failing to put out the smoke pot, grabbed it with his bare hands and threw it overboard. Because of Parle's quick thinking, and self-sacrifice, the enemy was not forewarned, but the brave ensign died a week later from the smoke and fumes he had inhaled.

**Johnnie David Hutchins**
Seaman First Class, U.S. Naval Reserve.
September 4, 1943

Japanese forces defending Lae, New Guinea, were throwing everything they had against the Allied amphibious assault. While stoically braving aerial bombardment and land-based artillery fire, the helmsman of one of the lumbering American LSTs bound for the enemy beach spotted a Japanese torpedo racing toward his ship. Just as he was about to alter course to avoid the torpedo, a bomb struck the ship's pilot house, and the resultant explosion dislodged the helmsman and left the LST at the mercy of the oncoming torpedo.

Seaman First Class Johnnie Hutchins, though mortally wounded by the bomb blast, used his last remaining strength to grasp the wheel and steer his ship clear of the torpedo. Moments later, Seaman Hutchins died at the helm of the ship he had saved—exactly one month after his twenty-first birthday.

# Glossary

| | |
|---|---|
| AK | Code letters for an Attack Cargo Ship. |
| AP | Code letters for an Attack Personnel Transport Ship. |
| APA | Code letters for transports converted from luxury liners. |
| APD | Code letters for transports converted from obsolete destroyers. |
| Amidship | Approximately the center of a vessel. |
| AVGAS | Aviation fuel. |
| AWOL | Acronym for Absent Without Official Leave. |
| BM 1/C | Abbreviation for the rating of Boatswain's Mate First Class. |
| BM 2/C | Abbreviation for the rating of Boatswain's Mate Second Class. |
| BM 3/C | Abbreviation for the rating of Boatswain's Mate Third Class. |
| Battleship | "Battleships are designed to deal out crushing blows, to receive and sustain punishment without complete loss of fighting power, to remain for long periods at sea without need to replenish stores or fuel and are the most self-supporting type of warship. They carry the largest naval guns, 14-plus inches in caliber, mounted two and three in a turret, and up to twelve in number. They are protected with armor belts 14-plus inches thick as defense against short range gunfire, and with armored decks sufficiently thick to be impervious to plunging shells of long range caliber, horizontal bombing and dive bombing...As secondary batteries they have the all-purpose medium caliber guns for use against speedy light surface craft and planes, and smaller caliber machine guns as additional anti-aircraft defense."* |
| Boats | Abbreviated term for the rating of boatswain's mate. |
| Boot Camp | Initial phase of military training for sailors and Marines. |
| Bosun | Boatswain. |
| Bow | Forward-most portion of a vessel. |
| Brig | Punishment confinement quarters, or Navy jail. |
| C-47 | Twin engined cargo/passenger aircraft (military version of the DC-3). |
| Chief | Chief Petty Officer. |
| Conn | The area aboard a vessel where the navigation takes places. |
| Corpsman | Enlisted naval medical specialist. |
| Courts Martial | Military judicial proceedings. |
| Coxswain | Naval rating for a boat pilot; the senior member of a boat crew responsible for the lives and property of the passengers and equipment. |
| Cruiser | "The development of the cruiser type seems always to be in a state of flux, with the heavier ones tending to usurp the characteristics of battleships and the smaller ones being little more than oversize destroyers. The main characteristic of all cruiser design seems to be speed, and more speed; and to obtain this superspeed the characteristic most apt to be reduced is armor protection...As the war proceeds a type of cruiser of greater displacement, and more heavily armed than the (disarmament) treaty 10,000 tonners, |

may be expected. These ships will have cruiser speed and in attaining this speed they will either be less heavily armored than battleships or will carry a fewer number of heavy guns. They will be thoroughly armed with anti-aircraft defense, both light guns and top armor, and one of the main functions of the type will be to chase down the new and speedy carrier types which are in production by all of the seapower belligerents."*

| | |
|---|---|
| DUKW | Commonly called a "Duck," this is the acronym for an amphibious two-and-one-half-ton truck. The code letter "D" stood for year of design (1942), "U" for amphibious, "K" for all wheel drive, and "W" for dual rear axles. |
| Davit | "Shipboard crane that can be swung out over the side; used for hoisting and lowering boats and weights. Often found in pairs."# |
| Destroyer | "Destroyers have become the all-purpose ships of the Navy. They are a gradual development from the small speed boat, which was envisioned as the logical torpedo conveyor when the torpedo was invented...With the establishment of the torpedo boat, the destroyer was developed, originally termed the torpedo boat destroyer...Destroyers range in displacement from 1,000 to 2,500 tons. They do not have as great a cruising radius as the larger types but are valuable as anti-submarine, anti-aircraft and anti-torpedo screens for them. Against aircraft and light surface vessels they use their guns, against heavy surface vessels their torpedoes in night attacks, and against submarines, depth charges."* |
| Ditty Bag | Small cloth bag for toiletries and small possessions. |
| Dogtags | The unofficial name given for the metal identification disks worn by all military personnel. |
| Exec | Executive Officer—second in command. |
| F 1/C | Abbreviation for the rating of Fireman First Class. |
| Fantail | Upper deck at the rearmost portion of a vessel. |
| 1st Class | Abbreviated term for the rank of Petty Officer 1st Class. |
| Flagship | A vessel under the command of a Commodore, or above. |
| Flak | Anti-aircraft guns and/or gun fire. |
| Fo'c's'le | Abbreviated term for forecastle—"upper deck in the forward part of the ship."# |
| 40(s) | Short for forty-millimeter anti-aircraft gun. |
| .45 | The caliber of cartridge used in the M1911 semi-automatic service pistol. ".45" was often used in lieu of saying the name of the pistol. |
| General Quarters | "Calls the ship's company to battle stations."* |
| Grinder | Naval term for an area on land designated for formations, training, etc. |
| Hawser | "Heavy lines used for towing, mooring ship to dock, or for other purposes where great strength is required."* |
| Head | Naval term for a toilet. |
| Higgins | Andrew Jackson Higgins—renowned manufacturer of landing craft throughout the war. During Prohibition, Mr. Higgins' company sold fast motor boats to both smugglers and law enforcement officials. |

| | |
|---|---|
| Kamikaze | Piloted, Japanese naval aircraft intended to deliberately crash into, and destroy, Allied targets. |
| LCM | Landing Craft, Mechanized. "The LCM might be described as a large version of the LCVP. It carries more cargo, has more power, and is more difficult to handle. Its purposes, however, are the same: to pound through the breakers, beach, unload, retract, and return to the ship for another load."# |
| LCP(L) | Landing Craft, Personnel (Large). |
| LCP(R) | Landing Craft, Personnel (Ramp). |
| LCVP | Landing Craft, Vehicle, Personnel. "The LCVP was designed to run through the surf to a beach, lower a ramp, unload men and cargo, retract through the breakers, and return to its transport."# |
| Liberty Ship | Mass-produced wartime cargo vessel. |
| Liberty | Official leave from duty. |
| Lorry | Truck, in British parlance. |
| LST | Landing Ship, Tank. Shallow draft oceangoing ship capable of landing tanks, other vehicles, personnel and cargo directly onto a beach. |
| MP | Military Police—Army or Marine Corps. |
| MoMM 1/C | Abbreviation for the rating of Motor Machinist's Mate 1st Class. |
| MoMM 2/C | Abbreviation for the rating of Motor Machinist's Mate 2nd Class. |
| Motor Mac | Unofficial abbreviation for the rating of Motor Machinist's Mate—A Navy rating for one whose specialty is the operation, maintenance and repair of engines and shipboard machinery. |
| '03 | Bolt-actioned model 1903 service rifle. |
| Onboard | A term given for indicating presence on a vessel. |
| P.O. | Acronym for the rank of Petty Officer—naval non-commissioned officer. |
| PT Boat | Patrol Torpedo Boat, or Motor Torpedo Boat. "The motor torpedo boat is a reversion to the original conception of a torpedo conveyor; it is small, swift and able to get close enough to launch the torpedo before being discovered. The present type is a development from the familiar sport and racing types of high speed boats. They are best adapted to night attacks in waters which are not too rough. Due to their small cruising radius they are operated from shore bases or from tenders. They carry torpedoes in deck tubes and a battery of machine guns for use against planes and small craft."* |
| P-38 | Also known as the Lockheed "Lightning,"—a twin-fuselage American fighter aircraft. |
| Points | A point system devised by the high command for determining an individual's eligibility for discharge. Points were awarded for time in the service, time overseas, number of awards and decorations, number of children, etc. When an individual reached a certain number, he could be released from further service. |
| Port side | Left side of a vessel. |
| Prop | Abbreviated term for a Propeller (also known as a screw)—shaft driven |

| | |
|---|---|
| | bladed device for moving a vessel through the water. |
| QM 2/C | Abbreviation for the rating of Quartermaster 2nd Class. |
| Rangers | Elite U.S. Army Infantry personnel. |
| Rate/Rating | Rank or grade of a naval enlisted man. |
| SP | Acronym for Shore Patrol. |
| Scouts/Raiders | Elite naval commando personnel—forerunners of today's Navy Seals. |
| SeaBees | Actually C.B.s—Acronym for Naval Construction Battalion personnel. |
| 2nd Class | Abbreviated term for the rank of Petty Officer 2nd Class. |
| Shore Patrol | Naval Military Police. |
| Small Boat | Name given to any one of the lesser landing craft. |
| Starboard side | Right side of a vessel. |
| Stern | Rearmost portion of a vessel. |
| Submarine Net | Large net stretched across a relatively narrow body of water for defense against submarines. |
| Suicide Boats | Manned, Japanese boats loaded with explosives—usually intended to smash into Allied craft and detonate upon impact. They were literally boat versions of the Kamikaze aircraft. |
| Swamp | "To sink by filling with water."* |
| Transports | "Transports are passenger ships especially conditioned from luxury liners to accommodate the maximum number of troops in the space available."* |
| 20(s) | Short for twenty-millimeter anti-aircraft gun. |
| UDT | Acronym for Underwater Demolition Team. Specially trained naval personnel who handled explosives, removed beach obstacles, reconnoitered enemy beaches and otherwise assisted in beach landings. |
| Underway | A term indicating a vessel in the process of movement. |
| V-1 | One of Germany's pilotless guided rockets. The V-1 was a short-winged missile propelled by a pulse jet engine. |
| Whaleboat | "Double-ended boats which are convenient for a wide variety of light duties. Large ships are supplied with the open type for use as lifeboats in addition to the pulling whaleboat."* |

* *The Bluejackets' Manual*, 1943, Eleventh Edition. United States Naval Institute, Annapolis, Maryland.

# *The Bluejackets' Manual*, 1950, Fourteenth Edition. United States Naval Institute, Annapolis, Maryland.